HEALTH-SEEKING BEHAVIOR IN ETHNIC POPULATIONS

HEALTH-SEEKING BEHAVIOR IN ETHNIC POPULATIONS

Edited by
Tyson Gibbs and Sue Gena Lurie

With a Foreword by
Erma Lawson

The Edwin Mellen Press
Lewiston•Queenston•Lampeter

Library of Congress Cataloging-in-Publication Data

Health-seeking behavior in ethnic populations / edited by Tyson Gibbs and Sue Gena Lurie ;
  [with a foreword by Erma Lawson].
    p. cm.
  Includes bibliographical references.
  ISBN-13: 978-0-7734-5842-0
  ISBN: 0-7734-5842-5 (hbk.)
    1. Ethnic groups--Health and hygiene--United States. 2. Minorities--Health and
  hygiene--United States. 3. Ethnicity--Health aspects--United States. 4. Health
  behavior--United States. I. Gibbs, Tyson. II. Lurie, Sue Gena.

  RA448.4.H426 2006
  613.089--dc22

                                                              2006042049

hors série.

A CIP catalog record for this book is available from the British Library.

Copyright © 2007 Tyson Gibbs and Sue Gena Lurie

            The Edwin Mellen Press   The Edwin Mellen Press
                    Box 450   Box 67
            Lewiston, New York   Queenston, Ontario
            USA 14092-0450   CANADA L0S 1L0

                        The Edwin Mellen Press, Ltd.
                        Lampeter, Ceredigion, Wales
                        UNITED KINGDOM SA48 8LT

                    Printed in the United States of America

Contents

Foreword by Erma Lawson   i

Chapter 1   1
Ethnicity and Health-Seeking Behavior
Tyson Gibbs and Sue Gena Curie

Chapter 2   13
Health-Seeking Behavior in a Mexican-American Community
Sue Gena Lurie

Chapter 3   31
African Americans and Health
Tyson Gibbs

Chapter 4   41
Cultural Apects of Health-Seeking Behavior for the African Population
in Katutra, Namibia
Debie LeBeau

Chapter 5   93
Nigerian Americans and Health
Doug Henry

Chapter 6   111
Arab Americans
Alice Reizian

Chapter 7   135
Native Hawaiians
Lisa Henry

Chapter 8   153
Resettled Refugees of Southeast Asian Ethnicities: Health-Seeking Behavior
Lance A. Rasbridge and Charles Kemp

Chapter 9   173
Ethnicity and Health-Seeking Behavior in India
Vijayan K. Pillai and Hector L. Diaz

Chapter 10   193
Big and Little Moon Peyotism as Health-Care Delivery Systems
Dennis Wiedman

Chapter 11   219
Culture and Health Behavior in Three Asian Communities in Singapore
Stella R. Quah

Chapter 12   241
Telemedicine: Health-Seeking Behavior in the Information Age Among
Affluent Americans
Arushi Sinha

Chapter 13   261
Conclusion
Sue Gena Lurie and Gordon Lurie

Foreword

Health is the product of both the environment in which we live and the social fabric of various cultures. Although the initial impact of a disease can be mediated (i.e., participating in disease prevention behavior) by eating the right foods, exercising, controlling stress, and exercising, ill-health is influenced by social factors. Specifically, disease is a biological explanation of a specific condition. However, "disease" does not exist until there is agreement that it does, by perceiving, naming, and responding to it. Disease must be treated as a condition that has its origins within the political and economic realities of the social structure and culture within which it exists.

This book is important because it focuses on the ways in which individuals and cultures seek health care. The book also discusses cultural variations in the way individuals respond to ill health. Examples from different cultural groups ranging from African Americans to Mexican culture to cultures in the Pacific Rim are presented. These studies illustrate that cultures vary in the way they treat a sick person as well as demonstrate that cultures differ in their definitions of an illness.

This book focuses on Health Seeking Behavior. It presents studies that explore health-seeking behavior within various social and cultural contexts. It also focuses on the concept of ethnicity. Critical to this book is the bridging of two concepts that have traditionally appeared in disparate places within the literature on health, i.e., ethnicity and health-seeking behavior. This book brings these concepts together to emphasize their impact on understanding the cultural and social influences of how individuals respond to ill health.

I ask the reader to consider the various cultural responses to the sick person as you read this book. It is my hope that the reader will come to understand the importance of cultural factors in which health-seeking behavior occurs. Finally, the reader must understand that different ways of seeking help for an illness have been successful because there are cultures older than Western civilization, that do not utilize medical treatment for care. The information provided in this book brings together material from various ethnic groups to transcend traditional understanding of health-seeking behavior. The reader will more accurately understand the impact of social and cultural factors of ill-health. Examining health-seeking behavior from a broader perspective offers not only a unique insight, but is an invaluable asset to an increasingly global health-care community.

Erma Lawson, Ph.D.
Congressional Fellow
United States Congress
Washington, D.C.

Ethnicity and Health-Seeking Behavior

Tyson Gibbs PhD. Associate Professor, Department of Anthropology, University of North Texas, Denton, Texas.

Sue Gena Lurie, Ph.D. Assistant Professor, Department of Social and Behavioral Sciences, School of Public Health, University of North Texas Health Science Center, Fort Worth, Texas.

Definitions

The purpose of this book is to provide information about the importance of ethnicity in the behavior of persons seeking to maintain equilibrium with their environment. This equilibrium is called health. To begin the discussion about ethnicity and health-seeking behavior, it is important that the terms are described. The concept of ethnicity is recent. Prior to the 1950s most people in the United States were thought to have specific behavior traits that were linked to race, breeding, class, socioeconomic standing, or level of intelligence. Race was defined in the simplest of terms. Race related to places of origin, Europe, Asia, Australia, and Africa being the common areas. People were referred to as European, Negroid, Mongoloid, or Asian. People other than Western Europeans were considered less than first-class citizens. Even those from certain parts of southern Europe were not always welcomed in the United States. After the 1950s, ethnicity became a catch-all term to provide a way of linking characteristics to human behavior.

The concept of Health-Seeking Behavior, on the surface, appears to be easily defined. Mascie-Taylor (1995, 101–102), quoting Talcott Parsons, who

2

defines health as "the state of optimum capacity of an individual for the effective performance of the roles and tasks for which he has been socialized." The term "seeking" is defined as "2: to go in search of: look for: try to discover." "Behavior" is defined in this way—"anything an organism does involving action and response to stimulation. c: the response of an individual, group or species to its environment." Therefore, the concept of "Health-Seeking Behavior" can be summed up as the actions of individuals or groups, in search of *something* to affect their performance, in their social roles, at the optimal level. Implicit in this definition, therefore, is that individual decision-making activities are the core processes that drive the attempt at discovery of the optimum capacity of individual performance.

However, complicating this definition is that health-seeking behavior has been defined and explored from various perspectives in medical, cultural, and psychological anthropology, medical sociology, medical psychology, public health, medicine, nursing, and social work (Chrisman 1977). Indeed, the very definition of "health" can be viewed from a number of perspectives. For example, research describing actions of individuals toward their health has been cited under many topic areas, such as Health-Seeking Behavior, Health Behavior, Health Beliefs, Health-Belief Model, Health-Decision Behavior, Help Seeking, Care Seeking, Care-Seeking Behavior, Self-Care, Self-Care Behavior, Self-Medical Care, Self-Medication, Folk-Medical Beliefs, and Folk Medicine. Medical sociology defines health-seeking behavior one way, whereas cultural anthropology defines it another. Other fields outside what would be normally considered the social sciences, such as public health, also have definitions for this type of behavior.

What makes such a list of definitions important is its use in gaining an understanding of the definition of health-seeking behavior. This requires that attention be given to a range of research domains and discipline-based concepts that are applied to understand human behavior and performance in social roles.

The perspective represented in the topical area chosen by the researcher can explain the various issues that are linked with health-seeking processes of individuals or groups. The definition of health-seeking behavior implies that individuals and groups can detect differences in personal functioning within a given environment and that noticeable changes within themselves require attention. Such attention is an action taken by the individual or group to change the difference that has been noticed, and that the person or persons involved sense must be acted upon, in other words, self-medication and care. Mascie-Taylor (1995) describes this behavior in the following manner:

> The general view of nature in which events must obey impersonal laws is one that produced the idea of regularity, the constancy or uniformity of nature that sustains the division between what is thought possible or impossible. It influences what kind of attention is paid to rare or extraordinary events. . . . Selective attention is strongly influenced by what is understood of possibility and impossibility. People try to make sense by looking for patterns or relationships between the things they notice. Over illnesses, (or change in function within their environment), it might be the search for patterns in body signs or in events or events surrounding illness: syndromes of disease or syndromes of circumstances explaining cause (Illness and disease defined as the absence of health) (103).

In summary, a definition of health-seeking behavior has three major components: (1) it requires that individuals have a sense about changes within themselves or within themselves in relationship to their environment; (2) that the sensation of change requires that a decision be made; and (3) that the decision requires that either action or no action be taken in an attempt to positively affect the change and reinstate equilibrium.

Health-Seeking Behavior Model

The models developed to describe these decisions cover the range of topical areas. Models for health-seeking behavior have come from studies of populations throughout the world and each has the same goal of describing how decisions are made when changes in health are detected by the individual.

Early in the 1970s Weaver (1970) developed a model that describes various phases of health-seeking Behavior. His data was derived from a study of 600 persons living in a village in Northern Mexico. These phases are described as follows:

- Self-Address Phase. Perception of Change
- Advice-Seeking Phase. Seeks Advice from friends, relatives or health system.
- Redefinition Phase. Advice is reevaluated to determine next step.
- Action Phase. Based on the reevaluation phase, person will act.
- Redefinition Phase. Individual "up-dates" status to determine next step.

Another model described by Loudell Snow (1974) is one that suggests that "Folk Beliefs" determine the behavior that individuals follow in the face of a detection of change of health status. She describes this system as follows:

> Three major themes emerge . . . first, the world is a hostile and dangerous place; second, that the individual is liable to attack from external sources; third, that the individual is helpless and has no internal resources to combat such an attack but must depend on outside aid. The individual as potential victim of attack must be wary of the world of nature, of a punitive god, and of malice of his fellow man. The latter is imbedded in pessimism about the nature of human relationships and the bedrock conviction that most people will do ill when it is in their interest that doing ill is more natural than doing good. Life is a constant hustle, and success in interpersonal relationships may be seen as the ability to manipulate others (81).

She further states: "The folk medical system under scrutiny here is not, however, restricted to Black Americans. Portions of it are to be found among groups as diverse as the: Pennsylvania Dutch, the Hutterites, Amish, Appalachian Whites, the Cajuns of Louisiana, Kansas farmers, Puerto Ricans in New York and the

Mid-West, and Mexican Americans wherever they are found." (page 81).Young (1980, 106) uses a model based on the concept of "natural decision-making" proposed by Gladwin and Gladwin in 1971. His study was conducted in Michoacan in west-central Mexico. This model attempts to describe the linkage between cultural knowledge and subsequent "purposive action." Young describes this model as: "A decision making study usually addresses three general questions. First, what are the alternatives members of a group view as open to them in regard to the particular problem at hand? Second, what are the criteria they use in selecting among these alternatives—what information is considered? Third, what is the decision process—the principles whereby the information is used or manipulated in making a choice? These findings may be formalized in a model that specifies the different ways in which considerations of relevant criteria lead to the choice of each alternative" Tanner, Cockerham, and Spaeted (1983) presented several determinants that predict whether or not a particular individual will seek health care. These include: (1) visibility and recognition of symptoms; (2) the extent to which the symptoms are perceived as dangerous; (3) the extent to which the symptoms disrupt family, work, and other social activities; (4) the frequency and persistence of the symptoms; (5) the amount of tolerance for the symptoms; (6) available information, knowledge, and cultural assumptions; (7) basic needs to denial; (8) other needs competing with illness responses; (9) competing interpretations that can be given to the symptoms once they are recognized; and (10) the availability and physical proximity of treatment resources, as well as the psychological and financial costs of taking action. Closely associated with their model is the idea that behavior operates at two levels: other-defined and self-defined illness.

Safer and colleagues (1979, 13) discussed three stages in the process of seeking or delaying health-care activities at the individual level: (1) appraisal delay, (2) illness delay, and (3) utilization delay. The premise is that at each stage of illness, the individual will either increase the speed of resolution of a medical problem or will continue to deliberate. The appraisal delay stage involves ascertaining of the number of days that passed between symptom identification and symptom definition. At this stage the person perceives a change in body functions. During illness delay the patient must decide whether the medical problem needs professional help or self-treatment. This stage is characterized by the assumption on the part of the individual that home remedies will not treat or cure physical or mental ailments. The final stage, utilization delay, is defined as the lapse in time between the decision to seek more formal treatment for a problem and the actual visit to a medical facility. At this stage factors such as cost and timing become crucial in confirming the resolution to confront medical problems.

The Health Belief Model grew out of psychological research conducted in the 1950s. It was first developed to help explain the preventive health practices of individuals, specifically the use of screenings for tuberculosis detection. The distinct beliefs expressed by an individual regarding susceptibility to a disease, perceived severity of the disease, and perceptions of the availability of both detection and therapy for the disease were all felt to influence the adoption of a particular health behavior, in this case disease detection. Since its inception, the Health Belief Model has also been applied to general health-care seeking and compliance with therapeutic regimens, as well as other areas in health with distinct behavioral connections. The goal of such a model is not only to understand the health-care action taken by an individual but also to predict the likelihood of a particular action occurring.

Kleinman (1980, 184) describes a model for health-seeking behavior derived from studies of Chinese medical practitioners living in Taipei's Lung-Shan district. He lists the various determinants of health-care–seeking behavior. These are type and severity of symptoms; course of sickness; type of sick role; specific sickness labels and the etiologies they implicate; evaluation of specific therapeutic interventions; age, sex, family role, occupation, and educational level of patient; the family's socioeconomic status, ethnic background, orientation to Western or traditional values, and past experiences with health care; urban or rural setting; the proximity to particular treatment resources; and the nature of patient's social network and lay referral system.

Research on health and medical decision-making processes tends to analyze a person's initial efforts to obtain health care and/or social support, and social and cultural determinants or influences. Despite current interest in narrative in medical anthropology, the focus in health decision-making is on one's choice of options available at one point in time, as contrasted with longitudinal and cumulative experiential processes.

Within the study of health-seeking behavior, theoretical models and research approaches range from health psychology that applies cognitive and cultural health belief models in the direction of individual decision making to anthropological and sociological analyses that give prominence to community, socioeconomic, family, and kinship determinants. Medical anthropological models explore clinical diagnostic "explanatory models" of illness that integrate psychological and cultural elements (Kleinman 1980, 1982; ; Anderson, Rafael, and Hazam, 1982; Sargent 1989). Ethnomedical models study the choice of folk, alternative, or complementary care and healers as contrasted with cosmopolitan medicine (Snow 1993; Finkler 1985; Harwood 1987), which include studies of decision making for self- and preventive care (Chrisman 1983; Eisenberg et al. 1993). Models for the significant roles of family and kin in influencing health seeking through social support have also been developed, such as "therapy management groups" in cross-cultural research in Zaire (Janzen 1987).

The current attention in the United States to health service access and utilization coincides with redefinition of health-seeking behavior in cross-cultural research as choice of care. In a recent study in Guatemala, two models of "treatment-seeking" were compared across six communities, to predict choice of health-care source: a sociobehavioral model of health services research with multivariate analysis of predisposing, enabling, and need factors; or a decision model of treatment actions, from descriptive interviews (Weller, Ruebush, and Klein 1997). Although this study did not include ethnicity as a variable, both approaches found similar key variables such as severity of illness, with the first model more able to predict choice of care. Medical anthropological research in a Mexican village found decision models of treatment choice provide an understanding of cultural rationality, but their use to predict treatment should be integrated with individual, cultural, social, and cognitive constructions of the meaning of illness (Garro 1998-). Comparative research in an Ojibway Native-American community in Canada found cultural meanings of illness and treatment based on assumptions that vary from those in decision-models (Garro 1998).

Significance of Research on Ethnicity and Health-Seeking Behavior
Ethnicity in the United States is popularly identified with race, which tends to be treated as an indicator of cultural patterns of health behavior and health seeking, despite critiques of the concept of race in public health and medical anthropology (King and Williams 1995; Singer and Baer 1995; Dressler 1993; Hahn 1994). Race and ethnicity are often compounded with social class, life-style, migration, and/or "acculturation" factors influencing health-seeking behavior. The rationale for the study of ethnicity and social class in medical care has been integrated (Harwood 1981), and race and social class analyzed in community mental health research (Dressler 1990). The current public health emphasis on the implications of cultural diversity for health behavior, illness, and prevention parallels concern with patients' ethnicity and cultural diversity in nursing (Spector 1991; Galanti 1991) and family medicine (Like, Steiner, and Rubel 1996).

Although income, employment, and access to care are associated with inequality in health status of different groups in a society and economic inequality with societal decline in health (Marmot et al. 1993), education has been selected by health policy makers and administrators in the United States as the basic cause of increasing inequality in health care of various ethnic groups. Education is also associated with mothers' health-seeking behavior for their children in developing countries.

Health-seeking behavior can be viewed as an intervening variable in differences in health status among individuals and groups. For analyzing health-seeking behavior across and within ethnic groups and social classes, several questions may be posed: is education an independent or dependent variable in health-seeking behavior, as related to income, health resources and access to care? That is, does education determine patterns of health-seeking, as well as income, health resources and access or do income, knowledge of health resources and access determine health seeking? How are ethnicity, culture, social support systems, health education, and experiences related to these variables? More specific questions on the process of health seeking can then be addressed: decision-making for self- or alternative/complementary care, the relative significance of acute or chronic illness, and responses of healers, health-providers, and social groups.

These questions should be considered in the context of the renewed significance of health-care changes in the United States toward managed care following attempts at health-care reform. The focus of social research on health has shifted to issues of access, prevention, the use of outcome measures, and economic accountability of medical care systems. These issues have been refocused in current efforts to extend managed care to groups formerly dependent on the public sector and/or nonprofit private organizations—the uninsured, persons receiving Medicare, and those on Medicaid. At the same time, political and legal changes in immigration policies and eligibility for health and social benefits mandate consideration of the political economy of health and options for care.

The ethnic diversity of U.S. society, the need to extend comprehensive managed care to diverse social and ethnic groups, and recognition of the importance of culturally sensitive or "competent" health care for prevention, treatment "compliance," and efficacy all have practical implications for applied research on health-seeking behavior. These include goals of understanding variations in self-care; interventions to change behavioral patterns; encouraging the use of prevention and primary care; and discouraging delays in acute care and emergency room visits for non emergencies. In order to make such changes effective, analyze reasons for health inequality, attend to the essential social conditions of health, and assess the consequences of chronic illness for various groups, more contextualized research is needed on the processes of health-seeking behavior. Multidisciplinary models and methods can provide a more balanced perspective and contribute to the development of a unified model of health seeking to effectively address policy implications.

11

REFERENCES

Anderson, B., T. Rafael, and N. Hazam. 1982. An approach to the resolution of Mexican-American resistance to diagnostic and remedial pediatric heart care. In *Clinically Applied Anthropology,* ed. N. Chrisman and T. Maretzki, 325–50. Dordrecht, The Netherlands: D. Reidel.

Chrisman, N. 1983. Popular health care, social networks and cultural meanings. In *Handbook of health, health care and the health professions,* ed. D. Mechanic, 569–81. New York: Free Press.

————. 1977. The health-seeking process: An approach to the natural history of illness. *Culture, Medicine, and Psychiatry* 1(4): 351–77.

Dressler, W. 1993. Health in the African-American community: Accounting for health inequalities. *Medical Anthropology Quarterly* new series, 7 (4): 325–45

————. 1990. *Stress and adaptation in the context of culture: Depression in a Southern black community.* Albany: State University of New York Press.

Eisenberg, D., R. Kessler, C. Foster, F. Norlock, D. Calkins, T. Delbanco.1993. Unconventional medicine in the United States: Prevalence, costs, and patterns of use. *New England Journal of Medicine* 56(4): 379–87.

Finkler, K. 1985. *Spiritualist healers in Mexico: Successes and failures of alternative therapeutics.* South Hadley, Mass.: Bergin and Garvey.

Galanti, G-A. 1991. *Caring for patients from different cultures: Case studies from American hospitals.* Philadelphia: University of Pennsylvania Press.

Garro, L. 1998. On the rationality of decision-making studies: Part I. Decision models of treatment choice. *Medical Anthropology Quarterly* new series,12(3): 319–40.

————. 1998. On the rationality of decision-making studies: Part II. Divergent rationalities. *Medical Anthropology Quarterly* - new series, 12 (3): 341–55

Hahn, R. 1994. Race and ethnicity in public health surveillance: Criteria for the scientific use of social categories. *Public Health Reports* 109(1): 7–15.

Harwood, A. 1987. Spiritist as needed: A study of a Puerto Rican community. In *Mental Health Resource.* Ithaca, NY: Cornell University Press.

Harwood, A., ed. 1981. *Ethnicity and medical care.* Cambridge, MA: Harvard University Press.

Janzen, J. 1987. Therapy management: Concept, reality, process. *Medical Anthropology Quarterly* new series, 1: 68–84.

King, G., and D. Williams. 1995. Race and health: A multi-dimensional approach to African-American health. In *Society and Health,* ed. B. Amick et al., 93–130. New York: Oxford University Press.

12

Kleinman, A. 1980. *Patients and healers in the context of culture.* Berkeley: University of California Press.

———. 1982.Clinically-applied anthropology on a psychiatric consultation-liaison service. In *Clinically applied anthropology,* ed. N. Chrisman and T. Maretzki, 83–116. Dordrecht, The Netherlands: D. Reidel.

Like, R., P. Steiner, and A. Rubel. 1996. Society for Teachers of Family Medicine Core Curriculum Guidelines. Recommended core curriculum guidelines on culturally sensitive and competent health care. *Family Medicine* 28: 291–97.

Mascie-Taylor, C. G. N. 1995. *The anthropology of disease.* New York: Oxford University Press.

Marmot, M., S. Levine, A. Tarlov, D. Walsh. 1993. Explanations for social inequalities in health. In *Society and health,* ed. B. Amick et al., 172–210. New York: Oxford University Press.

Safer M., Q. Tharps, T.. Jackson, H. Leventhal. 1979. Determinants of three stages of delay in seeking care at a medical clinic. *Medical Care* 17: 11–29.

Sargent, C. 1987. *Maternity, medicine and power: Reproductive decisions in urban Benin.* Berkeley: University of California Press.

Singer, M., and H. Baer. 1995. *Critical medical anthropology.* Amityville, N.Y.: Baywood.

Snow, L. F. 1993. *Walkin' over medicine.* Boulder, CO: Westview Press.

Spector, R. 1991. *Cultural diversity in health and illness.* 3rd ed. Norwalk, CT: Appleton and Lange.

———. 1974. Folk beliefs and their implications for the care of patients: A review based on studies among Black Americans. *Annals of Internal Medicine* 81: 82–96.

Tanner J. L., W. C. Cockerham, and J. L. Spaeted. 1983. Predicting physician utilization. *Medical Care* 21: 360–69.

Weaver, T. 1970. Use of hypothetical situations in the study of Spanish illness referral systems. *Human Organization* 29: 140–154.

Weller, S., T. Ruebush, and R. Klein. 1997. Predicting treatment-seeking behavior in Guatemala: A comparison of the health services research and decision-therapeutic approaches. *Medical Anthropology Quarterly:* new series, 11(2): 224–45

Young, J. 1980. A Model of illness treatment decisions in a Tarascan town. *American Ethnologist* 94: 106–35

Health-Seeking Behavior in a Mexican-American Community

Sue Gena Lurie, Ph.D. Assistant Professor, Department of Social and Behavioral Sciences, School of Public Health, University of North Texas Health Science Center, Fort Worth, Texas.

Introduction

This chapter analyzes health-seeking behavior in Mexican Americans in one of the of the fastest growing Latino communities in North Texas. Over 80 percent of Latinos in Texas are of Mexican descent. The Latino population in this city and county has more than doubled since the 1990 census. A state population of 33 million, including 45 percent Latinos, was projected in 1996 (Murdock 1996). This projection surpasses the estimated 12% of the national population identified as Hispanic in 2000 (U.S. Department of Health and Human Services, 2003). The Latino population in the state and metropolitan area is generally disadvantaged due to poverty, unemployment, a low level of education, and lack of access to health care, although there is a growing middle class. Mexican-American workers tend to be employed in the service, farming, and construction industries with minimal or no health insurance. The eligibility of immigrants for Medicaid or other federal health and social programs is problematic.

Nationally, Latinos and Mexican Americans vary in socioeconomic and cultural patterns, as well as health status, behavioral health risks, disease, causes of morbidity and mortality, and health-care utilization (Trevino 1990). Diabetes and obesity are becoming health issues for various Latino groups (Himmelgren, Martinez, and Berry 2002), yet Latino immigrants tend to be healthier than most

Americans, including long time Latino residents. Mexican Americans also have lower rates of cardiovascular disease than Puerto Ricans. Health is attributed to culture, behavior, and lifestyle—specifically, a nutritious diet, physically strenuous work, expanded family for social support, and low alcohol and tobacco use. Latino immigrant women also have the lowest rate of low-birth weight babies, and Mexican Americans have lower infant mortality than Anglo- or African Americans. In Texas, the age-adjusted death rate for Latinos (primarily Mexican Americans) was 420 per 100,000, contrasted with 489 for Anglos (Torrez, A., 1998).

Priorities for health promotion and disease prevention have been identified for urban, rural, and migrant Latinos, including Chicanos, Puerto Ricans, and Cuban Americans (U.S. Department of Health and Human Services 1997; Texas Department of Health 2000). National public health planning emphasizes the need for culturally sensitive, accessible, bilingual health care and prevention, which would involve the local community in participatory research, service planning, implementation, and evaluation. Accessible, culturally appropriate mental health care remains inadequate, as reflected in use of public mental health services (Hu et al. 1991; Everbach 1996).

Socioeconomic, educational, and cultural differences influence health-seeking behavior and self-care. In Latino communities, individual health beliefs and self-care vary in the patterns of decision making whether to seek formal health-system care or use healers and folk treatments for illness. Mexican-American health beliefs and behavior combine modern treatment with folk beliefs and practices (Anderson, Toledo, and Hazam 1982; Finkler 1985; Spector 1996). Some of the folk concepts of related to Mexican-American health beliefs and behavior are hot and cold theory of disease; dietary regimens; cultural syndromes (*empacho, susto, mal de ojo*); beliefs in *brujas* (witches) as causing illness; folk remedies and medicines; use of *curanderos* (spiritualists or holistic healers)

(Trevino 1990); *parteras* for childbirth; religious healing rituals; and attitudes of fatalism, related to culture or poverty and social isolation.

Acculturation and lifestyle changes influence health behavior. Although this is a complex process, the concept of *acculturation* itself is subject to criticism as unilinear and one-dimensional. Concepts such as *cultural consonance* have been recently used to analyze the relationship between lifestyle, social support, and health indicators such as blood pressure (Dressler and Rindon 2000). Research on health risk and behavioral consequences of Mexican-American acculturation and family cohesiveness has pointed to social policy (Balcazar, Peterson, and Krull 1997).

Cultural beliefs, practices, and language use interact with barriers to health care, such as the lack of Spanish-speaking health professionals and the restriction of access due to lack of health insurance, eligibility, or immigrant status. Current system efforts to overcome barriers include training health professionals in cultural sensitivity for patient care and state licensing of paraprofessional *promotores de salud* to serve their communities.

Ethnic Identity and Community
This pilot study on health problems and health-seeking behavior was conducted in an urban, Mexican-American neighborhood in North Texas through a community-oriented primary care project designed to promote integrated, effective preventive and primary care. The project collaborated with private family medicine clinic physicians and nurse practitioners (Lurie and Jones 1990). The study was done prior to the establishment of an area clinic by the county public hospital. The study explored actual and perceived community health needs, sociocultural health beliefs and behavior, and family and social relationships. It was conducted several years before the local health department developed the "Healthy Neighborhoods" and "Community Health Assessment" household surveys in 1998 and 2003 for this city.

This community has its own identity and a dynamic culture that is both similar to and different from traditional Mexican-American culture. The study gathered preliminary information on health practices and priorities of families and their use of health and social services as the context for community empowerment to increase preventive health-seeking behavior. Empowerment was assumed to be correlated with individual control and self-care for prevention associated with life-style change. The informal care system was expected to function as a significant influence on health attitudes and practices through support networks of family, friends, and community members.

Study interviews were to complement previous sociodemographic and morbidity research by nursing students and faculty. Responses from adults in a sample of local households were to be compared. Topics included health-seeking behavior; self-care; accessibility and need for health and social services; family roles; social networks; and perceived neighborhood strengths and weaknesses. Subsequent assessment of older residents' help-seeking behavior found that most were unaware of the availability of local social services (Torrez, D., 1995. It was anticipated that residents varied by place of origin (Massey et al. 1987), length of residence, socioeconomic situations, and needs for health care. Family and social roles (Williams 1990), individual and family life cycles, and lifestyles were proposed to influence and reflect health behavior and participation in community problem-solving. Based on the literature on Mexican-American ethnicity and health-seeking behavior (Kay 1979; Romero 1983), it was expected that although families combined traditional and modern health and mental health providers and practices, the problems for which each was used and sequence of choices, varied within the community.

The residential neighborhood, bounded by the four streets surrounding the clinic, provided a convenient sample of households, although a number of those residents could not be contacted directly. The nineteen households in which interviews were conducted comprised a total of sixty-nine residents. Several respondents were interviewed on their porches; others invited interviewers in to avoid the summer heat. Most residents contacted were willing to be interviewed about their health; two declined, and a man on his way to work made an appointment but did not return home at that time.

Neighborhood streets ranged in appearance from blocks with poorly kept, unpainted frame houses protected by barred windows and doors, ringed by trash or cars in need of repair, to adjacent blocks with well-kept yards, flowers, and frame or brick homes. Separate homes intermingled with garage apartments; a number of children were playing in yards or on the street. Although most respondents liked the neighborhood and considered it safe, there were several reported recent crimes, including homicides. A teenager had been shot playing Russian roulette on a street corner; the son of a respondent was shot in his front yard by someone who followed the young man's girl friend to their home; the friend of another respondent, who lived in the next block, was also shot. One man who kept a loaded gun in every room displayed an unloaded pistol. An elderly woman reported a robbery next door; a young woman's car had been stolen.

Of the Anglos who were interviewed, three had lived in the neighborhood for many years, the longest 44 years; half were natives of the city and owned their own homes. By contrast, Mexican Americans interviewed fell into two groups: families who had lived in the neighborhood from three months to one year, and those who had lived in the same house 15–17 years or more. Origins of Mexican-American respondents ranged from Juarez to Zacatecas to Allende Coahuila. Only two, both female, were primarily Spanish-speaking: one, aged 50+, was a recent immigrant; the second, aged 30+, had lived in the area for fourteen years. One man who grew up in the area had returned there after his father died and remained for 30 years.

Demographics

The majority of households in the sample (thirteen) were single-family, four with one other family member; one household had multiple related families. Individual interviews using a semi-structured questionnaire were conducted with an adult member of each household by two Anglo female researchers with one bilingual male interpreter for respondents who were monolingual in Spanish. One respondent had a friend translate. Of the total, ten Mexican-American and four Anglo respondents were interviewed in depth; partial interviews were done in five additional households. The age range of respondents was 17–87 years. One adolescent working at the neighborhood recreational center politely declined but referred interviewers to his grandmother attending a seniors' program at the center because she had "a lot of health problems." The average age for Mexican-American respondents was younger; Anglos ranged in age from 58 to 87 years (Table 2-1).

Table 2-1. Ethnicity, Gender, Age

Ethnicity and Gender	Age
Mexican-American:	
Male	60+, 30 (2), 18
Female	50, 33, 23, 22, 18, 17 (2)
Anglo:	
Male	87
Female	58, 65, 83

Those Mexican Americans who had resided in the area a considerable length of time tended to be non-Spanish speaking with the exception of a woman who had lived there fourteen years and spoke only Spanish; her mother lived with her and one of her three children, fluent in English, asked the interviewer for a business card while they waited for his mother to return home. Most of the long-term residents reported their parents spoke little Spanish and had no ties to Mexico, except that their families had come from there. In one household of sixteen members (thirteen children), the mother, who spoke no English, said she and her husband had returned to the United States a year ago to stay; none of the young adults spoke English but one was working in a restaurant.

The LACEA Acculturation Scale (Burnam et al. 1987) was administered to eight persons. Scores ranged from 32 to 108, depending on length of residence in the United States, and use of Spanish (see Table 2-2).

Table 2-2. LACEA Acculturation Index

N=8

Age	Years of Residence	Language	Score
60+	35	bilingual	77
50	1	Spanish only	34
33	14	Spanish only	32
30	2	bilingual	42
23	23	English only	108
22	(4 months)	bilingual	70
17	17	English only	97
17	15	English only	88

Major Diseases and Health Concerns

Most respondents perceived themselves as healthy, although this varied with age. Older Anglo respondents reported they did not feel healthy or their health fluctuated: a 65-year-old woman said, "I'm not healthy; one thing goes wrong all the time"; a 58-year old woman said, "It comes and goes with me; in summer, I am big and healthy, winter doesn't agree with me." Major health problems were related to age and family life-cycle. For example, elderly respondents reported more heart problems; younger ones placed priority on children's health services. Chronic health problems among other respondents ranged from ulcers and skin infections to hemophilia of a teen-aged Mexican-American father. Frequently mentioned health problems included dental, vision, children's health problems, injuries, and lack of safety. Thirteen households reported vision problems, injuries, and children's health problems.

Among older respondents in the sample, the majority said they were healthy. However, a 65-year-old Anglo woman had insulin-dependent diabetes, and others reported chronic illnesses or disabilities such as diabetes, emphysema, heart disease, gall bladder, vision, and dental problems. One elderly Mexican American, a retired independent businessman who was partially disabled with serious chronic health problems, was proudly caring for his profoundly retarded adult son. He received assistance from his married daughter following the son's release from a local residential institution for the mentally retarded at the age of 21. The institution was subsequently closed. Health problems within sample households and members' concerns that could have been alleviated by preventive health behavior and care are reported in Table 2-3.

Health-Seeking Behavior
Most respondents tended to seek help when ill rather than as a preventive measure; they thought seeking preventive care was primarily for children. Questions to elicit definitions of health or descriptions of what a person must do to be healthy found a general attitude that health can be improved by individual actions. Eating proper foods was particularly important, although there was an apparent lack of knowledge about other specific activities to promote health. That is, "health" generally meant a healthy diet in contrast with other health promotion and prevention concepts; some responses also included lack of stress and positive social relationships.

The response of a 50-year-old Mexican-American woman who spoke only Spanish revealed a perception that health is integrally tied to behavior, lack of stress, and positive or supportive family and social relationships: "No smoking.

No drinking. Have a peaceful life. *La Familia* is very important. Help each other and have respect for elders. If a young person goes astray, the family can talk to them and bring them back."

Table 2-3. Health Problems and Concerns

N=14 households

Health Problem or Concern	Number with Problem	Percent with Problem
Vision	12	86
Child health	11	78
Injury	9	63
Heart/blood pressure	8	57
Dental	7	50
Weight	7	50
Exercise	7	50
Alcohol	6	42
Nervousness/conditions	6	42
Fatigue	6	42
Allergies/asthma	5	36
Depression	5	36
Pregnancy	5	36
Teen pregnancy	4	28
Diabetes	4	28
Hearing	4	28
Smoking	4	28
Homicide	4	28
Hearing	4	28
High fat diet	3	21
MR/learning problems	2	13
Neurological	2	13
Drugs	2	13

Comparison by ethnicity and language use found similar perceptions of health:

Mexican-Americans

Bilingual

- Decrease stress, take care what you eat, take naps, not have financial problems, have a good attitude.
- Exercise, eat well, and don't smoke. It is a gift.
- Believe it is a gift. Have to eat right, exercise, don't worry.
- Exercise. Lack of worries about job.

Spanish-speaking

- Not being a compulsive eater.

English only

- Feeling good about yourself and eating a good diet.
- Take care of yourself, eat the right foods.
- Eating right and taking care of yourself. Not born with it; have to work and control it.

Anglos

- Fix a nice meal with two-three vegetables daily. Drink milk and juice.
- Gift from the Lord, but need to not do things to mistreat your body.
- Eat a lot of vegetables.

Respondents also reported they engage in a variety of activities to relax, such as watching television, listening to the radio, gardening, or crocheting. None mentioned exercise or socializing for relaxation. Social relationships appeared mainly informal, although bilingual or Spanish-speaking older women were actively engaged in crafts, quilting, and ceramics groups at the neighborhood Seniors' Center. Children and parents participated in Head Start; teenagers participated in recreational and sports activities at the center.

With respect to the social environment, the majority of respondents felt the neighborhood was safe and liked living there, despite their reports of four homicides in the area surrounding the clinic. There was one complaint that neighbors had been recently harassed by immigration officials—this was verified in an interview with a local social service agency director.

Specific preventive health practices to reduce risk of illness or injury were also elicited: most households in which the respondent was a driver reported they use of seat belts "because it's the law." The majority reported that neither they nor anyone else in the household smoked; four persons cited smoking as a concern for a family member.

Regarding pregnancy, two Mexican Americans reported early prenatal care-seeking. However, in two households in which a teenager was or had been pregnant, the mother received late or no prenatal care. A 23-year-old woman said she received prenatal care from the second month on and a prescription for oral contraceptives from Planned Parenthood. She stated that "Women should not drink, smoke, or use drugs when pregnant; they should exercise but not 'overdo,' and be around other people to stay happy and not feel left out." A 22-year-old bilingual woman who had not received prenatal care with her third child expressed similar thoughts: "Women should not smoke, use alcohol or drugs during pregnancy." A 50-year-old Spanish-speaking woman said a member of her household who was two months pregnant had not sought care because she was unsure of available resources and concerned about the cost. One teenaged mother had received care from a private doctor through health insurance her mother, who was a clinic employee, provided.

Self-care practices for illness in this sample were found to be focused on food and eating, as described by several Mexican-American respondents:

"Fruits are best; eat a lot. If you have the flu, give cold fluids like orange juice; if you have chills, give bowls of rice and soft foods." (50-year-old female, Spanish-only)

"When ill, you should orange juice, soup, drink a lot of fluids, and eat a lot of fruit." (23 year-old female, English-only)

"Chicken soups, strained foods when ill; when a child has a temperature, give cold foods and drinks; wash with cold water." (30 year-old male, bilingual)

Healers and Practitioners

Based on anecdotal information from a bilingual Mexican-American family physician that directs another private clinic in the area, the majority of his patients use both traditional and modern medical practices. These include herbal or pharmaceutical products from Mexico, purchased at the local Mexican market held each weekend near his clinic, or on trips to Mexico. Patients tend to reveal these practices when rapport is established with the physician and combine them with treatments he recommends.

When asked about their use of alternative healers during this study, the majority of Mexican-American respondents acknowledged knowing about such practices but said they did not personally believe in them. Only bilingual respondents reported knowledge of alternative healers and several laughed when asked about *curanderas*. Identification of interviewers with the local clinic could have biased responses or contributed to reluctance to reveal such information. For example, an elderly retired businessman replied, "Why do you want to know? They would be in competition with the clinic."

Those who did respond affirmatively reported knowing a local alternative healer who lives in a nearby neighborhood. A 22-year-old bilingual woman, the wife of a recent immigrant who spoke only Spanish, said her husband had visited a *curandera* there for his swollen ankle but the treatment did not help him. Her Mexican-American mother-in-law also treated all their children but the wife did not think this did any good. Another man reported that his mother-in-law treated his children whenever she visited but his son, who had cerebral palsy, used the care system; he had been seen at the city's developmental diagnostic center for children.

Access and Use of Health-Care System

This study was completed prior to the entrance of managed care or the Children's Health Insurance Program into the state or community. The majority of persons interviewed at the time reported members of their households used private doctors and clinics at public and private hospitals. Seven used private doctors; three used the public and/or a private hospital; neither group associated with the local clinic; two used the local and other clinics; one used both the local clinic and hospitals. One Anglo woman used only the local clinic with a specialist from the affiliated hospital. Health problems for which Mexican-American respondents used this clinic in combination with other health-care services included blood pressure checks for seniors and children's health care.

Nine respondents reported they never received checkups when they were not sick; three respondents reported childhood immunizations, vision screening, and dental care. Some said household members had received immunizations, prenatal care, or services for teenage mothers provided at the neighborhood recreational center next to the clinic. Two others used the gym at the center; two seniors said they use center services infrequently.

An unanticipated finding was lack of general familiarity with the local clinic, despite the increase in overall patient visits since the previous year. One 22-year-old Mexican-American mother with two children, who lived two blocks from the clinic, did not know what services were available, but wanted to learn more. The 50-year-old mother of thirteen children was eager to learn about comprehensive, low-cost, convenient services; one of her daughters, who was two months pregnant, needed prenatal care, and services of the Women's, Infants' and Children's (WIC) program.

The largest concern expressed by respondents was cost of care. A 23-year-old mother of three said she preferred the local clinic, but could not afford it. On a recent visit for nervousness, sleeplessness, and somatic complaints, she was told her problems were caused by stress and a tranquilizer was prescribed. Blood and urine analyses were done, and she was asked to pay for them after being interviewed on her financial situation. However, she could not take the tranquilizer because she had to care for two young children and an infant. Her son had been seen at the public hospital for less than one-fifth the cost of a clinic visit, and she was concerned about expense.

Some respondents reported they had tried the local clinic but did not return for various reasons. For elderly persons with chronic illnesses, the decision was influenced by the need for specialized medical services. A diabetic Anglo woman distrusted the medical students at the clinic and always asked for her primary care physician. A 19-year-old Mexican-American woman said she would not return after taking her sick infant to the clinic and was told to come back later. It turned out that the child was diagnosed with meningitis as the public hospital. However, she had used the prenatal care and WIC services available through the health department at the neighborhood center adjoining the clinic.

Socioeconomic Differences in Health-Seeking Behavior
The small sample in the pilot study represents a relatively lower income group in which cost is perceived as a barrier or important consideration in obtaining health care for both adults and children. Anecdotal evidence from a current study on health insurance of Mexican Americans in this community indicates many are undocumented aliens and ineligible for Medicaid or CHIP. This is constant with national data at the time of the pilot study, indicating Latinos were least likely to have employer-sponsored medical insurance and most likely to be uninsured (Seccombe, Clarke, and Coward 1994).

The pilot study included members of at least three population groups in the community distinguished by age, ethnicity, and language use. Older persons in the sample, regardless of ethnicity, who tended to have chronic health problems, were more likely to need care by medical specialists. The need for medical care for older Mexican Americans was confirmed in a later study of 46 elderly clients for a local social service agency. They reported health problems of diabetes, arthritis, vision problems, and high blood pressure (Torrez, D. 1995). Although these older adults were in contact with their children, they were not able to obtain adequate health and social services without assistance by case workers.

The range of variation in education within the sample, indirectly measured by frequency of bilingual language use, is assumed to be associated with diversity in health-seeking behavior. Although this would require further investigation within a larger, stratified sample, it is hypothesized that income and education interact with lifestyle, family, and social networks to determine variations in patterns of health-seeking behavior. In this study, families with members who had recently immigrated to North Texas or had relatives who visited them from Mexico were especially familiar with traditional healers and medications. However, the majority of these families sought formal health care for serious or chronic illness for themselves, their children, and other household members and desired to gain increased access to the health-care system.

Community access to the public hospital outpatient services, medications, and referral to inpatient care has been increased by the opening of an area clinic managed by and linked to that hospital. Planning is underway for a new federal clinic that would serve undocumented Mexican-American patients under newly developed guidelines. Assessment of perceived priority of using such primary care as a component of current health-seeking behavior of Mexican-American families in this and nearby communities is a topic for future research.

28

REFERENCES

Anderson, B., R. Toledo, and N. Hazam. 1982. An approach to the resolution of Mexican-American Resistance to diagnostic and remedial pediatric heart care. In Clinically *Applied Anthropology,* ed. N. Chrisman and T. Maretzki, 325–50. Dordrecht, The Netherlands: D. Reidel.

Balcazar, H., G. Peterson, and J. Krull. 1997. Acculturation and family cohesiveness in Mexican American pregnant women: Social and health implications. *Family and Community Health* 20(3): 16–31.

Burnam, M. A., R. Hough, M. Karno, J. Escobar, C. Telles. 1987. Acculturation and lifetime prevalence of psychiatric disorders among Mexican Americans in Los Angeles. *Journal of Health and Social Behavior* 28(March): 89–102.

_____ Dressler, W., and J. Rindon. 2000. The health consequences of cultural consonance. *American Anthropologist* 102(2): 244–60.

Everbach, T. 1996. MH/MR fails Hispanics, panel finds. *Dallas Morning News.* November 4, sec 17A.

Finkler, K. 1985. Spiritualist healers in Mexico: Successes and failures of Alternative. *Therapeutics.* South Hadley, MA: Bergin and Garvey.

Himmelgren, D., D. Martinez, and B. Berry. 2002. Acculturation and lifestyle changes as factors in obesity among Latino adults. Paper presented at Society for Applied Anthropology Annual Meeting. Atlanta, Georgia.

Hu, T., L. Snowden, J. Jerrell, T. Nguyen. 1991. Ethnic populations in public mental health: Services choice and level of use. *American Journal of Public Health* 81(11): 1429–34.

Kay, M. 1979. Health and illness in a Mexican-American barrio. In *Ethnic medicine in the Southwest,* ed. E. Spicer. Tucson: University of Arizona Press.

Lurie, S. G., and M. E. Jones. 1990. An exploratory study of health beliefs and practices and health care usage by residents in the Northside Clinic service area. Community Partnership Primary Care project preliminary report (unpublished).

Massey, D., R. Alarcon, J. Durand, H. Gonzalez. 1987. *Return to Aztlan: Social process of international migration from western Mexico.* Berkeley: University of California Press.

Murdock, S. 1996. Presentation to the Texas State Legislature. Unpublished report.

Romero, M. 1983. Institutionalization of folk medicine: The mental health profession and *curanderismo*. In *Third world medicine and social change,* ed. J. Morgan. Lanham, MD: University Press of America.

Seccombe, K., L. Clarke, and R. Coward. 1994. Discrepancies in employer-sponsored health insurance among Hispanics, Blacks and Whites: The effects of sociodemographic and employment factors. *Inquiry* 31(Summer): 221–29.

Spector, R. 1996. *Cultural diversity in health and illness.* 4th ed. Stamford, CT: Appleton and Lange.

Texas Department of Health. 2000. *Texas healthy people 2000: Health status indicators by race and ethnicity, 1989–1993.* Bureau of State Health Data and Policy Analysis. Austin, TX.

Torrez, A. 1998. Recent Hispanic immigrants generally are better medically than those who have been in Texas for years, studies show. *Fort Worth Star-Telegram,* Metro., October 14.

Torrez, D. 1995. Health and social service utilization patterns of Mexican American older adults. Unpublished paper.

Trevino, F. 1990. Hispanic health and nutrition examination survey, 1982–84: Findings on health status and health care needs. *American Journal of Public Health* 80(Supplement): 1–72.

U.S. Department of Health and Human Services. 1997. *Developing objectives for healthy people 2010.* Washington, DC: Government Printing Office.

_____2003. *Health,* United States, 2003. Washington, DC: Government Printing Office.

Williams, N. 1990. *The Mexican-American family: Tradition and change.* Dix Hills, NY: General Hall.

3

African Americans and Health

Tyson Gibbs, PhD. Associate Professor, Department of Anthropology, University of North Texas, Denton, Texas.

Introduction

One does not have to look diligently to find studies that demonstrate that African Americans have less access to and less utilization of health care (Elixhauser, Harris, and Doffey 1994; Blendon et al. 1989; Sullivan 1992; Sandman, Simantov, and An 2000; Williams 1999). Moreover, virtually any analysis of health status also indicates a disparity dependent on race (Aday 2001; Healthy People 2000, 1998). As Smith (2000) argues, this disparity in modern U.S. medicine reflects the inequality created by slavery and sustained by such legal decisions as *Plessy v. Ferguson* and the Jim Crow laws. This chapter on African Americans will explore several factors to enhance understanding of the African-American experience of health and health care.

Demographics

According to the most recent release of U.S. Census data (2003), African Americans comprise 12.9 percent of the U.S. population. African-American females make up 52.43 percent of African Americans with African-American males constituting the remaining 47.57 percent (U.S. Census 2000). These figures are closely in line with Whites wherein females comprise 50.90 percent of the population and males comprise 49.10 percent. However, the median age provides more a striking difference. The median age for Whites is 37.3 years whereas the median age for African Americans is 29.5 years (U.S. Census 2000). In addition,

19.3 percent of African-American households are headed by single females (female householder, no husband present, with own children under 18 years) compared to 5.2 percent of the White households (U.S. Census 2000). Approximately one-third of African Americans live below the official poverty line, a rate that is three times the poverty rate for Whites (Spector 2000).

Of all ethnic minority groups, African Americans continue to experience higher residential segregation (U.S. Census 2000). Over 85 percent of African Americans resided in metropolitan areas (U.S. Census 2000). These metropolitan areas are frequently characterized by the associated conditions of poverty: inadequate housing, poor schools, higher crime rates, and inadequate medical facilities (Spector 2000). In addition, African Americans are more likely to be concentrated in the southeastern region of the United States. In some Mississippi counties, for example, African Americans constitute 50 percent or more of the population. As in urban regions, higher rates of poverty, with its attendant social problems, occur in the south (Centers for Disease Control [CDC], conference proceedings, 1998).

Traditional/Folk Healing and Healers
Prior to examining how African Americans access and experience traditional U.S. medicine, we must begin with an understanding of African Americans' perception of health. Studies have shown that members of ethnic groups may have different definitions of health, illness, and health care and beliefs regarding the causes of disease or illness that vary from traditional Western understanding (Wilson and Simson 1991). Understanding these differences in belief systems is fundamental to understanding the difference in experience.

For many Africans, the traditional definition of health revolved around the process of being in harmony with nature, stressing the importance of process over state (Spector 2000). The traditional African healer known as a "conjurer," "sorcerer," "juju man," or "witchdoctor," not only cured with herbs and other plants but also acted as an intermediary with divinities and forces (Mathews 1987). As Africans became enslaved and were brought to what would become the United States, these beliefs became integrated with Christianity. This system of belief has been referred to as rootwork. Rootwork refers to the role of plant roots in disease causation, primarily through magical spells (Mathews 1987; Ness and Wintrob 1981). However, rootwork also recognizes that there is a struggle between good and evil or between God and the Devil. Natural illnesses occur when there is a violation of harmony with either the physical or spiritual world. Unnatural illness occurs when a spell is the cause of illness (Mathews 1987; Snow 1974). Health is about the relationship with the environment, not simply the presence or absence of disease. Therefore, traditional understandings of health do not separate mind, body, and spirit but recognize an interconnection, requiring health-care processes to address all three areas (Spector 2000).

Health-protection activities include a nutritious diet, adequate rest, and prayer (Spector 2000). Home remedies are often used, including the use of turpentine, poultices, and herbs (Spector 2000). The inclusion of prayer is not limited to health protection activities but is included as a primary health maintenance behavior (Spector 2000).

Traditional beliefs regarding health and illness are predicated on a view that the world is a hostile place—with harm potentially coming from nature, fellow human beings, and God or the Devil (Snow 1974).

Access to Health Care
The concept of access to health care is a complex one. What is access? Is access simply a place to go? Some social scientists characterize health care received primarily via hospital emergency room as "access to high quality medical care" (Henderson 1999, 2). Others recognize that there are a variety of components that make up access, including geographical availability, financial resources, transportation, cultural considerations, and competing needs. Aday and others

(1998, 200) frame the discussion of access in terms of equity. "Equity" to be concerned not only with health disparities but also with the fairness and effectiveness of the solutions that are intended to address the problem.

Barriers to care include facility location, transportation, lengthy waiting times, inconvenient office hours, and lack of privacy in facilities (Aday et al. 1998; Airhihenbuwa 1995). African Americans often face barriers to care that Whites do not. These factors include physician refusal to treat indigent or self-paying patients and refusal to treat African Americans (Airhihenbuwa 1995). African-American women are more likely to be the head of a household with children present than are White women, presenting a potential barrier to receiving needed health services (Blendon et al. 1989).

Four out of ten African Americans reported no regular physician in 1997, compared to one in four Whites (Healthy People 2000 1998). African-American children are twice as likely as White children to not have a regular source of care (Healthy People 2000 1998). African Americans have statistically significant lower average annual number of physician visits compared to Whites. This is particularly troubling because African Americans are more likely to experience major and chronic illness (Blendon et al. 1989). African Americans are also more likely to be unable to afford prescribed medications than Whites (Healthy People 2000 1998). Blendon, Scheck and others (1995) reported that 32 percent of African-American respondents indicated that they faced financial difficulties in not only paying for prescriptions but also paying other medical costs, including physician and hospital visits, home health care, and nursing homes, whereas 17 percent of Whites reported such difficulty. African Americans are twice as likely to report not receiving health care for economic reasons than Whites (Blendon et al. 1989). The presence of a serious health condition did not mitigate the disparity. For example, Blendon and others (1989) reported that 30 percent of African Americans diagnosed with hypertension did not have an annual blood pressure check compared with 19 percent of Whites.

Given the current system of health-care delivery in the United States, the most significant structural barrier to access for African Americans is the lack of health insurance (Commonwealth Fund Minority Health Survey 2002). Although minority adults are more likely to be employed than White adults, minority adults are less likely to have health insurance (David 1995). Specifically, in 1995, over 31 percent of minority adults did not have health insurance compared with 14 percent of White adults (Davis 1995). African Americans are not only less likely to be covered by private health insurance, but they are also more likely to reside in states that have the least generous Medicaid programs (Blendon et al. 1989).

In 1979 the U.S. government began a national health policy strategy with the adoption of the Healthy People Report and the establishment of the Office of Health Promotion and Disease Prevention (Aday et al. 1998). This led to the formulation of Healthy People 1990 Objectives and Healthy People 2000 Objectives (Aday et al. 1998). The Healthy People 2010 objectives were eventually added. The Healthy People Review 1995–1996 found that although much improvement had been made toward meeting targeted health goals, major health disparities between minorities and nonminorities persisted (Aday et al. 1998). According to Hayward and others (2000), the health disparities between minorities and nonminorities are so wide that life expectancy estimates for Black Americans is 66 years compared to almost 74 years for White Americans. Moreover, the years lived by Black Americans are more likely to be beset with chronic and/or disabling health conditions (Hayward et al. 2000).

Relationship to Health-care System

Blendon, Scheck and others (1995) reported that 46 percent of African Americans characterized available health services as fair or poor compared to 23 percent of the Whites. In addition, the researchers reported that 42 percent of African Americans believe that the health-care system in this country needs to be completely rebuilt, compared to 31 percent of Whites. African Americans report greater dissatisfaction with the quality of care received than do Whites. Blendon and others (1989) reported that African Americans indicated significantly less satisfaction with inquiries regarding pain, instructions on medications, explanations of test and examination findings, and length of hospitalizations compared to Whites. Interestingly, African Americans were more likely to report satisfaction with the extent of information regarding prevention than Whites.

Institutional discrimination may well play a significant role in the negative characterization of the U.S. health-care system. Byrd (1990) argues that the on-going focus on culture-of-poverty theories or cultural-deficiency theories incorrectly places analysis of disparity on individual characteristics, such as ignorance, noncompliance, and life-style factors, rather than structural deficiency factors such as institutionalized discrimination. Weitz (2003) also suggests looking at structural characteristics for insight into the relationship between ethnic minorities and the health-care system. Link and Phelan (1995, 80) also argue against an overemphasis on individually based risk factors and argue for analysis of what puts individuals at risk of risks and at the socioeconomic cause of disease.

Socioeconomic Differences in Health Behavior
Blendon and others (1989) conducted a national survey regarding access to health care for African Americans and Whites. This study demonstrated that across all income levels there was a significant gap in access between African Americans and Whites. Moreover, when the researchers controlled for income, health status, age, sex, and presence of one or more chronic illnesses, a statistically significant difference in mean number of ambulatory visits was reported. The same study reported, again controlling for income, that African Americans were less likely to have seen a physician during the previous year.

Otten and others (1990) demonstrated that African Americans had a significantly higher mortality rate compared to Whites. Controlling for life-style factors (e.g., alcohol consumption, smoking) and other risk factors (e.g., cholesterol level, diabetes), the authors concluded that low income accounts for 54 percent of excess mortality of African Americans (Otten et al. 1990).

Hayward and others (2000) confirmed the importance of socioeconomic status in explaining the racial gap in chronic health conditions. They found that health stratification originates not in personal health risk behaviors but in socioeconomic conditions. Moreover, they found no significant difference in African Americans' ability to transform socioeconomic resources into health resources.

Illness and Disease Affecting African Americans

In 1990, Congress passed the Disadvantaged Minority Health Improvement Act, acknowledging that racial and ethnic minorities' health status is significantly lower than that of the general U.S. population. Moreover, Congress recognized that racial and ethnic minorities suffer disproportionately higher rates of major chronic illnesses, infant mortality, and other diseases and disorders (Pickney 2000). In 1998, President Clinton announced an initiative with the goal of eliminating health disparities between racial/ethnic minorities and Whites by 2010 (U.S. Department of Health and Human Services 1998). Six key areas were identified: cancer, cardiovascular disease, immunizations, diabetes, HIV/AIDS, and infant mortality. In a 1998 update of Healthy People 2000, it was reported that progress toward the goals for breast cancer deaths, tuberculosis, early prenatal care, syphilis infection, and some vaccinations for African Americans was moving too slowly to meet the goal. Moreover, it was reported that goals for asthma, maternal mortality, diabetes related deaths, end stage renal disease, lower extremity amputations, and HIV/AIDS were not only not going to be met, the rates were actually increasing (Healthy People 2000 1998). Although African Americans have, overall, experienced an improvement in their health status, a disparity continues to exist in their overrepresentation in morbidity and mortality rates for major chronic illnesses (Pickney 2000).

38

Conclusion

Racial stratification and the requisite supportive ideology can be seen in every segment of U.S. life—and the structure of health care is certainly no exception. Link and Phelan (1995) describe socioeconomic stratification as the social cause for disease. Socioeconomic stratification affects "stress, social ties, diet and health-risk behaviors, the nature of work and the work environment, and the availability of health care" (Hayward et al. 2000, 913).

Adding to the complexity of research into health disparities is methodological. Andersen, Mullner, and Cornelius (1994) found that African Americans show greater health deficits when the mode of measurement was objective—such as observation, clinical examinations, mortality rates and health provider records; self-reports of illness tended to indicate that African Americans were relatively well-off as compared to Whites (Andersen, Mullner, and Cornelius 1994). The concern here is that reliance on self-reports may actually underestimate the disparity of health outcomes.

REFERENCES

Aday, L. A. 2001. *At risk in America.* San Francisco: Jossey-Bass.

Aday, L. A., C. E. Begley, D. R. Lairson, and C. H. Slater. 1998. *Evaluating the healthcare system.* Chicago: Health Administration Press.

Airhihenbuwa, C. O. 1995. *Health and culture: Beyond the Western paradigm.* Thousand Oaks, CA: Sage.

Andersen, R. M., R. M. Mullner, and L. J. Cornelius. 1994. *Black-White differences in health status: Methods or substance:* In *Health Policies and Black Americans,* ed. David Willis. New Brunswick, NJ: Transaction.

Blendon, R. J.and A. C. Scheck 1995. How White and African Americans view their health and social problems. *Journal of the American Medical Association* 273(4): 341–46.

Blendon, R. J., L. H. Aiken, H. E. Freeman, and C. R. Corey. 1989. Access to medical care for Black and White Americans: A matter of continuing concern. *Journal of the American Medical Association* 261(2): 278–81.

Byrd, W. M. 1990. Race, biology, and health care: Reassessing a relationship. *Journal of Health Care for the Poor and Underserved* 1(3): 278–96.

Centers for Disease Control. 1998. Conference Proceedings. Office of Minority Health.. Atlanta, Georgia. Centers for Disease Control.

Commonwealth Fund Minority Health Survey. 2002 .Princeton Survey Research Associates. Methodology: Survey on Disparities in Health Care Quality: Spring 2001. Princeton, NJ: Princeton University Publishing.

Davis, JG . 1995. Minority Adults and Life Insurance. *Life/Health/Financial Services* 99(14): 58.

Elixhauser, A., R. Harris, and R. Coffey. 1994. Trends in hospital procedures performed on Black patients and White patients, 1980–1987. *Agency for Health Care Policy and Research Publications* No. 94–0003, Provider studies research note 20. Rockville, MD: Public Health Service.

Hayward, M. D., E. M. Crimmins et al. 2000. The significance of socioeconomic status in explaining the racial gap in chronic health conditions. *American Sociological Review* 65: 910–30.

Healthy People 2000, 1998. Hyattsville, MD: National Center for Health Statistics.

Henderson, J. 1999. *Health economics and policy.* Cincinnati, OH: South-Western College Publishing.

Link, B. G., and J. Phelan. 1995. Social conditions as fundamental causes of disease. *Journal of Health and Social Behavior* (Extra issue): 80–94.

Mathews, H. 1987. Rootwork: Description of an ethnomedical system in the American South. *Southern Medical Journal* 8 (7): 885–91.

Ness, R., and R. Wintrob. 1981. Folk healing: A description and synthesis. *American Journal of Psychiatry* 138(11): 1477–81.

Otten, M. C.and S. M. Teutsch . 1990. The effect of known risk factors on the excess mortality of black adults in the United States. *Journal of the American Medical Association* 263: 845–50.

Pickney, A. 2000. *Black Americans.* 5th ed. Upper Saddle River, NJ: Prentice-Hall.

Sandman, D., E. Simantov, and C. An. 2000. Out of touch: American men and the health care system." *Commonwealth Fund Men's and Women's Health Survey Finding.*

Smith, G. D. 2000. Learning to live with complexity: Ethnicity, socioeconomic position, and health care in Britain and the United States. *American Journal of Public Health* 90(11): 1694–98.

Snow, L. F. 1974. folk medical beliefs and their implication for care of patients: A review based on studies among Black Americans. *Annals of Internal Medicine* 81: 82–96.

Spector, R. E. 2000. *Cultural diversity in health and illness.* 5th ed. Upper Saddle River, NJ: Prentice-Hall.

Sullivan, L. 1992. Foreword. In *Health issues in the black community,* ed. R. Braithwaite and S. Taylor. San Francisco: Jossey-Bass.

U.S. Bureau of the Census. 2000. *Statistical abstract of the United States.* Washington, DC: Government Printing Office.

U.S. Bureau of the Census. 2003. *Statistical abstract of the United States.* Washington, DC: Government Printing Office.

U.S. Department of Health and Human Services. 1998. Eliminating racial and ethnic disparities in health. Grant Makers in Health. Conference Proceedings. Washington, DC. Government Printing Office.

Weitz, Rose. 2003. *The sociology of health, illness and health care.* Belmont, CA: Wadsworth/Thomson Learning.

Williams, D. 1999. Race, socioeconomic status and health: The added effects of racism and discrimination. *Annals of the New York Academy of Sciences* 896: 173–88.

Wilson, L. B., and S. P. Simson. 1991. Planning minority health programs to eliminate health status disparity. *Evaluation and Program Planning* 14: 211–

4

Cultural Aspects of Health-Seeking Behavior for the African Population in Katutura, Namibia

Debie LeBeau, PhD. Senior Researcher, University of Namibia, Africa.

Introduction

The focus of this chapter is health-seeking behavior in Katutura, the large African settlement located approximately five kilometers northwest of Windhoek's Central Business District (CBD).[1] The chapter will focus on health-seeking behavior and a model for the hierarchy of resort between Western and traditional medicine for the four main ethnic groups living in Katutura, as well as factors that influence urban patients' traditional health-care utilization.[2]

Research on health-care utilization patterns was undertaken in an urban setting (Katutura) due to the availability of both Western and traditional health-care options.[3] In addition to diverse Western and traditional medical practitioners, there is a wide variety of other health-care alternatives such as self-medication,

---

[1] The term "African" refers to the Black indigenous African population. Although it is recognized that this term can be used to identify white persons who have been born on the African continent, it is felt that the term "Black" was used under the apartheid regime and still carries a racist connotation.

[2] Although it is recognized that the rural/urban dichotomy is simplistic in that there is a web of interrelationships and a gradation in population attributes between the two, this dichotomy is used for the sake of convention.

[3] Many healers involved in the research are not "traditional" in that they practice faith healing. It is acknowledged that the concept of "tradition" is problematic in that it can be misunderstood to mean a static, precolonial set of attitudes and practices (Barfield 1997, 470). However, the word "traditional" in this chapter is not meant as a static term to describe precolonial practices, but to describe a paradigm of beliefs and practices based on culture.

health care from friends and relatives, and various homeopathic remedies. Given that all types of health care are available in Katutura, the utilization of traditional medicine represents a conscious choice by patients and is not due to the lack of other alternatives. The use of traditional medicine can, therefore, be attributed to social, cultural, and personal factors such as ideology rather than access, cost, and distance to modern health-care facilities that has been assumed by rural researchers of traditional medicine (Good 1996, 12; Slikkerveer 1982, 1859).

The focus of this research is cross-cultural in that part of the analysis examines differences in traditional beliefs, which influence health-care use patterns by the four main ethnic groups that live in Katutura. However, the analysis is presented in a relatively dualistic manner based on Western and traditional health-care beliefs and behaviors. This dualism is necessary due to the co-existing ideologies upon which these two health-care systems are based. For both the patient and the healer, the gap between Western and traditional medicine is far greater than the gap between the various ethnic groups' traditional health practices. There is what can best be described as a general African paradigm that categorizes causes of illness in much the same way. In Katutura, where there is significant mixing of these four ethnic groups, there has also been a great deal of mixing and borrowing in order to consolidate traditional health beliefs and practices. Patients in Katutura exhibit cross-cultural health-seeking behavior, which makes a wider range of treatment options available.

Participant observations with several different traditional healers over a two-year period (1996–1998) form the primary basis for the analysis.[4]

---

[4] It is necessary to introduce some of the cast of characters for the forthcoming discussion. Katrina is a Nama/Damara/Sothu herbalist and spirit medium; Fillipus is an Owambo herbalist and spirit medium; Fanuel is a Herero herbalist and spirit medium; Aline is a Herero faith healer and herbalist; Selma is a Damara/Herero faith healer, herbalist and spirit medium; Tara is a Xhosa/Zulu sangoma; "Dr." Michael is a Nyanja herbalist; from Tanzania and "Dr." Toni is a Zulu sangoma. Some traditional healers in Namibia use the title "Dr." (doctor) when referring to themselves, whereas other healers do not consider this term appropriate. Although not technically correct, the term is used to refer to those healers who refer to themselves in such a manner. This

Quantitative research in the form of a questionnaire was conducted within the Katutura population with a stratified systematic sample of 377 respondents in order to provide important supplemental health beliefs and practices data.[5] The use of a combination of qualitative and quantitative research methods is deemed appropriate for this study, given the complex yet sensitive nature of the topic under consideration.

Historical Background

Namibia, commonly known as South West Africa until independence in 1990, lies on the southwestern part of Africa, and covers an area of 824,269 square kilometers. It is bound by two major deserts. The Namib Desert is found along the west coast of Namibia and the Kalahari Desert is along the southern and central-eastern border between Namibia and Botswana. The Namib and the Kalahari deserts cover 22 percent of Namibia's total land area. Namibia shares its borders with Angola and Zambia to the north, South Africa to the south, Botswana to the east and the Atlantic Ocean to the west (Department of Women Affairs [DWA] 1995, 1).

Political History

The first Europeans to come to Namibia were travelers and missionaries. Many of these early explorers published accounts that described the "native tribes" they encountered (Vedder 1966; Andersson 1856). Much of the early ethnographic accounts can be attributed to these writings. Many of the first missionary stations in Namibia were built at the time of first colonial contact and often consisted of a

---

practice has been given several explanations of its origins. Some healers claim that it means "traditional doctor," other say they also doctor (treat) patients and still others have a certificate issued by an alleged African Traditional Doctors' Association which states that the bearer has the right to use the title "Dr." or "doctor."

[5] These data are referred to as the 1996 Tradition and Health Survey (THS). For the purpose of clarification, the conventional use of "informant" to indicate a person involved in qualitative research and "respondent" for persons participating in quantitative research will be used.

church and school, as well as hospital or clinic (Green 1962). Due to these early missionary influences, contemporary Namibia has a high percentage of Christians.

Namibia was colonized by Germany in 1884. German colonial rule lasted until 1915 when its government was defeated by an army from the Union of South Africa during World War I. In 1918, the League of Nations assigned Namibia to South Africa as a Class C mandate, which required that Namibia be administered in a manner that promoted the social, material, and moral well-being of its inhabitants (Katjavivi 1988, 13).

In 1945, the United Nations succeeded the League of Nations that requested South Africa to place Namibia under its trusteeship. Instead, South Africa refused and introduced apartheid policy into the country. As in South Africa, the basis of apartheid policy was the appropriation of African land for White settlers through forced removals and the confinement of Africans to small reserves commonly called "homelands." In addition, Africans were denied political rights, whereas professional employment opportunities were reserved mainly for White people. This land policy was the basis of a colonial economy that hinged on the Contract Labor System[6] and the underdevelopment of family-based subsistence agriculture in African settlements. Under this system, the role of the "homelands" economy and the contract labor system was to supplement the wages of workers, support them during old age and sickness and sustain the conditions necessary for the reproduction of a cheap labor force (DWA 1995, 1).

After a prolonged guerilla war lasting nearly thirty years and an intensive diplomatic campaign by the United Nations Security Council a peaceful

---

[6] The notorious Contract Labor System under apartheid recruited males from the rural areas who temporarily migrated for contract employment to the "white" areas. Africans were forced to stay on "native reserves" (homelands) unless contracted to work elsewhere. The pass system prevented women from traveling and living with their husbands who were contracted to work in the "white" areas (Hishongwa 1992, 60).

settlement in Namibia was negotiated. Namibia officially became an independent country on March 21, 1990, after more than 100 years of colonization.

Health and Health-Care History

Namibia's history has been one of suppression, discrimination, and disenfranchisement of African populations, which severely affected their health. Namibia's long periods of colonial rule and subsequent unequal development in health-care services led to health problems in the African population. These influences include inadequate health care, as well as unhygienic living conditions with a lack of proper housing, sanitation, and limited access to potable water.

In Namibia, colonial health-care provisions were racially based and urban centered (Indongo 1984, 1). In addition, medically sophisticated technologies were primarily reserved for the Whites, further inhibiting African health-seeking behavior (LeBeau and Marais 1997, 91). Health care was almost exclusively curative in nature and only marginally offered Africans preventative health-care measures such as childhood immunizations.

Under colonial rule many Western health facilities were run by missionary organizations. Many missionary run facilities offered better health care than that of the colonial facilities; however, they also offered competing ideologies. Many users of the missionary health facilities in Namibia were either compelled out of necessity or pressured to convert to the religion offered by the local missionaries. In Africa, including Namibia, missionaries offered health care and education, primarily for the purpose of religious conversion.

The 1989 Namibian Demographic and Health Survey (NDHS) found a correlation between high infant mortality and unavailability of infrastructural support such as hygienic toilets, potable water, and electricity (Rossouw and Van Tonder 1989, 7–8). A dependable source of potable water and hygienic sanitation is essential for the maintenance of good health. The water supply in Katutura is erratic and often polluted. Some households must fetch water from distant sources; thus, a variety of water sources must be utilized (LeBeau and Pendleton 1993, 12). Prior to independence, about one-half of all Namibians did not have access to potable water and hygienic sanitation (Department of National Health and Welfare [DNHW] 1989, 8). Statistics at independence indicate that 47 percent of Namibian households had access to potable water and only 23 percent had hygienic sanitation (World Health Organization [WHO] 1990). With independence, one of the Namibian government's priority areas has been the improvement of Western health care for sectors of the Namibian population that had previously been marginalized. Namibia adopted policies and practices meant to address matters such as the transformation of Namibia's Western medical system from an urban-based, curative focus to a community-based preventative focus (LeBeau and Marais 1997, 94). Other policies adopted by the new Ministry of Health and Social Services (MoHSS) include providing all communities with affordable and appropriate health-care programs that target the rural African populations, capacity building at the national level for more effective health-care planning, and the implementation of programs specifically directed at woman and child health (Ministry of Health and Social Services [MoHSS] 1993[NOTE: It is 1993]). Since independence the MoHSS has attempted to address many of the Western health-care provision problems. However, the lack of adequate Western health care has had a direct impact on health-seeking behavior within Katutura's African population. The impact of previous colonial and missionary intervention has, to some extent, continued to influence health and health care in Namibia. An inferior form of Western medicine, as well as its inability to address the spiritual aspects of health care, has caused many people to continue to use traditional African medicine.

Ethnic Identity and Definitions
Namibia has a total population of about 1.8 million people, with over a dozen language groups and both Bantu and non-Bantu click languages spoken, as well as European derived languages such as English, Afrikaans, and German (DWA

1995, 119). The five most commonly spoken languages in Namibia are Oshiwambo (51%), Khoekhoegowab (Nama/Damara 13%), Rukavango (9%), Afrikaans (9%), and Otjiherero (8%) (CSO 1994, 10).[7]

The most numerous and geographically widespread ethnic groups in Namibia are the Nama, Damara, Herero, and Owambo, who together make up over 90 percent of the population in Katutura (Frayne 1992, 154–55).[8] The other African ethnic groups of Namibia, the Lozi (Mafwe and Basubia from the Caprivi), Kavango (five related groups), San (eight distinct groups), Tswana, and Ovahimba (ethnically related to the Herero), but are only marginally represented in Katutura. There is also a small population of foreign Africans living in Katutura, although they rarely appear in official statistics because they are for the most part illegally residing in Namibia. Given their numeric majority in Katutura, this discussion will concentrate on the Owambo, Herero, Nama, and Damara.

Geographic Location and Community

Katutura was built in the 1950s as part of a resettlement program aimed at removing the African population from the Old Location to Katutura.[9] There have been three temporal and spatial phases in Katutura's development. The first section of Katutura, frequently referred to as the "old section" (or "old Katutura"), is the original area developed for people relocated from the Old Location. This section consists mostly of four-room cinder block houses with water taps and pit

---

[7] People who are ethnically Damara or Nama speak variants of what is popularly termed the "Nama/Damara" language; however, the official name of the language is "Khoekhoegowab" (Haacke and Eiseb 1999. The Owambo are a set of ethnically related communities who speak Oshiwambo and the Herero are ethnically related people who speak Otjiherero.

[8] Ethnicity is defined here as a group of people who have come to accept a common identity based on similar values, beliefs, history and language (LeBeau 1991, 3).

[9] The "Old Location" was the original area where Africans lived when they first moved to the Windhoek area. However, in the 1950s the apartheid government decided to build a new African location (Katutura) further from Windhoek because it was felt that the African population was living too close to the Whites, and under apartheid policy this situation was deemed unacceptable.

48

latrines located outside of the house but on the property. The old section of Katutura was stratified into subsections for residents according to their ethnicity. The second development phase of Katutura occurred in the 1970s and took place mostly in a suburb designed to house the more affluent African population without ethnic subdivisions. Houses in this area are substantially better than in the old section, given that they are larger and usually have water taps and toilets inside the building. The third phase of development began approximately at independence in Hakahana, Okuryangava, Goreangab, and Big Bend. These areas consist of National Housing Enterprise (NHE) (government-sponsored) houses, self-built houses, and shanty houses (informal structures without electricity, water, and toilets) on site-and-service plots. Although the NHE has tried to provide housing to all the people who move to Katutura, immigration has been too rapid and the municipality has only been able to provide a plot of land and communal water taps to most people living in the shanty sections. When one visits these sprawling shanty areas the smell of open sewers, wood burning fires, and dust fill the air. There are no streetlights, household cooking is done with small wood burning fires, and candles provide household lighting. Toilets and bathing facilities are self-built and usually consist of four sticks pounded into the ground with black plastic or cardboard wrapped around for privacy. However, there is usually no pit or any means for disposing of human waste.

Migration Patterns
As previously mentioned, one of the major focuses of German colonization and South African apartheid was the recruitment of White settlers to occupy African-owned land (Hishongwa 1992, 6). The loss of land due to White occupation and the defeat of the Herero and Nama by the German occupying forces caused many Africans to move to the Old Location in Windhoek (5–6). The Damara were the first to move to Windhoek in the mid-1890s to escape the German War.[10] Most

---

[10] Germany waged a war against the Herereo and the Nama with the stated purpose of exterminating everyone from these ethnic groups.

Owambo migration to the towns was due to the aforementioned contract labor system (52). However, due to South Africa's extension of apartheid policies to Namibia, urban migration was limited until the 1980s when apartheid regulations were being abolished. Katutura has experienced considerable growth since the 1980s, primarily due to labor migration from the rural areas. However, the rate of immigration has increased substantially since independence.

Currently, immigration is the most significant transformational factor influencing the structure and composition of Katutura's population (Iipinge and LeBeau 1997, 23–24). The overall population growth rate for Namibia is 3.1 percent, whereas the population growth rate for Katutura is approximately 6 percent per annum (Tvedten and Mupotola 1995, 9). This differential growth rate is due solely to immigration. Migrants to Katutura tend to be young men looking for work and the amenities of the city. However, recent data indicate that women are also beginning to migrate to Katutura for the same reasons. The impact of immigration on Katutura's demography is reflected in the 1996 THS with 61 percent of those interviewed saying that they grew up in the rural areas, whereas only 14 percent grew up in Windhoek. About one-half of the population has moved to Katutura within the first ten years after independence. Again, as is consistent with other research findings, 92 percent of the THS population has family in the rural areas that they visit. These data indicate that immigration is not unidirectional from rural areas to Katutura but is cyclical in nature with migrants sending money home to their rural families and visiting them during holidays. In turn, rural families come to stay with their Katutura relatives when there is the need to use Windhoek's amenities, such as medical services and schools. There is a substantial support network between Katutura residents and their rural families linked by a web of relationships that can be called upon in times of need. It is important to note that recent migrants with links to the rural areas are more likely to participate in traditional health care than "town" people.

Demographics

Katutura's population density is much higher than the rest of the Greater Windhoek area (Tvedten & Mupotola 1995, 5).[11] The population of the Greater Windhoek area is estimated to be 200,000, of which 60 percent reside in Katutura (7). The average household size for Katutura is 5.7 people; the rest of the Greater Windhoek area has an average household size of 3.4 people (CSO 1996, 209). About 12 percent of the households in Katutura cook without electricity or gas, 17 percent light their houses without electricity, and about 1 percent have no toilet and no piped water within a five-minute walk of their domicile (226). However, given the municipality's inability to keep up with high rates of immigration, shanty houses have the highest rate of increase in Katutura. It is estimated that between 25,000 to 30,000 people live in informal settlement areas and shanty dwellings in Katutura (Tvedten and Mupotola 1995, 12). Given that Katutura's population is estimated at 120,000, these data indicate that about 25 percent of Katutura's people live in substandard shanty conditions.

Katutura residents have a socioeconomic status substantially lower than the rest of the Greater Windhoek area (Frayne 1992, 5). It has a much higher unemployment rate (32%) than the rest of Greater Windhoek (7%) (CSO 1996, 221). Moreover, the per capita average annual income in Katutura is N$4,300, compared to the rest of Greater Windhoek, which has an annual per capita income of N$27,000 (CSO 1996, 229).[12] The 1996 THS data indicate that about 37 percent of the people make less than N$1,000 per month, 39 percent earn from N$1,000 to N$2,000 per month and 24 percent of the people earn more than N$2,000 per month.

---

[11] The term "Greater Windhoek area" refers to all of the suburbs that were previously classified as "white" areas, Khomasdal which was the previous "coloured" area and Katutura, as well as all new subdivisions that have come into existence since independence.

[12] October 2002, the exchange rate is N$6.3 (Namibian Dollars) to US$1 (U.S. Dollar).

The population in Katutura is somewhat younger than the rest of the Greater Windhoek area (CSO 1996, 209). About one-third of the Katutura population is under 15 years of age (216). There is also a gender imbalance in that Katutura characterized by a large and growing population (Frayne 1992, 10). There are more men (53%) than women (47%) in Katutura, reflecting male immigration patterns (Tvedten and Mupotola 1995, 10). However, the 1996 THS, which only surveyed spouses and heads of households, has 57 percent women and 43 percent men with about one-fourth under 30 years of age and an additional 50 percent between the ages of 30 and 43 years old. Thus, the 1996 THS population is older and more likely to be female in keeping with the age/sex distribution of the adult population rather than the general Katutura population (Frayne 1992, 154). As is common throughout the world, there is a higher attrition rate for young men in Katutura, who tend to participate in social and health risk-taking behaviors.[13]

The THS indicates that 64 percent of respondents are the head of the house and 36 percent are spouses of the head of the house. Of these households, 12 percent are headed by males, 22 percent are female-headed, and 32 percent are traditional African extended families. About one-third of the survey population is married, one-third is living together, and just under one-third are not married. About 8 percent of the 1996 THS population has no education, one-third has a primary education, and 60 percent have secondary or higher education.

Religion is an important factor in the daily lives of Katutura's people and has a significant impact on traditional beliefs and behaviors: some Christian sects have forbidden (upon threat of excommunication) the use of traditional healers. Although this dictate is difficult to enforce, it does have a psychological impact

---

[13] The sample population for the 1996 THS also over-represents women due to purposeful selection criteria. Adults older than 16 years of age who were either the head of the house (whether male or female) or the spouse of the head were selected because they are more likely to make health care decisions for their families. Thus, women had the ability to be selected as either the head of the household or the spouse of the head, whereas men are only represented as heads of the household, because in Namibia a man is not considered the spouse of a household head.

on parishioners' use of traditional medicine. The 1996 THS data indicates that over one-half of respondents are Lutheran, 15 percent are Roman Catholic, 7 percent are Anglican, and about 9 percent of the population is affiliated with indigenous churches such as Oruwano or Apostolic.[14]

The preceding demographic indicators paint a picture of Katutura as a place with high percentages of young, unemployed, and undereducated people. Many of these young people are recent arrivals from the rural areas in search of money, jobs, and the amenities of the city. Due to substantial immigration from the rural areas, as many as 30,000 people live in overcrowded, unhealthy conditions in Katutura, a situation which has serious repercussions on their health and health-seeking behavior.

Major Diseases

The leading cause of adult mortality in Namibia is AIDS. In 1997, 18.6 percent of all deaths were attributed to AIDS. Tuberculosis (TB) (10.2%) and malaria (8.7%) are also major causes of adult mortality (United Nations Development Program [UNDP] 1998, 126). In 1997 the Greater Windhoek area had the highest number of new HIV-positive cases and the fifth highest prevalence rate (16%) for HIV-positive pregnant women for all of Namibia (UNDP 1998, 127; UNDP 1997, 34). Katutura has been "hard hit" by the AIDS pandemic: "We are burying 10–20 people every weekend in Katutura. The cemeteries are filling up. At the Katutura Cemetery on the weekend it is chaos because there are so many funeral services at the same time" (Tom Agnes, AIDS counselor, quoted in United Nations Joint Program on HIV/AIDS [UNAIDS] 1998, 3). There are few families in Katutura who have not experienced the death of a family member due to AIDS. Katutura

---

[14] In southern Africa many Christian-based independent churches ("indigenous churches"), broke away from missionary and Christian churches. Although some indigenous churches denounce traditional healers as "demonic," some indigenous churches incorporated traditional aspects of healing into their ceremonies (Dillon-Malone 1988, 1160).

already has many AIDS orphans and AIDS babies (MoHSS 1998, 6).[15] In addition to its social impact, AIDS is having a significant impact on the state hospitals: "the number of HIV related admissions has grown from approximately ten inpatients at any point in time, to over forty at present. We have at least one HIV-related death every 24 hours. . . . It's a tremendous burden on both hospitals in Windhoek" (Dr. David Uirab, Medical Superintendent of Katutura State Hospital, quoted in UNAIDS 1998, 5, 17).

In addition to AIDS, alcohol abuse is a leading contributing factor to adult morbidity and mortality within the Katutura population. A significant proportion of people in Katutura consume alcohol, mostly over weekends and on paydays, with expenditures on alcohol taking up a large proportion of household finances (CSO 1996, 232). Many health providers working at the Katutura State Hospital have identified alcohol-related illnesses (e.g., liver disease) and alcohol-related injuries (e.g., gunshot and stab wounds) as taking up a significant portion of the hospital's financial and healing energies. For example, one male patient admitted with a nonfatal upper-torso stab wound costs the hospital approximately N$3,000 and takes up a hospital bed for five to seven days. In addition, alcohol has been found to be a significant contributing factor to the incidence of domestic violence and the spread of HIV, which also absorbs state resources.

In general, the people of Katutura are healthier than those in many of Namibia's rural areas; however, health indicators suggest that they are less healthy than the rest of their Greater Windhoek counterparts. Women who responded to the 1992 Namibia Demographic and Health Survey (NDHS) were asked about their experience of childbirth and maternal health. Katutura women who gave birth were less likely to be attended by a doctor than the rest of the women in Greater Windhoek. In addition, women in Katutura experienced many more complications during labor and delivery such as bleeding, high fevers,

---

[15] Children whose parents have died of AIDS but are HIV-negative are "AIDS orphans," whereas HIV-positive infants are termed "AIDS babies."

convulsions, and extended labor. Children born to mothers from Katutura had lower average birth weights than children born in the rest of Greater Windhoek. Overall, immunization rates for all children were high for first vaccinations, but rates for second and third vaccinations declined for Katutura children, which resulted in fewer children being fully immunized in Katutura than in the rest of Greater Windhoek.

For children, the leading causes of mortality nationwide are prematurity, pneumonia (Acute Respiratory Infection [ARI]), malaria, and AIDS. In addition, dehydration from diarrhea is a significant co-indicator for infant and child deaths (UNDP 1997, 37; MoHSS 1993, 75). Rates of childhood deaths were lower in Katutura than in the rural areas. A 1990 Household Health and Nutrition Survey (HHNS) found infant mortality rates were significantly lower in Katutura (43 per 1,000 live births versus 70 in the northern more rural areas) (Tvedten and Mupotola 1995, 13). However, infant and under-5 childhood deaths were higher in Katutura than in the rest of the Greater Windhoek area. In Katutura, childhood mortality is less likely to occur due to malnutrition and malaria than in the rural areas, but again, diarrheal disease is a significant contributing factor in morbidity and mortality for Katutura's under-5 population. Children in Katutura are significantly more likely to experience severe diarrhea, diarrhea of long duration, and diarrhea with blood in the stool. Children in Katutura also experienced slightly higher incidence rates of measles, coughs and colds, shortness of breath, and other minor ailments than children in the rest of the Greater Windhoek area. The majority of Katutura children experienced coughs (possibly ARI) for an average duration of eight days and diarrhea for an average of five days. These averages were several days longer than children in the rest of Greater Windhoek. In addition to experiencing poorer health than the rest of their Greater Windhoek counterparts, Katutura children who had anthropometrical measurements taken as part of the 1992 NDHS were on the average shorter, weighed less, and had smaller mid-upper–arm circumferences than children in the rest of the Greater

Windhoek area. These data show that children in Katutura were more likely to have low height-for-age (an indication of stunting) as well as low weight-for-age and low weight-for-height (indicating acute and chronic under-nutrition, respectively).

The overall health picture that emerges from the preceding discussion indicates that although residents of Katutura have lower morbidity and mortality rates than their rural counterparts, their overall health status is worse than the rest of the population in Greater Windhoek. The leading causes of adult mortality in Katutura are AIDS and tuberculosis; alcohol and violence are contributing factors to morbidity and mortality.

Culture and Language

Based on the 1996 THS, the Owambo comprise about 57 percent of the Katutura population. The Owambo traditionally[16] are the most economically diverse of the Namibian ethnic groups, raising cattle and cultivating crops (Malan 1995, 24–25).[17] The Herero constitute about 15 percent of the Katutura population and are traditional cattle pastoralists. The Damara precolonially were hunters and gatherers but have always kept some small livestock whenever possible and make up about 15 percent of the Katutura population. The Nama, who have always kept goats and sheep, constitute approximately 6 percent of the Katutura population.

The Owambo[18]

The Owambo have a matrilineal descent system whereby a mother's brothers are responsible for the well-being of her children (Becker 1993, 63). Although still

---

[16] The term "traditional" refers to those attitudes and practices that are handed down from generation to generation, are embedded in cultural beliefs and derived from the history of the ethnic group, whereas the term "precolonial" is used in this text to describe traditional practices that have been extinguished or changed significantly due to colonial contact.

[17] Although all ethnic groups in Namibia are incorporated to a greater or lesser extent into the global capitalist system, traditional subsistence activities are still carried out in the rural areas.

[18] Differences in Oshiwambo terms in the text represent variations in sublanguage orthographies.

practiced, this social arrangement is slowly changing, especially in Katutura where fathers are taking more financial and disciplinary responsibilities for their children. Traditionally the Owambo live in northern Namibia between the Etosha Pan and Angola in what was formerly known as "Ovamboland."[19] The Owambo did not face relocation during the colonial period due to the remoteness of their traditional lands (Wellington 1967, 141–42). However, due to participation in the contract labor system, Owambo people can be found throughout Namibia, including Katutura. Today, many Owambo still migrate to towns and mines in search of employment.

The Owambo believe that the spirits of the dead (*aathithi*) roam the earth. These ancestor spirits can be either good or evil. Evil spirits are those that come out at night (*omukwamhungu*), whereas good spirits are those that are around during the day (Vedder 1966, 75; Tönjes 1996, 181). Ancestor spirits usually affect a close friend or relative of the deceased and are easily appeased with small animal sacrifices and traditional ceremonies (Möller 1974, 133). However, a more feared spirit is that from a living being (*owanga*), which comes from a witch (*omulodhi* or *omulodi*) and can cause serious illness or even death (Hahn, Vedder, and Fourie 1966, 5; Möller 1974, 127). The spirit of a dead witch (*oshiluli* or *okanikifa*) is particularly dangerous because it comes out in the evening and will "eat" (*okuloga* or *okulya omunhu*) the spirit of whomever it catches (Hiltunen 1986, 29; Tönjes 1996, 180–82). The precolonial Owambo appear to have believed in a witch (*omulodhi* or *omulodi*), a person who had inherent powers to bewitch, as well as a sorcerer (*omutikili* or *omhule*), a man who had learnt how to employ magic to injure others (Hiltunen 1986, 27; Tönjes 1996, 180, 192).

The Owambo traditional healer is generally referred to as an *ondudu* or *onganga* (but also *onganga yeanekelo*) and he or she divines or "smells out"

19
The people are known as the Owambo; however, their former "homeland" is referred to as "Ovamboland."

(*eanekelo* or *okunyanekela*) witchcraft (Hiltunen 1986, 28; Hiltunen 1993). The traditional healer is greatly respected in Owambo culture and most precolonial headmen had a traditional healer whom they alone consulted (Hahn, Vedder, and Fourie 1966, 3–5).

In contemporary Katutura the belief in witchcraft (*okutikila*), performed by the *omutikili* or *omhule,* is still central to Owambo cosmology. *Athithi* still wander around Owambo households causing illness. The breaking of cultural taboos (pl. *iidhila;* sing. *oshidhila* or *oshidila*) is a significant source of illness and misfortune to the Owambo. Many of the Owambo traditional taboos relate to childbearing and sexual relations (Hahn, Vedder, and Fourie, 1966, 2–3). The *ondudu* or *onganga yeanekelo* are the primary traditional healers recognized by the Owambo. However, after repeated questioning, no Owambo—traditional healer or patient—was found to have any knowledge of witches in their precolonial sense of inherited and accidental use of witchcraft. Informants say that on rare occasions, people can be born an *omulodhi,* but that when the *omulodhi* bewitches someone, it is deliberate. Informants repeatedly say that if a person is bewitched it is because someone meant to do it and there is no witch who bewitches by accident (without knowing what he or she is doing). Tara (Xhosa/Zulu *sangoma*) says, "Oh, no . . . they know exactly what dirty things they are doing." This change in cultural beliefs from the precolonial to the present is probably due to the consolidation of Owambo traditional spiritual beliefs after much interaction with missionaries and other cultures' belief systems.

The Herero
The Herero people account for approximately 8 percent of the Namibian population. The Herero have a double descent system that on the surface appears highly contradictory; however, the lineages have two different functions (Malan 1995, 71–72). The matrilineage (*eanda* or *eyanda*) is responsible for social and

economic issues and the patrilineage (*oruzo*) is responsible for political and religious functions (Becker 1993, 64; Malan 1995, 71).

Precolonially, the Herero occupied most of what is today central Namibia (including where Windhoek is located), to the north almost as far as the Ugab River, and as far eastern as the Waterberg area (Hahn, Vedder, and Fourie 1966, 155). Although the number of Herero and Nama killed under German colonial rule is difficult to estimate, some scholars estimate that 80 percent of the Herero people were massacred by the Germans; a significant number fled to Botswana and the remaining Herero were placed in native reserves that became known under apartheid as "Hereroland East" and "Hereroland West" (Bley 1971, 150; Soggot 1986, 9). These areas topographically form part of the Kalahari zone (Iipinge and LeBeau 1997, 50). Although many Herero people have come to Katutura in search of employment, the Herero have always had populations living in and around Windhoek (Wallace 1997, 66).

Traditionally, the Herero are cattle pastoralists who precolonially followed a more-or-less nomadic way of life (Becker 1993, 60). Today, as in the past, the Herero value nothing above cattle. Cattle are classified into either sacred cattle (*ozongombe zamuaha*), which are the cattle owned by the matrilineage, or secular cattle (*ozongombe uririkazondere*), which a man owns himself. The Herero have a true cattle complex in that they claim that cattle give them all they need in life. The dung of the cattle is used to build their houses; they drink sour milk (*omaere*) for food, precolonially used they the leather for clothing, and occasionally use their cattle for meat.

One of the central features of the Herero homestead is the sacred ancestral "holy" fire (*omuriro omurangere*) and the place where it burns in the open (*okuruuo*). The *omuriro omurangere* (ancestral fire) is tended by the head wife. Prayer, healing, and other spiritual practices take place around the *omuriro omurangere* and disrespect of the holy fire or the breaking of taboos (*kazukarere* or *otjisere*) relating to the holy fire cause illness, misfortune (*ovipo*), and death.

Some of the Herero healing practices emphasize the use of ash (*omutue*) from the *omuriro omurangere* for medicinal purposes or to ensure good luck (Becker 1993, 48). Related to this is a particular Herero illness, *okuripura navi*: if a transgression is committed against cultural norms thereby angering the ancestors, illness and misfortune can occur. In addition, ghost (*omawi* or *oviruru*) infestations are only healed when treated at the ancestral fire. Herero cosmology is mainly centered on the importance of the ancestors (*ovakuru* or *ovihuha*), ancestor worship (*okurangera*), and the ancestral fire (*omuriro omurangere*). However, breaking taboos is also a Herero explanation of misfortune (*ovipo*) or illness. Finally, an accusation of witchcraft may be employed (Green 1962, 154; Hahn, Vedder, and Fourie 1966, 156; Vedder 1966, 47–49). Frequently, witchcraft (*ovirovero*) among the Herero takes the form of contagious magic. In order to perform witchcraft, the witch must have something that belonged to or had been in contact with the intended victim (Hahn, Vedder, and Fourie 1966, 173). If bad luck befalls someone, they go to a "lot caster" (*ombetere*) who can divine the source of the problem; however, the "professional" traditional healer is the *onganga* (pl. *ozonganga*) is also a skilled herbalist (*otjimbanda*) and does divination (Hahn, Vedder, and Fourie 1966, 174). In addition to the *onganga,* there is the *ozombuke,* who is generally considered a fortune teller (Hahn, Vedder, and Fourie 1966, 175).

In contemporary Katutura, the Herero still center many of their beliefs and practices around ancestor worship and the ancestral fires. It has been stated that the Herero "do not take care to keep them burning [in Katutura]" (Malan 1995, 83). Wallace (1997, 209–10) indicates that the question of whether or not ancestral fires burn in Katutura is a hotly debated topic. However, I have been to an ancestral fire in Katutura that was said to have been rekindled from a family's *omuriro omurangere* from their rural homestead, "so long ago that people do not now remember when it [that particular fire] was brought to Katutura" (Herero traditional leader). This family's *omuriro omurangere* is still tended with all of the diligence accorded its status. Other Herero informants claimed that the ancestral fires in Katutura were never extinguished, but "hidden from the whites." Although this claim cannot be proven, it is in line with the importance placed on the ancestral fire in Herero cosmology. There are also many Herero traditional healers (*ozonganga*) residing in Katutura. A new and significant aspect of contemporary Herero healing is the abundance of Herero faith-healing churches (as well as the indigenous *Oruwano* Church, which does not do faith healing) in Katutura. In fact, the majority of faith healing churches in Katutura are Herero (although there are also a fair number of Owambo faith healers). This phenomenon is unique to the Herero because of the large number of Herero who went into exile in Botswana after the German-Herero war.

The Nama[20]

The Nama speak a variant of a language commonly referred to as Nama/Damara. Nama/Damara is, in fact, one language with distinct variants for Nama speakers and Damara speakers. Approximately 4.5 percent of the Namibian population is Nama (Iipinge and LeBeau 1997, 50). Due to their physical appearance (short, light skinned, with "peppercorn hair"), as well as their non-Bantu click language, it has been commonly believed that the Nama are related to the San (Malan 1995, 114–16; Hahn, Vedder, and Fourie 1966, 109–12). The Nama, unlike the Herero and Owambo, have a patrilineal descent system in which livestock traditionally belongs to and is inherited by the male members of the lineage (Becker 1993, 64; Wellington 1967, 139; Vedder 1966, 54).

Precolonially, Nama territory extended from as far south as beyond the Orange River and as far north as the Swakop River. However, some historians

---

[20] The Khoekhoegowab language (also know as Nama/Damara) has four click sounds that are represented as / "dental click," // "lateral click," + "palatal click" and ! "alveolar click" (Haacke and Eiseb 1999). Orthographic corrections have been done as closely as possible to those suggested by Haacke (personal communication); however, any mistakes are strictly my own. Fewer Khoekhoegowab words appear in this text than for the Owambo or Herero due to traditional healers' inability to identify or spell the words.

assert that the traditional Nama territory spread further north to the Etosha Pan (Hahn, Vedder, and Fourie 1966, 109; Wellington 1967, 139). The Nama traditional ancestral land also included Windhoek, which was hotly disputed by the Herero, causing several wars to be fought between the two groups (Wallace 1997, 66; Hahn, Vedder, and Fourie 1966, 118–20). During the apartheid era, the Nama were relegated to the most extreme areas in southern Namibia. "Namaland" extended from the Rehoboth *gebied* (area) south almost to the Orange River. This area is an extremely dry and rocky part of the country. As with the other ethnic groups in Namibia, Nama people have migrated to Windhoek in search of jobs, although there have been Nama people inhabiting the area since precolonial times.

The Nama precolonially, as well as today in the communal areas, practiced a pastoral lifestyle that consists of keeping of small livestock, such as goats and sheep (with smaller numbers of cattle), and small scale farming of mostly *daaxab* (cannabis plants) and a form of traditional tobacco (Becker 1993, 61; Vedder 1966, 53; Möller 1974, 158).[21] Today, pensions of the elderly are the primary source of income for many Nama families in southern Namibia (Iipinge and LeBeau 1997, 50).

Due to their southerly location, the Nama have been in contact with Europeans and missionaries for far longer than the Owambo or the Herero. This extended contact has had a significant impact on the precolonial beliefs of the Nama because much of their precolonial knowledge has been lost; it has been claimed that all Nama were Christianized by the turn of the twentieth century (Becker 1993, 74). Precolonially, the Nama also had a less important version of the sacred fire than the Herero, but traditionally have a strong belief in witchcraft (Vedder 1966, 29–30). Witches (*!gai-aodi*) and sorcerers (*!gaidii-aon*) are considered active agents in causing misfortune (*tsuu!oob*) and illness.

---

[21] Long vowel sounds are represented in the text as double vowels, such as "aa" instead of a vowel with a line above it, due to computer limitations.

The most significant feature of Nama cosmology is the fear of ghosts and spirits (Vedder 1966, 55–56; Hahn, Vedder, and Fourie 1966, 133). The Nama believe in ancestor spirits who can be either good or evil, but are mostly portrayed as evil (Malan 1995, 126). The spirits of the dead (*//naosab*) can become extremely dangerous, especially if the graves of the dead are opened, from which spirits can escape (Vedder 1966, 55–56). Precolonially, after death the body was tightly bound and women threw scented powder (*sâ-i*) into the grave to hold the spirit in place. Huts were moved soon after the death of a family member to ensure that the dead could not find their way back to the family (55–56). As with the Owambo, spirits of the dead are most dangerous to close family members (55–56). However, ancestor spirits (*aboxan*) can also cause problems for descendants if the *aboxai* (sing.) is dissatisfied with certain actions of the descendants (Malan 1995, 127). Omens of the dead and ghosts also abound in Nama cosmology (Hahn, Vedder, and Fourie 1966, 133). Even today, the strongest element in Nama society is the fear of ghosts (*/noren* or */hai/noren*, or "foul ghosts"), and */hailnuun* (spooks, or "pale feet") (Hahn, Vedder, and Fourie 1966, 133; Vedder 1966, 55–56).

The Nama have a variety of traditional healers (*/khuu-aob* or *!guu-aob*) who can detect and treat witchcraft, quell evil spirits, foretell the future (*/khuu-aoqu*), perform sucking surgery,[22] or practice herbalism (*xoma-aob* or *//khama-aob*) (Hoernlè 1985; Hahn, Vedder, and Fourie 1966, 134). Central to Nama traditional medicine is the smoking of *daaxa-i* (dried cannabis) for medicinal

---

[22] When it is divined that a witchcraft poison or foreign object has been introduced into the patient's body the offending item is removed by means of sucking surgery. This is a procedure whereby small cuts (usually lateral) are made on the patient's body and the healer uses his or her mouth or some other suction device to suck the object out of the patient's body. Some healers use a tennis ball that has a hole cut into it. The sides of the ball are squeezed together and the hole is placed over the lateral cuts to create suction. It is believed that traditionally the Nama and Damara used the mouth as a sucking device, given that the Khoekhoegowab term (am+nûi/khaa) literally translated means "mouth place on body" (Haacke personal communication). However, traditionally many ethnic groups used objects (such as animal horns) to create the suction. The origin of the use of a tennis ball is unknown to the researcher.

purposes (Vedder 1966, 53). Due to their fear of ghosts and evil spirits, the Nama have a variety of amulets that can be worn to protect them from unhappy deceased relatives or to deliver them from evil spirits (Hahn, Vedder, and Fourie 1966, 134).

In contemporary Katutura the Nama are largely Christianized, but they still possess a lively cosmology that includes the use of spirits mediums, foretellers, and herbalists. However, Nama traditional healers also insist on going to church on Sunday and are strict Christians. Today, the Nama still use *daaxa-i* (cannabis) as a traditional medicine for a range of illnesses including calming the nerves, eating disorders, and treating mental illness. Nama traditional medicine includes divination and steaming to cleanse the patient from evil spirits.

As in the past, spirits of the dead including ghosts (*/noren* or */hai/noren*), spooks (*/hailnuun*), and spirits of ancestors (*aboxan*) are still frequently identified causes of misfortune (*tsuu!oob*) and illness. However, the Nama would not rule out witchcraft as the cause of an illness until a diviner has been consulted.

The Damara
The Damara make up approximately 8.5 percent of the Namibian population. The Damara also speak variants of the Nama/Damara (*Khoekhoegowab*) language, but are clearly not physically related to the Nama. The Damara are generally tall and possess physical characteristics similar to Bantu-speaking people. The paradox of a Bantu appearance with a non-Bantu click language has caused considerable speculation among scholars. Some scholars have claimed that the Damara were slaves or servants of the Nama thereby "losing their language" (Wellington 1967, 139–40). Other scholars contend that they are descended from the people of West Africa, but also suggest that they were subjugated by the Nama and Herero (Malan 1995, 129; Möller 1974, 153; Hahn, Vedder, and Fourie 1966, 39–41). None of these theories sufficiently explain the Damara mix of physical, language, and cultural attributes. However, Haacke and others (1997) assert that the Damara

were already in the Namibian territory and already spoke a Khoe language before they ever encountered the Nama.

Precolonially the Damara lived in the mountainous part of Namibia's western highlands. As with the Nama, the environment of the Damara was arid, rocky, and mountainous. Due to Apartheid relocation, the Damara have also lived in the central western part of Namibian that borders the Namib Desert. The former "Damaraland" was located in the contemporary designations of the Erongo and Kunene regions. Although some populations of Damara have always lived in the Windhoek area, the Damara have also begun to migrate to Windhoek looking for employment and to escape from poverty related to recent droughts.

As with language, the Damara shared many aspects of precolonial cosmology with the Nama (Hahn, Vedder, and Fourie 1966, 61). However, the Damara have different beliefs related to some spiritual aspects of their life (see below). The Damara also have spirits (//noren) who reside on earth. Some spirits stay on earth and wander around; other spirits return to earth to "pay it a visit." The wanderings of these recently dead spirits are the reasons why relatives sometimes die soon after the death of a loved one (Vedder 1966, 65). The ancestor spirits can also cause illness and misfortune for their earth-bound relatives by hiding deadly objects in the relative's body, in which case sucking surgery (am+nûi/khas) is required to remove the object from the victim's body (65–66).

It was said that the reason //Gamab (God) gave the Damara traditional healers (xoma-aogu, pl.) was so that they could find out when the heavenly ancestors were trying to do evil deeds against their earthly relatives and to have a medium through which //Gamab could communicate directly with his people (Vedder 1966, 66). Traditionally, the Damara have a healer (xoma-aob, sing.) who specializes in sucking surgery to remove objects placed in people by the ancestor spirits (65–66). As with the Nama, the Damara have witches (!gai-aodi), and a variety of traditional healers who can detect and treat witchcraft, quell evil spirits (*dii-aogu* or *!gài-aagu*), foretell the future, divine causes of illness and misfortune (*/khuu-aogu*), and practice herbalism (*xoma-aogu*) (Wallace 1997, 198). The Damara also have an elaborate form of ritual expression, including proverbs, songs, trance dancing, and funeral dirges. They previously used their hunting bow as a musical instrument and many of their dance-songs were a form of prayer with religious implications (Vedder 1966, 62).

In contemporary Katutura the Damara, like the Nama, still have a lively cosmology that includes the use of spirits mediums, foretellers, and herbalists. Witchcraft and ghosts are still the main sources for illness and misfortune (*tsuu!oob*). Nama and Damara traditional healers in Katutura tend to either work together or frequently refer patients to one another. Damara traditional healers are more frequently spirit mediums, whereas the Nama are more likely to specialize in herbs. This healing pattern appears to be a residual behavior based on the precolonial belief that Nama traditional healers are better with herbs whereas Damara traditional healers are best at spiritual problems, in particular sucking surgery (*am+nûi/khas*) (Green 1962, 166).

Interethnic Beliefs and Practices
In Namibia, colonialism, and more recently modernization and globalization, have done much to change traditional cultural beliefs, including beliefs concerning health and illness. Both the German and South African governments' laws and restrictions on cultural practices, including traditional medicine, had an impact on the various ethnic groups in Namibia. However, cultural beliefs still have a significant influence on a patient's health-care utilization choices. Today there are various cultural beliefs that are held by the different ethnic groups; however, it should be emphasized that there are many similarities between these various beliefs. The belief in witches and witchcraft, ghosts and spirits, ancestor spirits, and taboos all form the core of African explanations of illness causation. There are also similarities in the use of divination to determine the cause of illness and misfortune; the relatively common practice of "sucking surgery" to remove

witchcraft items from the body; the use of herbal decoctions and steaming as a means of cleansing a patient of witchcraft, misfortune, and other social or spiritual disorders. Just as several beliefs and practices tend to cross ethnic boundaries, ethnic boundaries are also crossed in search of health and healing.

Healers and Practitioners

Katutura is a medically pluralistic community: there are different medical systems within the same social system. The most important medical systems co-existing in Katutura are the Western government recognized system and the traditional nonformally recognized system.

The Western medical system in Namibia consists of hospitals, community clinics, pharmacies, nurses, doctors, private doctors, and other clinical staff. Katutura residents have access to the Katutura State Hospital, Windhoek Central Hospital, and several community clinics, which are all state-run facilities.[23] In addition, there is a wide range of private Western doctors, two private hospitals, and private clinics within the Greater Windhoek area for those with the ability to pay commercial rates or for those people who have medical aid through their work. Namibian law recognizes only medical practitioners within the Western system. They enjoy special status and more clearly defined rights than other types of healers. For example, health insurance only pays for medical treatment provided by Western medical practitioners, and only Western medical practitioners are allowed to treat patients at hospitals and clinics.

Although Western health-care services are available to most of the Katutura population, the services provided are often inadequate. This is partly due to the inequalities in the quality of Western health-care services provided by the

---

[23] There is a network of clinics and hospitals throughout Namibia that are owned and operated by the Namibian Government. In 2002, the fee for a state-run hospital or clinic was N$12 per visit, compared to the average cost for a visit to a private medical doctor which was about N$130. The N$12 hospital users' fee entitles the patient to medical examinations, some pharmaceuticals and auxiliary services such as x-rays.

state (for the Katutura population) versus privately provided Western health care (for the more affluent sectors of the Greater Windhoek population). The most frequently identified problems with state-run facilities are poor quality of patient care, nurses' negative attitudes, a shortage of vital drugs, and limited availability of specialized facilities. Although there is a wide range of services available between the two state-run hospitals, patients requiring certain specialized surgical procedures (such as a cardiac bypass) are referred to hospitals in South Africa.

The other co-existing medical system in Katutura is the traditional medical system, which has a wide range of traditional healers. There are Owambo, Herero, Nama, and Damara traditional healers who are herbalists, spirit mediums, faith healers, fortune tellers, and any combination thereof.[24] There are also several *sangomas* (spirit mediums/herbalists) from South Africa who are renowned for their ability to deal with imbalances in social relationships, as well as various traditional healers from all over the African continent. As previously mentioned in this discussion, the traditional healers of Katutura offer a variety of healing methods, most of which involve the use of herbs and divination. Within traditional medicine there is generally no distinction between physical and spiritual health. Misfortune, problems in social relations, and disease are all treated within the traditional health-care system. Although some traditional healers have a high status within their own culture and the African community, they are generally not recognized within the wider society and currently have an unclear legal status in Namibia.

---

[24] The terms "traditional healers," and "healers" are used to refer to the following types of people: a person who treats primarily with African traditional herbs (herbalist), a person who calls on God to heal (faith healer or prophet), a person who calls on the ancestor spirits to divine the cause of illness and to heal (spirit medium), a traditional midwife (Traditional Birth Attendant [TBA]), a person who tells fortunes and checks patients for misfortune and bad luck, or any other health-care person who is not trained in the Western medical tradition. Although there are a number of Chinese traditional healers, acupuncturists, Western homoeopathists, and reflexologists operating in and around Windhoek, these health-care persons do not fall within the definition of traditional healers used for this discussion.

When making traditional health-care choices, patients can select from a range of ethnic and/or traditional healing methods. Some ethnic groups in Katutura have different (as well as higher) utilization patterns of traditional medicine than other groups. It is widely known that Herero traditional healers are powerful and their services should only be used at great risk of the treatment "backfiring" and causing social or spiritual damage to the patient. (For example, it is said that if their "love potions" are too strong, it could have the negative effect of causing the intended recipient to "hate instead of love" the patient). There are Owambo TBAs who specialize in antenatal and postnatal care. Nama traditional healers frequently use traditional steaming and are considered good herbalists. Damara traditional healers specialize in the use of sucking surgery to remove witchcraft related objects from the patient's body. There are also a significant number of Herero (as well as some Owambo) faith healing churches to which patients can turn for healing from God. In Katutura, patients can use any type of traditional medicine and any type of traditional healer from any ethnic group thereby giving them a vast number of alternatives for traditional health care.

By far the most common type of traditional healer in Katutura is a spirit medium who usually treats patients with herbal decoctions. Traditional herbs are typically dried, ground, and stored for later use. There are no formal markets for traditional medicine in Katutura, other than a traditional pharmacy in Windhoek's CBD; most traditional healers have substantial private pharmacies. The majority of customers who go to the Windhoek traditional pharmacy are healers; however, patients can also go to the traditional pharmacy and request herbal medicines such as charms against misfortune, purgatives, and incense to ward off evil spirits.

The most common types of traditional treatments include purgatives (vomiting and diarrhea) to "clean" the patient on the inside; herbal mixtures to bath in, which "cleanse" the patient on the outside; herbal mixtures to be placed, sprayed, or burnt around the house to cleanse or protect against witchcraft; herbs mixed with Vaseline or cream to rub onto the skin; and herbal decoctions to ingest. Massage is practiced by several traditional healers to ease sore muscles and correct problems with internal organs.[25] Steaming, in various forms, is a frequent treatment for removing witchcraft or bad luck, as well as to treat any number of universally recognized illness manifestations.[26] Traditional steaming is a treatment method that requires patients to sit together inside a hut while hot stones are dropped into a pot with boiling water that contains an herbal mixture.

Family Illness Histories

The following section examines 1996 THS respondents' or their families' most recent illness episode.[27] About one-third of respondents say that they or a family member had been seriously ill within the three months preceding the survey, another one-third say that they or a family member had been seriously ill within the past four to twelve months and a further one-third indicated that they or a family member had been sick more than a year ago. Only fifteen people (less than 2%) say that there have been no serious illnesses that they know of in their immediate family.

Family illnesses described are primarily minor with symptoms such as ear problems, teeth pain, sore feet, coughs, and colds, although some respondents

---

[25] One traditional belief is that internal organs can move location in the body, become "sick," or get injured. In which case, massage puts the organs back into place or heal them.

[26] The term "universally recognized manifestations" refers to illness symptoms or disorders that are recognized by both traditional healers and Western medical personnel, whereas exclusively African manifestations, symptoms, or disorders are those that have no Western-defined equivalent and are, therefore, not recognized by Western medical personnel. A "social-spiritual" cause of an illness comes from the patients spiritual realm (including breaking cultural taboos, contamination, witchcraft, misfortune, and ancestor dissatisfaction). In contrast, a "natural" etiology comes from the Western concept that illnesses are biological phenomena (Foster 1976, 774–75). Most people in Katutura talk in terms of "African illnesses" and "Western illnesses." Therefore, this categorization of illnesses will also be used due to the categories used by the people.

[27] Although patterns may vary slightly by ethnic group, most Africans consider illness a family rather than an individual matter. Several family members usually participate in health-seeking behavior with an ill family member. Therefore, health and illness are discussed for the entire family rather than for individuals.

reported more serious illnesses such as heart problems, meningitis, and kidney failure, as well as injuries due to car accidents, broken arms, and hernias. Sexual and childbearing illnesses include uterus problems, "female organ problems," and male sex organ problems (e.g., sore testes). Some people report recent mental problems such as family members who wander around aimlessly, family members who run around and physically attack people, and family members who suffer from depression. In addition, some respondents identify witchcraft-related problems in the family such as "ghosts around the house," "face deformed due to ghosts," "ate witchcraft poisoned meat," and witch familiars in the house or in a family member's body.[28]

Respondents who say that they or a family member had been sick were asked what kind of treatment was first tried to get the patient well. The overwhelming majority say that the patient was first taken to a hospital, clinic, or private Western doctor. Only about 10 percent of respondents say they first went to a traditional healer. However, when the first health-care choice failed, a significant number of respondents then took the patient to a traditional healer. When asked what finally got the patient well, about one-fourth of respondents say the person was still sick, whereas another 9.7 percent say that the patient died. However, 41.6 percent say that Western medicine was successful, whereas about one-fourth of respondents say that it was traditional medicine that was successful in healing their sick family member. Given that there was a 22 percent increase in the use of traditional healers from first to second treatment and a corresponding 26 percent decrease for hospitals and clinics, it can be determined that about one-fourth of respondents switched from Western to traditional medicine, with positive results.

---

[28] A "witch familiar" is any animal (natural or supernatural), spiritual being, ghost, or other such creature that is used by a witch to carry out his or her deeds.

These data indicate that patients first try Western medicine for illnesses with universally recognized manifestations. However, when Western health care is unsuccessful, a large percentage of patients then turn to traditional medicine. Traditional healers, as well as their patients, say that patients tried Western medicine first but that it had been unsuccessful in curing them:

> The traditional healers are good because I suffered a long time from headaches. And the day that I decided to go to the traditional healer it didn't take a long time to be cured like at the hospital. After I went to that healer everything was successful and I haven't suffered again from that headache which was very painful every morning. So I believe in traditional doctors more than hospitals (Herero patient, 30 years old).

> In most cases I just feel that maybe a person has just gone to the hospital and then he does not see an improvement or a rapid improvement, then he decides to come to the traditional healer ("Dr." Toni, Zulu sangoma).

> Normally people come from hospitals. Mostly what I heal are the ones who are refused by the hospital, which the hospital finds them difficult to heal. Whether they are adults or children, I normally treat them (Fanuel, Herero spirit medium/herbalist).

Use of Traditional Healers

A large majority (70%; n=264) of respondents to the 1996 THS have, at some time in their lives, been to a traditional healer. Many respondents also report having gone to more than one type of traditional healer. Of those that have been to a healer, 40.8 percent (n=186) have been to an herbalist. In addition, respondents have also been to a TBA, a spirit medium, and a faith healer in about equal numbers. Qualitative data also indicate that herbalists or spirit medium/herbalists are the preferred types of healer.

Respondents who have been to a traditional healer were asked why they went. Respondents could give more than one reason for this treatment choice.[29]

---

[29] Data for this section come only from those respondents who say that either they or a family member has been to a traditional healer. Therefore, the total number of respondents for this section is 264 people.

Almost one-fourth (n=101) of respondents went to a traditional healer because Western medicine did not help them. However, most respondents went to traditional healers because they had an exclusively African manifestation (e.g., "smoke in legs," "witchcraft" or "misfortune caused by twins"[30]; had illnesses that were exclusively African in nature (e.g., "help to get a job," "jealousy between cousins," to "kill a court case"); or other cultural factors (e.g., "traditional healers are part of culture"). Therefore, patients go to traditional healers if they believe they have an illness that cannot be cured by Western medicine or if Western medicine has failed.

Respondents who have been to a traditional healer were asked if they go to Western doctors for the same illnesses for which they go to traditional healers. Respondents are divided as to whether these are different illnesses (42.9%; n=111) or whether there is no particular pattern (40.9%; n=106); however, 16.2 percent (n=42) of respondents have been to a traditional healer for the same illness as that for which they sought Western health care. Over one-half (59.3%; n=156) have been to a traditional healer from an ethnic group other than their own, whereas 40.7 percent (n=107) have only been to a traditional healer from their own ethnic group. Almost 40 percent of respondents indicate that the ethnicity of the healer is not as important as the healer's ability to cure. As Fillipus (Owambo spirit medium/herbalist) says, "[I treat] All the people—any tribe, races, even white people I can heal. So I do not have apartheid." In fact, when traditional medicine has not been successful, many patients go to other healers for a witchcraft-related problem, such as having been given traditionally poisoned food to eat during the night or someone threw witchcraft powder in the patient's path, which caused sores on the patient's legs. Respondents or their family members also went to the traditional healer for social-spiritual problems,

---

[30] In African cosmology the birth of twins is considered bad luck and the mother needs to go to a traditional healer to be cleansed from the bad luck. Without such cleansing the mother, her sexual partner and/or the children face serious illness and possibly even death.

such as "bad luck from birth of twins," "angry ancestor spirits" or witch familiars in the house, as well as mental illnesses (such as "from finding a dead body") and sexual or childbearing problems (such as "not having menstruation"). Moreover, respondents have been to traditional healers for minor disorders such as back injuries, rashes, and rheumatism, as well as serious illnesses (e.g., heart problems, malaria, and cancer). These data support previous findings that traditional health-seeking behavior is primarily for witchcraft, mental illness, and other problems identified as having a social-spiritual cause. However, patients also go to traditional healers for illnesses that have universally recognized symptoms with a natural etiology, which can be treated by either Western or traditional medicine.

Evaluation of Western and Traditional Medicine

The 1996 THS respondents were asked to evaluate traditional and Western health care, regardless of their use of traditional or Western medicine. Respondents' evaluation of traditional healers' skills were tested by asking them what illnesses they think traditional healers find difficult to treat. Respondents gave a wide range of illnesses. Interestingly, 21.6 percent feel that traditional healers cannot treat HIV and AIDS. This finding is important because many times rumors are spread that traditional healers can cure HIV or AIDS, which could contribute to the spread of HIV when HIV-positive patients have unprotected sexual intercourse, under the assumption that they have been cured. Many respondents identify a wide range of minor illnesses that have universally recognized manifestations such as dizziness, dental problems, earaches, and asthma, which they feel traditional healers cannot treat. Other more serious illnesses respondents say traditional healers cannot treat include malnutrition in children, tuberculosis, cancer, and high blood pressure. Many patients identify Western medical procedures such as x-rays and injections as healing mechanisms not available to traditional healers.

Conversely, respondents were asked which illnesses Western medical doctors find difficult to treat. A wide range of responses were given, with 20.9

percent indicating that Western doctors cannot treat AIDS and 8.5 percent saying they cannot treat cancer. Thus, respondents' knowledge of incurable diseases seems to be high. Respondents also identified a wide range of minor illnesses with universally recognized symptoms (e.g., stomach problems, diarrhea, and headaches) that they said Western doctors cannot successfully treat. As can be expected, the majority of responses to this question centered on illnesses with exclusively African causes or symptoms. Overall, 16.2 percent of respondents feel Western medical doctors cannot treat witchcraft caused illnesses, misfortune, "traditional poisoning," ghosts, "ribs changed position," and burning down a traditional hut.[31] In addition, social problems such as unemployment, alcoholism, and theft of property are not treated by Western doctors. Respondents also said that Western doctors cannot treat mental illness and epilepsy.

Health-Seeking Behavior in Katutura

Hierarchy of Resort for Universally Recognized Manifestations
When given a choice between traditional healers, home treatment, or Western medical personnel for a variety of universally recognized disorders, such as fevers, coughs, and diarrhea, they are most likely to *first* use home remedies, the majority of people go to Western medical personnel, although there are some interesting variations in health-care utilization patterns. People first try to use Western medicine for STDs, tuberculosis, malaria, and AIDS, followed by asthma, high blood pressure, and impotency. For help with a malnourished child, contraceptives, and male circumcision they are more likely to go to Western medical personnel. However, people are more likely to *first* go to traditional healers for epilepsy, intestinal problems, and mental illness, all of which are

---

[31] The burning of a traditional hut, which is common given that most people light their huts with candles and huts are typically made out of thatch, is usually thought to have a social-spiritual cause such as witchcraft. However, if a person dies in the fire, this can lead to haunting of family members by the deceased's spirit.

considered to have a social-spiritual cause, although they have universally recognized manifestations.

The choices people make when first going to traditional healers for illnesses with universally recognized disorders is best explained by the cause of the illness. For example, in the African paradigm there are two types of epilepsy. An Owambo key informant explains, "In our cosmology there are two types of epilepsy; one is natural and the other [oshinona] is contracted from an 'infected' person, inherited from a mother or father or caused by witchcraft. Epilepsy caused by witchcraft or contamination is treated by the administration of a purgative which causes diarrhea and vomiting to clean out the patient." Epilepsy of a natural origin may or may not respond to traditional herbal treatments (depending on the medicine and the healer), whereas oshinona is considered caused by witchcraft (a social-spiritual cause) and responds only to traditional treatment.

Within the African cultures of Katutura, especially the Owambo, there is an exclusively African illness caused by witchcraft that, if not treated, causes the intestines to burst open and the patient to die. This illness is also only successfully treated by traditional healers. In addition, mental illness is considered to be primarily caused by witchcraft. However, mental illness can result from universally recognized disorders (e.g., stress) or from several other social-spiritual causes (e.g., breaking taboos, ancestor dissatisfaction and contamination). "Dr." Toni (Zulu sangoma) explains:

> The mental illnesses are of different types because some people's [illnesses] are from stress of certain problems which they cannot overcome. That leads to mental disturbances. But other mental illnesses are from witchcraft where at night one is crying or having to run away, going to the bush and wanting to hang oneself. . . . Now that is the one of pure witchcraft where we can see a difference [when traditionally treated].

Utilization patterns change slightly for most of the illnesses when the treatment patients had sought the first time failed. Most people who first try home treatments indicate that if this does not work, they then go to Western medical personnel. It is interesting, however, that utilization rates of traditional healers, for all illnesses, increase for the *second* health-seeking attempt. Illnesses with the highest rates of increase for traditional health care are epilepsy and infertility, as well as headaches, bleeding from the nose and mouth, and stomach problems. In addition, illnesses such as impotency, intestinal problems, and asthma also exhibit an increase in traditional utilization rates from first to second health-seeking attempt. As can be expected, after a failed attempt to treat an illness at home, people are more likely to try either Western or traditional medicine. Unsuccessful attempts with Western medicine give mixed results, with people just as likely to continue using Western medicine as they are to try traditional medicine. However, unsuccessful attempts at traditional medicine do not cause respondents to change treatment types.

If the second attempt to cure an illness is unsuccessful, some interesting patterns emerge. In general, utilization rates for a *third* health-seeking attempt rise for traditional medicine and drop for home treatment and Western medicine. However, some people indicate that they would be more likely to turn to home treatments if Western medicine were unable to treat AIDS symptoms and more likely to turn to Western medicine for recurring fevers and persistent coughs. Illnesses that show the overall highest rates of increase for traditional healer utilization are stomach problems, headaches, sore eyes, diarrhea, menstruation problems, and impotency.

For most illnesses with universally recognized symptoms, people are likely to either first try to treat themselves at home or go to Western medical personnel. Only illnesses that are considered to have a clear social-spiritual cause are likely to first be taken to a traditional healer. However, as Western medicine and home treatment fail, individuals are more likely to turn to traditional healing for illnesses previously considered the realm of Western medicine.

Hierarchy of Resort for Social-Spiritual Needs

There are clear distinctions made for various types of social-spiritual illnesses and forms of health-seeking behavior. For social-spiritual needs (e.g., protection from witchcraft, misfortune, good luck, and love potions) people go to traditional healers. With some illnesses people are divided as to whether they would seek Western medical personnel or traditional healers. Some people are more likely to say that they would use both Western and traditional medicine for help getting pregnant, for the health of a mother and baby, for help with children born with deformities, and for sexual or marital problems. However, for problems such as alcohol abuse and worry or stress, they are divided as to whether they would seek Western help, traditional help, both, or neither.

People make clear distinctions between what types of health care they seek based on the type of illness. People most often go to traditional healers for illnesses with a social-spiritual cause, or when Western medicine has been unsuccessful in treating their illness. The following statements illustrate some utilization patterns identified by Katutura residents:

> I also heal skin sores by putting medicine in their drink. These are sicknesses where they might go to hospital first, but there are other sicknesses which people don't go to hospital for such as ghosts or *tokoloshes* . . . for ghosts they come to me first (Zulu healer).[32]

> I usually only go to a healer when the illness is not clear to the Western doctor or when it is other things like madness, craziness or bad luck. For a Western doctor you go for any pain, flues, etcetera, and sicknesses that are clear. You go to traditional healers for any illness which is not clear, complicated illnesses which are not clear for the Western doctor, deteriorating bad luck, etcetera (Herero patient, 50 years old).

---

[32] A *tokoloshe* is a witch familiar that is most often described as a small, hairy man-like being with large feet and large ears. The most distinctive feature of a *tokoloshe* is his large penis. *Tokoloshe* infestations most often take the form of sexually molesting female patients in Katutura, although a *tokoloshe* infestation can also have manifestations similar to other types of haunting by ghosts and spirits. The concept of a *tokoloshe* appears to be a South African concept, but fits neatly into the witchcraft ideology of other southern African ethnic groups and is now widespread throughout southern Africa.

> There are illnesses I will take to Western doctors and illnesses I
> will take to traditional healers. Illnesses like mental illness and
> cases like getting confused and bad luck go to traditional healers. I
> don't trust traditional healers in treating many illnesses like
> something that grows in the stomach. These things have to be
> operated on (Herero patient, 57 years old).

Patients who have illnesses with a social-spiritual cause and exclusive African manifestations will first use traditional medicine, but will not use Western medicine because they perceive that Western medicine will not help. Several categories of illnesses are identified with considerable variation in perceived causes. The same illness can be attributed to witchcraft, misfortune, and contamination, breaking of taboos or ancestor dissatisfaction, depending on divination. All of the types of social-spiritual causes identified for illnesses have in common the concept that they are attempts by humans to explain and influence the dark forces that hold sway over people's lives.

Witchcraft is the most common social-spiritual cause given for illness and misfortune within Katutura's African population. Many patients who present themselves to traditional healers with exclusively African symptoms are diagnosed as suffering from witchcraft. The manifestations of witchcraft exhibit significant variation in physical symptoms, social problems, misfortune, and mental illness. Witchcraft in the Katutura context is considered a deliberate attempt by one person or group of people to harm another person or group of people. There are a variety of illnesses that can befall a patient who has been bewitched. Types of witchcraft caused problems can range from minor illnesses and discomforts to death. The most common witchcraft related problems are mental illness (which could result in death), epilepsy (which may also afflict the entire family), financial losses (which could include the death or loss of cattle), various social problems with friends and relatives, infestations of witch familiars, and a variety of minor to serious universally recognized manifestations, some of which could lead to death due to unnatural or unknown causes. As one informant declares, "anything can happen to you when you are [be]witched."

Ethnic Variation in Health-Seeking Behavior

In addition to the perceived cause of an illness and previous health-seeking experience, individual health-seeking behavior, performed within the rubric of personal possibilities and social structural constraints, also exhibits variation between the four main ethnic groups in Katutura.

Witchcraft is the most common social-spiritual cause given for illness within Katutura's African population, regardless of ethnicity. Although the various ethnic groups have certain witchcraft types that they all experience, certain witchcraft types are unique to different ethnic groups.

In general, Owambo people are most likely to attribute unexplainable events to direct witchcraft attacks, although other ethnic groups also explain illness in terms of witch familiars. The Owambo are also more likely to attribute mental illness and epilepsy to witchcraft. In Owambo culture it is believed that if a person acts too rich, beautiful, or arrogant, he or she is risking bewitchment due to jealousy, which is likely to result in mental illness. Tara (Xhosa/Zulu *sangoma*) was asked if the different ethnic groups in Katutura come to her with different types of witchcraft. The following is an excerpt from an interview where she describes examples of the different types of witchcraft problems that different ethnic groups experience:

> There was one Herero man I treated when I was working from Grootfontein, who was afraid of looking at people. He would never leave his house. He had been [be]witched and I washed [cleansed] him and did all that was necessary and he got better.

> I also treated a 12-year-old Damara boy who was afraid of horses and he had grown up with them. He loved them but became afraid of them all of a sudden. I washed [cleansed] him with the medicine of the ancestors. It is a certain type of medicine that when you beat it [water mixed with this herb] it makes foam. I had him drink the foam only and he and horses were friends again.

> [The Owambo] eat the witchcraft while they are sleeping. Usually this is given to them by a tokoloshe. Some people are alert while they sleep, they have strong ancestors, so they know they are being

fed bad [spiritually poisoned] food and they will not eat it. Sometimes the witchcraft is put in food. In this case maybe the person doesn't mean to [be]witch someone. For example, maybe a woman wants to put love medicine into the man's food to make him love her, but the medicine is too strong. So it irritates his throat. Then he leaves that woman because she [be]witched him. Some of these love medicines can "back fire" because they are too strong and the person becomes [be]witched instead.

Misfortune is also a frequent health concern for people in Katutura and different ethnic groups have different ways of protecting themselves from mishap. Many Owambo people travel with an *omuounguuka* (good luck stick or charm) to protect them from misfortune (*omupya*) on long journeys. Nama and Damara patients are given Vaseline or a cream with an herbal mixture to protect them against misfortune and to make the patient more spiritually attractive to others. If a Herero person has been to a traditional healer to remove misfortune (*ovipo*), but the treatment is not successful, the next step will be *okuravaera* (an ancestors' ceremony). The patient goes to his or her eldest male relative and requests the relative to "talk" to the ancestors (*ovakuru*) and to request the ancestors' protection from the misfortune.

Sexual taboos are the most prevalent type of cultural taboo for Katutura's African population, especially in the Owambo culture. Taboos can prohibit sexual relations between specific categories of individuals, proscribe times when sexual contact should not take place, or indicate sexual behavior that is considered inappropriate.

Although all ethnic groups in Katutura have a belief in ghosts and spirits, the Nama, and to a lesser extent the Damara, have a particularly strong fear of spirits. In Nama cosmology a common source of ghosts are restless recently deceased persons or spirits of ancestors (*aboxan*). In the following short case study, a young man relates the story of how his dead mother came to him in his dreams because she could not rest. Rather than revering the dead mother's spirit, the boy was so petrified that he did not want to sleep at night. The focus of health-seeking behavior was to rid the child of the mother's spirit. Daniel is a 25-year-old Nama/Damara man who was raised in Windhoek. His father was Damara born in the Rehoboth area and his mother was a Nama born in the Gibeon area. Daniel tells the following story:

> When I was 5 years old my mother died from goitres. Three days later I started my primary school at the age of six. I was in grade two, two years had passed since my mother had died. This episode happened only at nighttime. While I was sleeping my mother came to me to fetch me [take him back to the spirit world]. I cried the whole night. I could not sleep very well at night. When the night arrived I was afraid to sleep because my mother was calling me. My father decided to send me to my aunt's house in Khomasdal. It was not successful because my mother kept coming to me. We went to the cemetery, to my mother's grave, to talk with her; that did not help. My father took me to a traditional healer in our location [in Katutura]. He was a Tswana healer. The healer threw the bones; he told my father that my mother did not die in peace and dignity. At the stage when she was dying she was thinking of me. She was worried about who was going to look after me and that is why she couldn't rest. The healer gave my father something; it looked like brown powder, to put into both of our bathing water. We were told to only bath at night. He [the healer] also took something and made a cross under my feet. From that day, my mother's ghost disappeared.

With the possible exception of the Herero, ancestor dissatisfaction is one of the least often given social-spiritual causes for illness within the Katutura population. Ancestors are seen as less active today than in the past, especially in the urban areas because "people do not know their ancestors today" (Tara, Xhosa/Zulu *sangoma*). Although it does occur, ancestor (*aathithi*) belief among the Owambo is particularly uncommon, one key informant says: "The Owambo do not really worship the ancestors in the urban areas, but in the rural areas they do it, but just a few of them. In most cases, the new generation does not even know about ancestors" (Owambo woman, 42 years old).

However, the Herero still have a fairly strong ancestor cult. As in precolonial Herero society, most traditional healing practices and ceremonies are supposed to take place at the sacred ancestral fire (*omuriro omurangere*) in the place where it burns in the open (*okuruuo*). Although there are ancestral fires in Katutura, many Herero travel to the rural areas for healing and to participate in ceremonies due to the presence of the ancestral fire. Some of the examples given for going to the *omuriro omurangere* are to ask for luck in general, when applying for a job, when writing exams, when getting married, to get healed from any illness, to exorcise an evil spirit, to celebrate a new born baby, to give the baby a name, or to celebrate the purchase of a new car in the family. In addition, traditional wedding ceremonies are celebrated at the ancestral fire, as well as celebrations of the survival of cattle during droughts or other unpleasant weather conditions. One Herero key informant explains that:

> . . . when a person is suffering from any illness, they must first ask permission to inform the ancestors about what they are going to do at the holy fire. Then they slaughter a cow or sheep, but not a goat. This animal should be a young female cow or sheep which has not yet mated. Then they take the blood and the intestinal contents of this sheep or cow and mix it and then wash the sick person with this mixture for any type of illness and at the same time the recipient asks for blessings from the ancestors.

Although the most commonly given social-spiritual cause for illness by all ethnic groups in Katutura is witchcraft, in general, the Owambo are most likely to explain illness as caused by witchcraft attacks and the breaking of sexual and childbearing taboos. The Herero, who still have a strong ancestor cult, are more likely to explain illness in relationship to the ancestors. Conversely, the Owambo ancestors are particularly inactive. The Nama and the Damara are more likely to attribute illness to being caused by ghosts, recently deceased ancestors and witch familiars.

Health-Seeking Behavior in an Urban Environment
Katutura is an urban area that exhibits high rates of social change. Immigration is the most significant force behind the changing social landscape in Katutura. Culturally isolated rural dwellers are moving to Katutura in large numbers. These

new Katutura residents face challenges previously unknown to them. In addition, their social world (physical as well as spiritual) is changing. Life is unpredictable. They are in contact with people and situations that are new and threatening. They are competing for Katutura's resources, which cannot keep pace with the growing population. For the newly arrived migrant Katutura is a place of strange sights and sounds, foreign experiences, and threatening situations. Katutura is highly unpredictable and spiritually dangerous. Social-spiritual attack is due to a number of external forces, over which the victim has no control. There are several ways in which the occurrence of illnesses with a social-spiritual cause is influenced by living in an urban area.

Many unsettling urban experiences can be managed through witchcraft accusations, a familiar and comforting way for individuals to explain the fearful and unknown. Witchcraft accusations explain an individual's utilization of traditional healers for exclusively African symptoms such as problems in social relationships. Social change, which affects individual behavior, has caused a rise in social disturbances within the Katutura community. How people attempt to deal with their new and threatening life experiences varies considerably. However, witchcraft accusations are an important component of managing social change and disequilibrium. Urban dwellers are also likely to be in competition with others for scarce resources and are therefore likely to experience jealousy, which can lead to witchcraft accusations. Competition in the work place as well as for other financial resources is seen as a primary motive behind witchcraft attacks, although competition for sexual partners can also lead to witchcraft attacks. Witchcraft attacks are perceived by those who succeed, out of fear of those who may be jealous of their success or competing for the same resources. Witchcraft accusations are also prevalent in the urban areas due to the close proximity of and distrust of people from other ethnic groups. As Dillon-Malone (1988, 1159–72) writes, "witchcraft is rampant in the urban areas."

Although the ancestors are considered less active today than in the past, especially in the urban areas, ancestor dissatisfaction can be attributed to the failure of urban dwellers to uphold traditions, ceremonies, and respect for ancestors or elders. Ancestor dissatisfaction is frequently associated with social problems between family members such as constant quarrelling among families, family members who steal, or an unnatural number of deaths in a particular family. Urban dwellers are also likely to break taboos (especially sexual taboos) while living away from their families because they are living "the modern life" and are therefore less likely to uphold cultural beliefs and behavior. Breaking cultural taboos can cause illness and misfortune directly, or it can cause the ancestors to become angry and remove their protection.

In the urban area, with widespread Western health information campaigns, the majority of Katutura's population associate contamination with the transmission of contagious diseases. However, contamination can also occur when people come into contact with others in the urban area with who they normally would not be in contact. Although contamination by virtue of contagious magic is a traditional African concept, in Katutura it is frequently converted into the idea of "cultural contamination," where it is believed that contamination comes from simply being in contact with people from an ethnic group other than one's own. Another type of "cultural contamination" can occur within ethnically mixed marriages and partnerships. "Cultural contamination" is more likely to occur in the urban areas due to the presence of various ethnic groups and the higher likelihood of mixed marriages. Illnesses from contamination are also attributed to a form of contagious magic. For example, a person who has been bewitched to have misfortune may, by virtue of association, pass on the misfortune to friends or family members. However, many respondents indicate that witchcraft, epilepsy, and death can also come from contamination. In Nama society, contamination or contagious illnesses (*+hii //oob*) come from contact with a contaminated person. For example, a woman who has been bewitched and who is breastfeeding a child can give the witchcraft to the child through her breast milk.

Conclusion

This chapter has examined the Katutura population's utilization patterns between and within the Western and traditional health-care systems. The focus of the study was to determine what factors influence an urban patient's choice between Western and traditional medicine.

There are many variables that influence a patient's health-care choices. At the societal level, Western health care is the only formally recognized medical system in Namibia. This lack of official recognition influences health-care choices in only limited ways, such as a patient's inability to use health insurance when paying for traditional health-care services, and people's perceptions of traditional medicine as a supplement rather than an alternative to Western medicine. Although formal recognition of traditional medicine would convey a sense of its legitimacy to the wider Namibian society, formal recognition does not significantly influence health-seeking behavior.

People from Katutura have access to all of the forms of Western and traditional health care discussed above. However, patients make choices based on their perception of the cause and origin (etiology) of the illness, rather than access related factors, such as time needed to obtain treatment and relative cost. Both the Western and traditional medical systems each have their understanding as to the causes and cures of illness. Just as there are two systems of healing, there are two etiologies of illness that roughly correspond to the healing systems. The most important variables in health-seeking behavior are cultural beliefs, which are expressed in the patient's perceptions of the cause of illness, and the patient's interpretation of illness symptoms (manifestations).

Patients classify disorders into either Western or African illnesses. This classification is based on a combination of two factors:

The perceived cause of the illness: an illness can have either a social-spiritual or a natural cause.

The manifestations of the illness: an illness can exhibit exclusively African symptoms (e.g., ghosts) or symptoms that are universally recognized in both the Western and traditional medical paradigms.

Health-seeking behavior depends on how these two classifications are combined to classify an illness as either a Western or an African illness. However, to view choices patients make as an either/or issue is to greatly simplify patients' decision-making processes. For example, health seeking can begin in the home or with pharmacy medications, change to herbalists and spirit mediums, then move to Western medical practitioners. Patients can consult one traditional healer and if that treatment does not work, they can go back to the same healer, go to another healer, or even go to a traditional healer who is considered an "expert" in the illness affecting them. Patients may also utilize both systems at the same time. Some patients engage in "double consumption" because the Western medical practitioner is seen as dealing with the universally recognized manifestation of the illness, whereas the traditional healer deals with the social-spiritual cause of the illness.

Some illnesses are considered exclusively African illnesses (with a social-spiritual etiology and exclusively African manifestation), whereas some are considered Western illnesses (with a natural etiology and universally recognized manifestation). In a case where the type of an illness is positively identified by the patient, a single-use pattern of health care is more likely to be employed. Some illnesses have an African (social-spiritual) origin but a universally recognized manifestation, in which case both medical systems may be used simultaneously, whereas some illnesses are of indeterminate origin until treatment begins, in which case a multifaceted use pattern will take place. For these illnesses, health-seeking behavior may be highly fluid and patients may drift between the various health-care options available. Based on the above discussion, a model with the three distinct patterns for health-seeking behavior can be identified:

Single medical system utilization occurs when:

> Illnesses are perceived as having a social-spiritual cause with exclusively African manifestations, causing patients to first and only seek traditional health care.

> Illnesses are identified as having a natural cause as well as universally recognized manifestations, causing patients to most often seek Western health care.

Simultaneous medical system utilization occurs when:

> Illnesses have a social-spiritual cause with universally recognized manifestations. Patients may seek traditional medicine to cure the cause and Western medicine to cure its manifestations.

Sequential or multifaceted medical system utilization occurs when:

> Illnesses have universally recognized manifestations, but are of indeterminate cause until treatment begins to show success. In this situation patients are more likely to go to Western medicine first, only to determine that the cause of their illness is social-spiritual and therefore needs traditional treatment.

Previous successes and failures with the various medical systems influence subsequent health-seeking behavior. If patients have been to Western medicine for an illness without success, they may seek traditional medicine either because they perceive that Western medicine is of poor quality and inadequate, or that they have an African illness and Western medicine was the wrong treatment. Less often, due to the holistic approach of traditional medicine, the reverse can be said of patients' experience with traditional healers: that either traditional medicine does not cure the particular type of illness or that they have a Western illness that needs Western medicine.

Personal attributes that also influence health-seeking behavior include circumstance and belief systems. Some people have never had an illness that they felt required the services of a traditional healer. Many people who do not use traditional medicine say it is because they either do not believe in it or that it is against their Christian religious convictions.

Cultural attributes also influence health-seeking behavior and are expressed in terms of different types of social-spiritual explanations for illness by the various ethnic groups in Katutura. In addition, the urban nature of the Katutura population also influences health-seeking behavior. Social-spiritually caused illnesses can attack due to a number of external forces such as breaking cultural taboos, dissatisfaction of the ancestors, contamination, and most notably witchcraft attacks.

89

REFERENCES

Andersson, C. J. 1856. *Lake Ngami; or Exploration and Discoveries, During four Years' Wanderings in the Wilds of South Western Africa.* London: Hurst and Blackett Publishers.

Barfield, T., ed. 1997. *The dictionary of anthropology.* Oxford: Blackwell.

Becker, H. 1993. *Namibian women's movement, 1988 to 1992.* Wissenschaftliche Reihe: Wissen.

Bley, H. 1971. *South-west Africa under German rule, 1894-1914.* London: Heineman.

Central Statistic Office [CSO]. 1994. 1991 *Population and Housing Census: Basic Analysis with Highlights.* Windhoek: National Planning Commission [NPC].

Department of National Health and Welfare [DNHW]. 1989. *Health status report 1988/89.* Windhoek, Namibia: Government of the Republic of Namibia.

Department of Women Affairs [DWA]. 1995. *Convention on the elimination of all forms of discrimination against women (CEDAW): First country report, Republic of Namibia.* Windhoek, Namibia: Government of the Republic of Namibia.

Dillon-Malone, C. 1988. Mutumwa Nchimi healers and wizardry beliefs in Zambia. *Social Science and Medicine* 26 (11): 1159–72.

Frayne, B. 1992. *Urbanisation in post-independence Windhoek.* Windhoek, Namibia: NISER/UNAM.

Good, B. 1996. *Medicine, rationality, and experience: An anthropological perspective.* New York: Cambridge University Press.

Ministry of Health and Social Services [MoHSS]. 1992. *Official national primary healthcare/community based healthcare guidelines.* Windhoek, Namibia: Government of the Republic of Namibia.

Green, L. G. 1962. *Lords of the last frontier: The Story of South West Africa and its people of all races.* Cape Town, South Africa: Howard Timmins.

Haacke, W., and E. Eiseb.] 1999. *Khoekhoegowab-English/Khoekhoegowab-English Glossary/Mîdi Saogub.* Windhoek, Namibia: Gamsberg Macmillan.

Haacke, W., and E. Eiseb. 1997. Internal and external relations of Khoekhoe dialects: A preliminary survey. In *Namibian languages, reports and papers, Namibian African Studies*, vol. IV, eds. W. Haacke and E. D. Elderkin. Cologne, Germany: Kôppe Rüdiger.

90

Hahn, C. H. L., H. Vedder, and L. Fourie. 1966. *The native tribes of south west Africa*. London: Frank Cass.

Hiltunen, M. 1986. *Witchcraft and sorcery in Ovambo*. Helsinki: Finnish Anthropological Society.

————. 1993. *Good magic in Ovambo*. Helsinki: Finnish Anthropological Society.

Hishongwa, N. S. 1992. *The contract labour system and its effects on family and social life in Namibia*. Windhoek, Namibia: Gamsberg Macmillan.

Hoernlè, W. 1985. *The social organization of the Nama*. Johannesburg, South Africa: Witwatersand University Press.

Iipinge, E., and D. LeBeau. 1997. *Beyond inequality: Women in Namibia*. Harare, Zimbabwe: SARDC/UNAM.

Indongo, I. 1984. *Forward in Namibia: Reclaiming the people's health*. Ed. T. Lobstein. London: AON Publications.

Katjavivi, P. 1988. *A history of resistance in Namibia*. Paris: UNESCO.

LeBeau, D. 1991. *Namibia: Ethnic stereotyping in a post-apartheid state. Research Report No. 5*. Windhoek, Namibia: NISER.

————. 2000. Seeking health: The hierarchy of resort in utilisation patterns of traditional and western medicine in multi-cultural Katutura, Namibia. PhD diss. Rhodes University, Grahamstown, South Africa.

LeBeau, D., and S. Marais. 1997. *Sociology of medicine for nurses*. Windhoek, Namibia: University of Namibia.

LeBeau, D., and W. Pendleton. 1993. A socio-economic and baseline desk-top study of health, water and sanitation. Research report prepared for the Engela Integrated Health Project and the Water Supply and Sanitation Project in Ohangwena Region. Windhoek, Namibia: NISER/FINNIDA.

Malan, J. S. 1995. *Peoples of Namibia*. Pretoria, South Africa: Rhino Publishers.

Ministry of Health and Social Services [MoHSS]. 1998. More than the love of a parent: Namibia's first study on orphan children. Windhoek, Namibia: Author.

————. 1993. *Namibia demographic and health survey 1992*. Atlanta, GA: Macro International.

Möller, P. 1974. *Journey in Africa: Through Angola, Ovamboland, and Damaraland*. Cape Town, South Africa: C. Struik.

National Planning Commission [NPC]. 1996. Living conditions in Namibia. Windhoek, Namibia: Author.

————. 1994. 1991 Population and housing Census: Basic analysis with highlights. Windhoek, Namibia: Author.

Rossouw, J. P. H., and J. L. Van Tonder, ed. 1989. *Southern African demographic and health survey: Namibia 1989: Infant mortality and child health.* Johnnesburg, South Africa: Human Sciences Research Council Press.

Slikkerveer, L. J. 1982. Rural health development in Ethiopia: Problems of utilization of traditional healers. *Social Science and Medicine,* 16: 1859–72.

Soggot, D. 1986. *Namibia: The violent heritage.* London: Rex Collins.

Tönjes, H. 1996. *Ovamboland.* Windhoek, Namibia: National Scientific Society.

Tvedten, I., and M. Mupotola. 1995. Urbanization and urban policies in Namibia. Social Science Division discussion paper #10. Windhoek, Namibia: University of Namibia.

United Nations Development Program [UNDP]. 1998. Namibia human development report 1998. Windhoek, Namibia: Author.

————. 1997. Namibia human development report 1997. Windhoek, Namibia: Author.

United Nations Joint Program on HIV/AIDS [UNAIDS]. 1998. Namibians speak out on HIV/AIDS. Windhoek, Namibia: Author.

Vedder, H. 1966. *South west Africa in early times.* London: Frank Cass.

Wallace, M. E. 1997. Health and society in Windhoek, Namibia, 1915–1945. PhD diss., University of London.

Wellington, J. H. 1967. *South west Africa and its human issues.* London: Oxford University Press.

World Health Organization [WHO]. 1990. Water supply and sanitation sector review. Windhoek, Namibia: Author.

5

Nigerian Americans and Health

Doug Henry, PhD. Assistant Professor, Department of Anthropology, University of North Texas, Denton, Texas.

Ethnic Identity and Definition

Nigerians are a particularly difficult people to generalize about. There is not one dominant Nigerian culture; over 200 different ethnic groups exist, each with its own language, customs, and traditions. In general, the Igbo are the largest group in the South and East of Nigeria, the Hausa and Fulani in the North, and the Yoruba in the South and West. Nigerians come to the United States for many reasons, some for economic opportunity, some fleeing political or religious persecution, some studying to obtain an advanced degree or certification abroad, and some simply joining family already here. Most arrive in the U.S. well educated (Reynolds 2002). Despite problems in Nigeria, interethnic relations among Nigerians in this country are more often cordial. It is common, however, to recognize kinship ties with members of one's same village, town, region, or ethnicity of origin; these relationships then become important mechanisms of material, social, and emotional support in times of instability in this country.

Demographics: Proportion of the Larger Population, Age and Sex Distribution

Nigerians represent the largest of West African immigrant groups living in the United States, with a U.S. population of approximately 100,000. They dwell especially along the eastern seaboard and in all major cities. The U.S. Census Bureau reports no data on age and sex distributions specific to Nigerian-

Americans, though if one may generalize from the data that exist for the general population of African-born immigrants, the median age is slightly younger than that of the native-born, and proportionately more male (U.S. Census Bureau 2001; see also Hansen and Faber 1997).

Major Diseases and Health Disparities Compared with the General Population

There is little research about the condition of Africans living in the United States,[33] and much less that considers diseases or health disparities related specifically to Nigerians. What exists considers the "brain drain" that having such an educated, professional class of immigrants represents to the country of origin (Reynolds 2002), or the somewhat paradoxical experiences of incorporation and discrimination that Nigerian immigrants to the U.S. face (Cordell *in press*). Concerning health care, there is research about the health status of a generalized population of mostly East-African–born residents (Siegel, Horan, and Tsferra 2001), the health of recent Nigerian immigrants or refugees (Early, McKinney, and Murray 2000), or the encounters of Nigerian-Americans or other West Africans with the U.S. health-care system (Leonard and VanLandingham 2001, Henry and Kemp 2002, Henry 2004).

Malaria may be especially common among recently arrived immigrants, refugees, or travelers from Nigeria. The classic symptoms are severe fever, chills, sweats, and headache. Schistosomiasis is also prevalent in some regions of Nigeria, caused by freshwater parasites (flukes) entering the body from contaminated rivers or streams. Also known as Bilharzias, it can cause fever, chills, tachycardia, diarrhea, or pain in any of the organs. Onchoceriasis, also called river blindness, is caused by the bites of black flies. Onchoceriasis may cause eye lesions and an itchy rash, especially in middle to older age individuals.

---

[33] For notable exceptions, see Stoller (1999, 2002), and the upcoming edited volume by Afolabi and Falola (*in press*).

Nigeria's HIV rate is increasing, and is estimated at between 3 to 6 percent of adults (UNAIDS 2006). Because of its large population, Nigeria has the third-largest HIV+ population in the world. AIDS carries with it considerable stigma among Nigerians (Alubo et al. 2002), therefore recommendations for HIV testing should be approached delicately by any practitioner.

Some researchers estimate that over 99 percent of Nigerian males, and 95 percent of females, are circumcised (Caldwell, Orubuloye, and Caldwell 1997; Igwegbe 2000). Female circumcision is often known in the U.S. as "female genital mutilation" (FGM). Among Nigerian women this can involve anything from a minor ritual cut on the hood covering the clitoris, excision of the hood, excision of part or all of the clitoris, excision of part or all of the labia minora, to (in the most extreme form, practiced only in a small area of Northern Nigeria) removal also of the labia majora, and stitching across the two sides of the vulva, which are then cut away upon marriage (Myers 1990). FGM has generally been strongly opposed by international women's groups and health practitioners on the grounds that the clitoral or labial mutilation may be considerably painful or sometimes life threatening, or that it is meant to reduce female libido, and is an example of the domination of women by men. For both men and women, the appropriate time for circumcision varies from 0 to 3 months after birth to puberty and adolescence. An equally passionate, often indigenous view sees the practice as controlled by women, for women. They view efforts to eradicate its practice as equivalent to Western, even male, imperialism (Adeleye-Fayemi 1994).

Nutritionally, a "healthy" body in Nigeria is conceived of as a large body, often described admiringly in terms like "plump," "full," or "fleshy." The Nigerian diet, especially in southern Nigeria, is high in palm oil, which has nutritious vitamins, but is also high in saturated fat. This may cause Nigerians in the United States to be at increased risk for cardiovascular disorders and diabetes.

Health-Seeking Behavior

When faced with sickness, Nigerians tend to be practical in their health-seeking behavior, but this practicality is defined by both the situation and the diagnosis made by the patient, the therapist, and the patient's family. Lay diagnoses and treatment are in turn impossible to understand without consideration of "traditional" health beliefs situated within Nigerian culture and religious thought, and the centrality of religion in Nigerian life. As with any broad survey, the statements that follow about "Nigerian culture" should be taken as generalizations subject to individual circumstance and change, not as steadfast "facts" applicable to every situation.

A Nigerian proverb says, "God is the medicine for everything." For the vast majority of Nigerians, religion is extremely important, permeating all aspects of daily life, including health and illness. Nigeria as a population is often labeled 50 percent Muslim, 40 percent Christian, and 10 percent "traditional"/indigenous religion, but this masks the complex ways in which aspects of traditional religious or spiritual beliefs enter and become a part of modern belief systems. Even those who consider themselves to be "good Muslims" or "devout Christians" may also follow "traditional" practices, such as prayers or sacrifices to the ancestors, the use of charms to ward off evil spirits or witchcraft, or traditional divination or prophecy.

Islam is everywhere in Nigeria, but is predominant among those from the North, especially the Hausa and Fulani. Christianity is most prevalent among those from the South, especially the Igbo. The most popular forms are similar to the Protestant denominations found in the United States, although many indigenous denominations are developing that incorporate Africanisms into their doctrines, such as an ease of restrictions on polygamy, incorporation of faith or spiritual healing, or the use of divination or charms.

Indigenous religions vary, though they share the idea that one supreme God created the world and is active in its everyday affairs. He must be prayed or sacrificed to vigilantly in order to maintain a good relationship. Many different lesser gods and spirits are also influential in daily life, and can even be mischievous in nature (Ezeji and Sarvela 1992). They are considered to be everywhere, and have domains in trees, water, rocks, rivers, or mountains. Finally, ancestral spirits are extremely important. Ever-present and particularly influential, they may intercede on one's behalf to the supreme God, if a good relationship with them is kept through prayers, sacrifices, or obedience to laws they may have set forth before their death (Kayode and Adelowo 1985).

"Sickness" to the Western practitioner typically refers to a problem with physical health, as in a disruption of the proper functioning of the body. The Nigerian concept is typically more inclusive, often considering not just the individual, but also the individual's social relationships with family, the community, and the moral order of existence. Likewise, "health" is more than just physical functioning: it is more the proper balance and well-being of the individual, and the state and order of the individual's relationships in society (Lambo 1999). Thus, "ill-health" is as much a social and moral dilemma as it is a personal one—the three realms are conceptually intertwined. For example, in Hausa, the word *ciwo* is usually used to describe "pain" or sickness in different parts of the body, yet can also mean "an offense," "a drawback," or "a discouragement." Likewise, *cuta* can mean a disruptive bodily function, but a derivative form means "an offensive act," or "to deceive" or "cheat" (Wall 1988). Sicknesses are generally thought to arise in one of two ways: from inanimate, natural forces in the physical environment, or as the result of the actions of some conscious, malevolent power. The first group are ailments that just "happen" as a normal part of everyday life, often caused by variations in the physical environment—especially irregular or excessive fluctuations in hot and cold.

Partly influenced by Islamic ideas of humoral medicine, Nigerians traditionally conceptualize the body's physiology in terms of a balance of fluids, like blood, water, urine, and phlegm (Abdalla 1997). Damp cold, for example, may be thought to enter the body and decrease the blood while increasing phlegm, and result in the common illness complaint of "low blood." As a condition, low blood symptomatically presents as malaise or a "weak body." Left untreated, low blood is thought to cause extreme tiredness, fever, or jaundice of the eyes. The prescription is usually to eat nutritious, often spicy foods, both "hot" and high in vitamins, iron, or protein. Nutrition must also be balanced—bodily health is traditionally seen as related to the proper balance of sweet, sour, bitter, or salty substances. If ingesting too much sugar is seen to cause a fever or stomachache, for example, bitter food or a bitter medicine is likely to be the popular prescription. A healthy appetite is seen as necessary to keep the blood "strong." Behavior must also exist in moderation: for example, eating too many sweet foods or having too much sex has traditionally been believed to cause impurities to settle in a woman's womb, capable of causing infertility. Thus, traditional treatments "wash" the womb to make it fertile again by causing the body to expel impurities in urine, feces, or menses (Renne 1996).

"Coldness," especially damp cold, is often considered causative of illness, and widely held responsible for coughs, colds, and acute respiratory infections (Iyun and Tomson 1996). Especially children are considered vulnerable to cold, exposed through a cold breeze, use of electric fans, or even air conditioning. Traditional remedies may be warm and soothing, especially as a warm tea or ointment, with the idea that the heat expels the cold from the chest.

The second cause of sickness is intentional, traditionally attributed to witchcraft, sorcery, or evil spirits. Particularly among children (whose souls are considered weaker and more vulnerable), chronic sicknesses and illnesses may be blamed on the malevolent actions of spirits or witchcraft. Witches are the personal embodiment of evil intent. Some people, recognized by their anti-social behavior, are thought to harbor witch spirits, capable of casting harm even without direct physical contact. If a sick person begins to lose weight and "waste" away, it is often said of them that a witch has "seized" their body or is "eating" them. It should be noted that witchcraft is rarely considered to be at the root of sickness among Nigerians living in the United States, though some may worry about the jealousy or ill-will harbored by contacts back in Nigeria.

For both kinds of sickness, there are a wide variety of medicines. "Medicine" to the Western practitioner usually represents something that can physically cure or relieve symptoms, and restore the health of a patient. In the traditional West African belief system, medicine may do more than just heal an illness: it can restore order, rightness, and balance (Asuni 1979). It can be a pill, leaf, drink, injection, prayer, charm, or even a ritual object used to bring about a certain desired end. It can be protective or curative, but can also potentially be used for bad purposes, depending on how it is manipulated by a practitioner.

If the Nigerian patient becomes sick or hospitalized, families become important sources for material, social, and emotional support, especially siblings, parents, uncles and aunts, and cousins. Individuals are rarely the lone decision makers during an illness; families often become involved as a "therapy-management group" in providing advice, diagnosis, or treatment to the sick person (Du Toit and Abdallah 1985, Ohaeri 1998). Traditionally, most Nigerian families are extended, although nuclear families are also common in the United States. Men, even if residing in this country, may have more than one wife. Men are the authority figures and generally direct household and decision making for the family, although women may play important advisory or advocate roles. In the Yoruba culture especially, paternal or maternal uncles will often be called "father" and the aunt "mother," especially if the "real" parent is absent or dead. It is also common for Nigerians living away from family at home to "adopt" fictive kin; hence younger people may thus call an older family friend or supporter "father," "mother," "uncle," or "auntie."

If the patient becomes incapacitated or unable to make decisions, decision-making authority usually passes to the eldest male family member present. If a woman is sick, her husband (if present) will have decision-making power, but decisions surrounding a sick husband usually are presided over by his brothers, sisters, or uncles. A woman may, however, have considerable input for health-care decisions concerning her own children or a member of her side of the family (Ohaeri et al. 1999).

Terminal illness may place particular stress on Nigerian patients and their families, and require major adjustments in their lives. In particular, recently immigrated families who may have to work several jobs to support themselves may be hard pressed to make adjustments, to mobilize support networks, or to develop coping strategies. A male patient will worry about his family, especially that his illness may cause an unmanageable financial burden on his wife or children. A female patient will likewise worry about family, particularly who will take care of her children or her husband upon her death.

If faced with a terminal illness, the Nigerian patient may decide it best to withhold knowledge of the illness from family members to prevent them from worrying. A man may choose to confide with a close male relative to outline a will. Alternately, depending on the patient's level of coherence or capacity, family members may decide to deliberately withhold some facts from the patient, especially if they judge it in his or her best interest. Most often, however, families should be helpful in communicating to the patient both information about the disease and the prescription for treatment. They could be actively solicited by Western-trained health professionals for their support, perhaps even serving as intermediary counselors. Realistic hope should be given, though practitioners may become frustrated by what seems to be a fatalistic attitude towards terminal illness. Terminal illness and death are sometimes seen as the will of God that cannot be changed (Buckley 1985). Nigerians particularly dislike "predictive" or time-determinant medical prognoses (e.g., "Person X has probably two months to live"), and such a statement would likely provoke much anxiety. "God's time is the best" is an often-heard quote, a statement both of spiritual devotion and a fatalistic admission of powerlessness before God's will.

At the end of life, death is almost always preferable at home, which usually implies passing occurred in peace. Upon death, all Nigerian religions favor burial; cremation almost never occurs. Many, especially the Igbo from the East, will spend over US$10,000 to ship the bodies of family members back to Nigeria for burial. Muslims are buried facing the holy city of Mecca. Otherwise, men are traditionally buried facing east towards the rising sun, women towards the west, and the setting sun. Both Muslims and Christians believe that, following death, the soul is released from the body and must be judged before God to enter Heaven. Traditional religions emphasize reincarnation, in which the deceased is often thought to be able to come back as a member of the maternal line. There may be complex rituals to prepare the body before burial, especially if the family decides precautions are necessary to prevent an illness suffered by the deceased from being passed on to the soul's next life. For instance, a person who was blind in one life may have special medicines placed over the eyes upon burial, to prevent blindness in the next life. Death is often especially difficult for surviving widows, as the deceased's male relatives are entitled to the material belongings of the estate. She may often take up residence with one of her former husband's brothers. Mourning can be quite emotional, especially when compared to conservative Western norms. Funerals are elaborate, especially for those of high social standing, and more so for men than for women or children. Additional ceremonies usually occur seven and forty days after death. It is often thought that the more music and dancing, the better a person's chances of beginning a successful afterlife.

Healers and Practitioners

In a society where healing represents the reestablishment of social, physical, spiritual, and material equilibrium, traditional healers represent important moral integrators in their communities. Different healers may prevent, diagnose, or cure illness, protect property, enhance productivity, set broken bones, detect ill intent from within the community, assist in politics or business, purge witches, and mediate between the living and their ancestors.

Indigenous traditional healers can be male or female, and often preside over secret knowledge of ritual or botanical lore, often passed down over generations or imparted to them by some spirit or ancestor figure. They may be consulted for a wide variety of ailments, from a cough, headache, stomachache, or sore throat, to more serious problems, like broken bones or psychiatric disorders. They are widely considered effective, undoubtedly in part because of their ability to communicate effectively, listen, and "connect" with the patient on both personal and cultural levels (Asuni 1979). Their medicines, too, beyond being innately effective, may produce fewer side effects than some Western drugs.

Herbalists are the most common of "traditional" Nigerian healers. Botanical knowledge among some is extensive, and there are literally thousands of known plants (including roots, stems, leaves, seeds, or bark) documented in current pharmacopoeia. Medicines may be made into a tea, an ointment, a poultice, or a water-based wash, depending on the diagnosis and prescription.

Muslim-based healers, almost always men, are common, especially among the Hausa and Fulani from the North. They may use combinations of Qur'anic or other sacred prayers or texts, divination, and "traditional" plants or herbs. Their medicines often include written passages taken from holy Islamic texts, sometimes mixed with substances made from vegetable, mineral, or animal origin. Christian-based "faith" healers are also popular, especially among the Igbo and Yoruba.

In Nigeria, traditional barbers may circumcise, tattoo, perform an uvulectomy, or practice "cupping," usually on the back or shoulders, in order to dispel "dead" blood, often considered at the root of localized subcutaneous swelling. Cupping is performed first by making a series of small incisions in the skin. A goat or cow's horn is then placed over each cut, and the air is sucked out, creating a vacuum inside that draws out blood. Dark blood coagulates inside the horn, comprising the "dead" blood to be disposed. Circumcisers of females are most often women; male circumcision is almost always performed by men.

Access To and Use of Health-Care System

Siegel, Horan, and Tseferra (2001) report that recently arrived African immigrants are at risk for reduced access to health care, being twice as likely to lack health insurance, and to have less contact with the health-care system. Leonard and VanLandingham (2001) collected data from Nigerians traveling to and from Nigeria to ask about health and health-maintenance before, during, and after a visit. They found that Nigerian travelers perceived themselves to be at risk for malaria while overseas, but were generally not concerned with its consequences, believing themselves to be physically adapted to handle it. Most preferred not to buy prescription medicine in the United States and start prophylaxis before the trip, but would wait to buy in Nigeria, as the price for prophylaxis was significantly cheaper. The cost of treating malaria is also significantly cheaper— between US$1–2 in Nigeria, versus $350 (if uninsured) in the United States (Leonard and VanLandingham 2001, 41). Barriers to accessing care before a trip were primarily cost, the limited availability of tropical medications that few U.S. pharmacies stock, and a skepticism about Western practitioners' limited knowledge and experience with tropical diseases, especially malaria. Posttravel, Nigerians worried most about falling ill with malaria in the United States, especially as it was felt that Western physicians would confuse malarial symptoms for allergies or the flu, or would order irrelevant or expensive tests that take days to receive results. Still others described embarrassing or humiliating experiences in which hospitals "isolated" them, fearing that their malaria was infectious, or suspected them of being HIV positive, and thus delayed time-sensitive treatment.

Most Nigerian patients have no problem using a mixture of traditional and Western medicines, sometimes in succession, but often synchronetically. There are even places of collaboration in Nigeria that are considered widely successful, particularly in treating psychiatric disorders (Offiong 1999). Although there is some debate as to whether the two systems should be considered complementary, the fact is that Nigerians themselves often patronize elements of both.

Although Nigerians living abroad may receive packages of traditional herbs or medicines from relatives living in Nigeria, they may be particularly sensitive to being questioned by a Western nurse or doctor about its use. Especially direct questioning about traditional medicines could be easily interpreted as a prejudicial accusation of Western arrogance that "being African" *must* equal "being primitive" or "backwards." Such questioning could also cause much offense in the patient or family, and certainly alienate the medical practitioner from the group. A health professional concerned about possible pharmacological contraindication can, however, still sensitively inquire about recent herbal medicine use. Questions can be carefully and appropriately worded (e.g., *"I don't want to give you a medicine that might react badly with something you've already been taking; can you tell me everything that you've taken or that people have given you by mouth over the past ___ days?"*). Family members may also be particularly helpful in this situation.

Other communication barriers with the Nigerian patient may easily exist, and may interfere with "what is spoken" and "what is heard" between patients and their providers. Barriers may be language or culturally based, but could easily be compounded by emotional distress. Disclosure of personal information to a nurse or physician may be further complicated by a patient worrying about accidental disclosure of potential visa or immigration problems. For example, though a male patient may have multiple wives, they are certainly aware of the legal implications of this disclosure. Thoughtful communication skills may be particularly useful for frank but considerate discussion of the illness at hand, with both the patient and the therapy management group. In addition, health-care workers in the United States would do much to put their patients at ease by respecting basic West African protocol. For example, long and effuse greetings are always important. Elders are particularly respected regardless of gender; consideration to important persons can be shown by shaking hands with the right hand while supporting the forearm with the left hand.

Socioeconomic Differences in Health-Seeking Behavior

Despite the length spent above describing "traditional" West African health beliefs, Western practitioners should be wary of an over-focus on "traditional culture" to understand or predict the health-seeking behavior of Nigerian immigrants. Nigerian patient noncompliance with a physician's or nurse's orders is less likely to be caused by a disjuncture between different cultural health beliefs than by other reasons—medicines may be expensive or have intolerable side effects, symptoms may disappear in mid-treatment, or the prescribed regimen or rehabilitation may interfere with a busy work schedule.

Like many immigrant groups in the United States, Nigerians sometimes have to work long hours for low wages. The fear of not being able to support one's family due to expensive or difficult to take medicine may prove stronger than the patient's desire to have a prescription filled. Sicknesses among immigrants, especially chronic ones, may cause severe financial burden. Adult children are likely to be expected to be able to provide material support for their parents. The U.S. Census Bureau reports that 30 percent of African-born residents of the United States are uninsured (compared to 14% of the general population) (2000). In their survey of over 500 African immigrants in Washington, D.C., Siegel, Horan, and Tseferra (2001) found that the leading reason for being uninsured was inability to afford coverage. They also found that income levels were low: 75 percent of respondents had an income below $25,000 (215). Almost 25 percent lacked a usual source of primary care (219). Among female respondents, 44 percent reported never having a mammogram; 34 percent had never had a pap smear (220). Among all respondents, 14 percent said they had been unable to see a doctor within the past twelve months due to cost; 20 percent came from households that had at least one member who could not see a doctor due to cost (220). The proportion who reported this was higher among persons more recent arrivals and women.

REFERENCES

Abdalla, I. 1997. *Islam, medicine, and practitioners in Northern Nigeria. Studies in African Health and Medicine, vol. 6.* Lewiston, NY: Edwin Mellen Press.

Adeleye-Fayemi, B. 1994. *Shinamania: Gender, sexuality, and popular culture in Nigeria.* Evanston, IL: Northwestern University Press.

Afolabi, N., and T. Falola, eds. In press. *African Minorities in the New World: Trans-Atlantic Migration and the Paradoxes of Exile.* New Brunswick: Rutgers Press. Expected printing fall 2006.

Alubo, O; A. Zwandor, T. Jolayemi, and E. Omudu. 2002. *Acceptance and stigmatization of PLWA in Nigeria. AIDS Care.* 14(1): 117-26.

Asuni, T. 1979. The dilemma of traditional healing with special reference to Nigeria. *Social Science and Medicine* 13B: 33–39.

Buckley, A. 1985. *Yoruba medicine.* Oxford: Clarendon Press.

Caldwell, J., I. O. Orubuloye, and P. Caldwell. 1997. Male and female circumcision in Africa from a regional to a specific Nigerian examination. *Social Science and Medicine* 44(8): 1181–93.

Cordell, D. in press. Paradoxes of Immigrant Incorporation: High Achievement and Perceptions of Discrimination by Nigerians in Dallas/ Fort Worth, Texas (USA). To appear in *African Minorities in the New World: Trans-Atlantic Migration and the Paradoxes of Exile.* Eds. N. Afolabi and T. Falola. New Brunswick: Rutgers Press: Expected printing fall 2006.

Du Toit, B., and I. Abdallah, eds. 1985. *African healing systems.* New York: Trado-Medic Books.

Early, M., S. McKinney, and J. Murray. 2000. Nigerian refugees and immigrants. Retrieved July 17, 2003, from www3.baylor.edu/~Charles_Kemp/nigerian_refugees.htm

Ezeji, P., and P. Sarvela. 1992. Health-care behavior of the Ibo tribe of Nigeria. *Health Values* 16(6): 31.

Hansen, L., and C. Faber. 1997. *The foreign-born population: 1996.* Current Population Reports. Washington, DC: Government Printing Office.

Henry, D., and C. Kemp. 2002. Culture and the End of Life: Nigerians. *Journal of Hospice and Palliative Nursing* 4(2): 111-115.

Henry, D. 2004. Liberia. In *Refugee and Immigrant Health: a Handbook for Health Professionals.* Eds. C. Kemp and L. Rasbridge. Cambridge: Cambridge University Press. Pp. 253-260.

Igwegbe, A. 2000. The prevalence and practice of female genital mutilation in Nnewi, Nigeria: The impact of female education. *Journal of Obstetrics and Gynecology* 20(5):520–29.

Iyun, F., and G. Tomson. 1996. Acute respiratory infections—Mothers' perceptions of etiology and treatment in Southwestern Nigeria. *Social Science and Medicine* 42(3): 437–45.

Kayode, J., and E. Dada Adelowo. 1985. Religions in Nigeria. In *Nigerian History and Culture*, ed. R. Olaniyan. Harlow, UK: Longman.

Lambo, T. 1999. *Psychotherapy in Africa*. Annual Editions: Anthropology. Guilford, CT: McGraw-Hill.

Leonard, L., and VanLandingham, M. (2001) Adherence to Travel Health Guidelines: The Experience of Nigerian Immigrants in Houston, Texas. *Journal of Immigrant Health*, 3(1): 31-45.

Myers, R. 1990. Female genital mutilation in southern Nigeria. *Women's International Network News* 16(2): 43–46.

Offiong, D. 1999. Traditional healers in the Nigerian health care delivery system and the debate over integrating traditional and scientific medicine. *Anthropological Quarterly* 72(3): 118–39.

Ohaeri, J. 1998. Perception of the social support role of the extended family network by some Nigerians with schizophrenia and affective disorders. *Social Science and Medicine* 47(10): 1463–72.

Ohaeri, J., O. Campbell, A. Ilesanmi, and A. Omigbodun. 1999. The psychosocial burden of caring for some Nigerian women with breast cancer and cervical cancer. *Social Science and Medicine* 49(11): 1541–49.

Renne, E. 1996. The pregnancy that doesn't stay: The practice and perception of abortion by Ekiti Yoruba women. *Social Science and Medicine* 42(4): 483–94.

Reynolds, P. 2002. An African Brain Drain: Igbo Decisions to Immigrate to the U.S. *Review of African Political Economy* 29 (92): 273-284.

Siegel, J., S. Horan, and T. Tseferra. 2001. Health and health care status of African-born residents of metropolitan Washington, DC. *Journal of Immigrant Health* 3(4): 213–24.

Stoller, P. 2002. *Money has no smell: The Africanization of New York City*. Chicago: University of Chicago Press.

———. 1999. *Jaguar: A story of Africans in America*. Chicago: University of Chicago Press.

Solanke, T. 1997. Communication with the cancer patient in Nigeria: Information and truth. In *Communication with the cancer patient*, ed. A. Surbone and M. Zwitter. New York: New York Academy of Sciences.

UNAIDS. 2006. Report on the Global AIDS Epidemic. New York: Joint United Nations Programme on HIV/ AIDS.

U.S. Census Bureau. 2001. *Broad age groups of the foreign-born population by region of birth and sex: 2000.* Washington, DC: Government Printing Office.

————. 2000. *Health care coverage of the foreign-born population by region of birth and sex: 1999.* Washington, DC: Government Printing Office.

Wall, L. 1988. *Hausa medicine: Illness and well-being in a west African culture.* Durham, NC: Duke University Press.

6

Arab Americans

Alice Reizian, DNSc. Professor, Adult Nursing Department, Faculty of Nursing, University of Alexandria, Egypt.

Ethnic Identity and Definition

Who are the Arab Americans?

Arab Americans form part of the United States' mosaic of ethnic people, and their numbers have increased considerably in the 1990's.Arab Americans are Arabic-speaking people, usually of Semitic origin, who were born in an Arab country and migrated to the United States, or whose parents were born in an Arab country and therefore consider themselves of Arabic origin (Lipson and Meleis 1983; Reizian 1984).

The Arab World extends over North Africa and Asia. It includes Algeria, Arab Emirates, Bahrain, Djibouti, Egypt, Iraq, Jordan, Kuwait, Lebanon, Libya, Mauritania, Morocco, Oman, Palestine, Qatar, Saudi Arabia, Somalia, Sudan, Syria, Tunisia, and Yemen. The population of this area exceeds 250 million inhabitants.

There are an estimated 3–4 million Arab Americans in the United States. Over half of them are well assimilated, being third and fourth generation descendants of Lebanese-Syrian immigrants who arrived between 1875 and 1948 (Naff 1980; Abraham 1981).

Arab Americans represent many nationalities and three major religions: Christianity, Islam, and Judaism; 78 percent are Christian, 21 percent are Moslem, and a small percentage are Jewish. Arab Christians represent several religious affiliations, including Lebanese Christians of Maronite, Melkite, Syrian and Greek Orthodox faiths, Eastern Rite Catholic Chaldeans, Roman Catholics, Protestants, and Egyptian Copts. There are Sunni (Shafei, Hanafi, Hanbali, and Malki) and Shia Muslims. Muslims of Ismaielities, Zeidi, Wahabi, Alawi, Bahaii, Ahmadi, and Durzi persuasions are also represented (Gold 2001).

Migration Patterns
Arab immigration to the United States occurred in several waves. The movement started as early as the middle of the nineteenth century until just before World War I coming predominantly from Greater Syria known nowadays as Lebanon, Syria, and Transjordania. A second wave of Arab immigration to the United States began after World War II and consisted of Syrians, Lebanese, Yemenis, and a large number of Palestinians displaced after the 1948 Palestine partition (Abraham 1981; Abraham and Abraham 1983). A final wave of immigration took place in 1967–70 after the Arab-Israeli war and the subsequent Lebanese political unrest. In the 1980s, approximately 150,000 Arab immigrants entered the United States. In the 1990s, the Immigration and Naturalization Service reported that the immigration rate has continued to grow by 3 percent annually (Zogby 2000; Orfalea 2005).

Early Arab immigrants were mainly nationals of the Ottoman Empire. These immigrants were single illiterate men who were employed as unskilled workers. Later on, the type of immigrants changed because they left their countries for political or religious reasons. In addition, a number of students and professionals from Iraq, Egypt, Syria, and Lebanon came to the United States as students or to work and preferred to remain (Abu-Laban 1980). The conflict in the Middle East, search of economic advancement, upgrading of life standards, escape of political pressure and personal threat, as well as religious challenges, were main causes for immigration. Another important factor was family unification. Palestinian immigrants, for instance, with greater networks and family

113

links overseas managed to join their extended family members in the United States. These more recent immigrants are largely unacculturated and unassimilated into the mainstream of U.S. society. Furthermore, they have limited English proficiency and a high degree of illiteracy ([Detroit] Free Press 2001).

Demographics, Geographical Location, Community, and Social Class
Though the United State's ethnic landscape includes a rapidly growing Arab population, it is still not identified nor addressed. It is classified within the category "other race," which makes up 5.46 percent of the total population in the United States (U.S. Census 2000).

Arab Americans live in all fifty states with the larger agglomeration in Michigan (Detroit), California (Los Angeles and San Francisco), New York, Illinois (Chicago), Maryland, Massachusetts, New Jersey, Ohio, Texas, and Virginia. The population density is variable. The Census 2000 Supplementary Survey reported that about over 1 million people reported Arab ancestry, distributed as follows: California (169,000), New York (107,000), Michigan (97,000), Washington, D.C. (30,000), Alaska and North Dakota (around 500), and Wyoming (fewer than 300 residents). Arabs of Lebanese origin account for 80 percent of the Arab population in the states of Maine, Vermont, and New Mexico, and accounting for at least 50 percent of the Arab population in eight additional states. The second largest group of Americans Arab originates from Egypt (11%), followed by Syrians (10%), Palestinians (6%), Jordanians (6%), Moroccans (4%), and Iraqis (3%).

It is worth noting that the greater Detroit area is home to perhaps the largest Arab settlement with 300,000 inhabitants. Southeast Dearborn's "Arab Village," adjacent to Ford's famous River Rouge plant, is home to a vibrant community. Approximately 40 percent of children in the city's schools are of Arab origin. Lebanese, Yemenis, Iraqis, and Palestinians continue to arrive in the region. A significantly large Yemeni population resides in Hamtramck, Michigan.

The Chicago Arab-American community is one of the three largest agglomerations in the United States. With a varied representation of the estimated 150,000 Arabs in the Chicago metropolitan area, the community includes Palestinians (57%), Jordanians (20%), Egyptians (7%), Iraqis (4%), Syrians (3%), Lebanese (2.6%), and Yemenis (2%). This community represents a young population; the majority are 14–19 years old.

Arab American's first, second, and third generations are well educated. The proportion of Arab Americans who attend college is higher than the national average. Compared to the norm, about twice as many Arab Americans earn degrees beyond the bachelor's degree, although this varies according to country of origin, length of time in the United States, and gender. Eighty-two percent of Arab Americans have at least a high school diploma; 36 percent have a bachelor's degree or higher degree; 15 percent have graduate degrees. Of the school-age population, 7 percent are in pre-primary school, 53.6 percent are enrolled in elementary or high school, and 39.5 percent are enrolled in college (Arab American Institute 2000).

Analysis of 1990 Census data for Michigan indicates that, as a group, Arabs are relatively well off, with a higher percentage of college graduates than Whites, relatively low rates of unemployment, and sub-poverty income. However, the community reveals significant economic variance, as some members are poor, whereas others are successful professionals (Gold 2001).

Arab Americans are found in every economic strata of U.S. life. They work in all occupations. About 60 percent are self-employed entrepreneurs, executives, professionals, office, and sales staff. Arab Americans are most likely to be executives in Washington, D.C., and Anaheim, California, sales people in Cleveland, and manufacturing workers in Detroit.

Famous Arab Americans have worked in the U.S. Senate, as Secretary of Health and Human Services, state governors, presidents of industrial companies, prominent lawyers and surgeons, White House Chief of Staff, and even a presidential candidate ([Detroit] Free Press 2001).

Culture and Language

Three important major aspects of Arab culture are family and its kinship ties, language, and Arab personality traits.

In Arab communities, the family is the most important prominent social unit; therefore loyalty to the family is highly valued. Racy (1970) has described this kinship system as the central, most durable, and most influential social institution in the Middle East. The family unit, which is the basis of all social relations, is patriarchal. Grouped in an economic unit around the father, who is the leader, are his male descendants and their wives and children, living together in several nuclear families. Within the extended family, uncles, aunts, and cousins, and immediate family members usually live in close proximity and maintain close ties. Affiliation follows the male line and women settle with the families of their husbands. The structure is characterized by masculine authority and subordination of women. In the past few years, this extended family has tended to give way to the nuclear family, which has made for increased individual autonomy and a more positive role for women (Rodinson 1981).

Although individual differences and variations exist from one country to another, early-arranged marriages, preferably to cousins in order to strengthen family ties, is favorably regarded in Middle-Eastern society. When in need, because of strong kinship and affiliation ties, one turns to a member of the family for assistance in almost any area, whether it be questions of health, financial need, the quest for a wife, or employment (Abu-Laban 1980).

Arabic is the common language spoken in the Arab World and is one of the great unifying modalities of Arab people. Colloquial Arabic is the spoken language with specific accents for each country in the region. Dialects from Morocco to Yemen to Iraq differ; Berber, Sawahili, and Amazigh are other spoken dialects. In the former French colonies, French remains the first language; however, the classical written and spoken Arabic language is the common denominator and the unifier of the Middle East. Arabic is a rich language, particularly apt for affective and descriptive expression. There is a tendency to overemphasis, hyperbole, and exaggeration: if not in the language itself, then in its expression (Racy 1970).

The most prominent aspects of the Arab personality are a strong affect, a deep narcissism, an anxious search for the approval of others, aggressiveness directed toward different objects and expressed in a variety of ways, hospitality toward strangers, generosity, courage, loyalty to one's group, family solidarity, and obedience to its leader (Racy 1970; Djait 1974).

The Arab-American population is heterogeneous in composition and differs in terms of religion, country of origin, and socioeconomic background. In addition to language, common bonds of cultural heritage, history, and religion are also evident. As an ethnic group, Arab-Americans are a self-perceived group of people holding in common a set of cultural traditions not shared by others with whom they come in contact. Such traditions typically include "folk" religious beliefs and practices, language, family values, food, music, art, literature, a sense of historical continuity, and common ancestry or place of origin (DeVos 1975).

Although the majority of Arab Americans are well assimilated in U.S. culture, they are bicultural. They have succeeded in keeping contact with their Arabic cultural heritage through social clubs, cultural, educational, and religious organizations. Arabic newspapers and magazines published in the United States with access to a number of Arab-American Web sites and the Arab American Institute keep them informed of current events in their homeland ([Detroit] Free Press 2001; Seattle Times 2002).

Health-Seeking Behavior

The culturally based system of health beliefs, which underlies Arab-American strategies for decision making and assists them with labeling, evaluating, and managing an illness and the problems created by it, affects their behavior and decision making. Their action-taken and health-seeking behavior will be examined below. In addition, the most prominent complaints presented by Arab-American populations will be identified and described, as well as the type of advice received from social networks, home remedies practiced, and self-care patterns used for treatment to manage the problems created by an illness situation. Furthermore, socioeconomic differences in health-seeking behavior and access to and use of health-care system will be described.

Cultural Definitions of Health and Illness

Every culture possesses its own philosophy, concepts, and practices in curative and preventive care. Within the Arab world there exists a vast body of beliefs and practices that are shared by different Arabic communities. It is commonly believed that a person is healthy as long as he functions normally, that is, as long as a person can go to work, live independently, and meet personal and family obligations. A person goes to a physician only when these responsibilities can no longer be performed effectively. For most Arab Americans, health equates with good luck and wealth, whereas disease equates with poverty and bad luck (Pillsbury 1978; Reizian 1981, 1984).

The Middle-Eastern cultural heritage is rich in proverbs and sayings describing health: "Health is a crown on the head of the healthy person" (Al seha tag ala roaus al asehaa); "A penny for prevention is better than a ton for treatment" (Derham wekaya wla kentar alag); and "The healthy mind is in the healthy body" (Al akl al saleem Fe al gesm al saleem).

Many Arabs believe that illness is sent from God as a punishment or a test, therefore, it is regarded as the will of God, the Afflicter, as well as the Healer (Pillsbury 1978; Maloof 1979). Patients and family mention that disease is in

"Allah's hands"; "It's Allah's will"; "Allah is testing me"; and "Allah will heal me."

This belief is a prominent causation of disease in Arab culture and is paralleled by acceptance to ones' destiny. (Nassib, el Maktoub—destiny, subjecting oneself to God's will, His judgment, and justice). An example of this attitude is the death of a young person, which is interpreted as God's choice to "spare him unexpected suffering in the future." People are likely to say, "This is his destiny" or "God wanted it this way."

Other illness causations are believed to be natural-physical or supernatural in cause. Two of the most common beliefs about illness are exposure to heat and cold and the evil eye. Exposure to cold weather late at night or early in the morning and the change of weather is believed to cause illnesses, such as gastrointestinal problems, chest conditions, coughing, sore throat, and body aches. Patients often seek care complaining of dampness in their bones (routouba). Also, drinking ice water when warm, sweating, exposure to drafts after bathing, and exposure to too much sun are other factors thought to be related to disease causality (Reizian 1981).

As for supernatural causes, people believe that the "Evil eye" (Ein el Hassoud or el Ein el Wehshah) causes disease and is preceded by envy (Hassad), the prime cause of being subjected to the evil eye. In this situation, illness is thought to be caused when a person looks admiringly, but enviously, at another (Meleis 1981; Shiloh 1968). A healthy, attractive child is susceptible to envy, as are male children and pregnant women. As a preventive measure and to distract the evil eye, a blue bead and amulets are worn and incense is burnt. Illness is also believed to be put willfully on another person by means of a Hex (el Aamal). It is commonly believed those most victims of a hex die.

Physical and mental fatigue is another cause of illness reported by Arab Americans. Many believe that work, with its long hours of physical and mental stress, has caused their illnesses (Reizian 1984). Others attribute stroke, heart attack, hypertension, circulatory problems, stomach trouble, and liver and gall bladder problems to what is called Fawaran el dam (heating, boiling, or effervescence of the blood). This condition is caused by nervousness, tension, and sudden fear, such as witnessing an accident or receiving bad news (Reizian 1981).

Great emphasis is placed on matters related to death and dying. A family member who is hospitalized for a terminal illness and is about to die will often be discharged at the request of the family, who prefer that the person spends the last moments of life in an environment surrounded by loved ones (Meleis 1981; Reizian 1981).

Healers and Practitioners
In Middle-Eastern rural communities, the majority of people consult indigenous health practitioners depending on the type and perceived severity of illness. These health practitioners are the village health barber (*Halak El Seha*), the bone healer {*Megabaraty*), and the herbalist (*Attar*). They prescribe and administer folk cures and herbal treatments, perform cautery wound care, treat conditions such as muscles sprains and dislocations, and perform male circumcisions. Others are traditional midwives (*Daya*), who are involved with women's health, labor and delivery, and newborn care. In addition, holy sheikhs and priests act as counselors on health matters (Pillsbury 1978).

Folk Health Practices
Treatment performed by Halak El Seha, "Heat cautery of skin" (Kawye) over diseased organs or parts of the body, is a well-known method of treatment in rural communities, especially for chronic conditions. This method sometimes works well in alleviating pain by acting as a counterirritant. However, this temporary relief sometimes makes people believe in and accept cautery as a magic treatment for all chronic conditions that cause pain or edema (Gadalla 1962).

Another form of healing practice is Zar, where drumbeats are danced to by patients with violent movements, often ending in trancelike convulsions, fainting, and ultimate release from whatever possessed them. Illness is overpowered by the influence of this Djinn (Pillsbury 1978).

Another folk health practice is "Doll charm treatment." A piece of paper is cut into the shape of a doll, which is then pierced as many times as needed with a pin for its symbolic piercing of the Evil Eye. The names of everyone—relatives, friends, or strangers—who looked at the person are mentioned. The doll is passed several times over the head of the sick person while reciting verses from the Qur'an or a prayer and is then burnt. The belief is that the effect of the Evil Eye is burnt with it (Gadalla 1962).

In addition, "alum charms" may be used. In this type of treatment, a piece of alum added to incense is burnt in a container placed on the floor while the patient is asked to cross over it seven times. The burning alum forms different shapes that are believed to be the face and eyes of the Evil Eye. In addition, the sound made by burning alum is symbolic of an eye burning and cracking. Amulets also are made of paper folded in triangles on which different sayings and verses from the Qur'an or Holy Bible are written (Gadalla 1962; Pillsbury 1978).

Another common practice is "hand lying," which is performed by religious persons regardless of the religious denomination. It is also common to wear as charms, amulets, with verses of the Qur'an. Medals of Saints, such as St. Rita, St. Theresa, or the Virgin Mary are worn for everyday protection and St. Christopher medals are used for safe traveling. Although many performances are still used among the rural and urban poor, Western medicine is well accepted and valued. People who fail to find relief under one type of remedy will often try another (Pillsbury 1978).

Major Diseases; Health Disparities

Perception of Symptoms and Symptoms Reported

The reaction of the individual to illness depends on the type of symptoms and their severity. In other words, the more the symptom appears to be serious and interferes with the individual's ability to carry on usual activities, the more likely the individual experiencing these symptoms will become concerned about their presence and take action for relief.

To Arab Americans, several symptoms seem to be the triggering factor for health-care seeking: pain in the chest, lump in the breast or abdomen, fainting spells, blood in urine, persistent headaches, shortness of breath, and chronic fatigue are symptoms needing medical attention. Moreover, other symptoms, such as loss of weight or loss of appetite, are not of lesser importance (Reizian 1984). The outpatient clinics most used by Arab Americans are gastro-intestinal, infectious disease, tropical medicine, ear nose and throat, orthopedics, cardiac, chest, ophthalmology, surgical, medical, diabetic, hypertension, medical screening, dermatology, and allergy. As for in-patient settings, Arab Americans were hospitalized in neurosurgery, kidney transplant, medical, orthopedics, and surgical units.

It can be noted that the major physical complaints presented by these patients were physiological, mainly related to symptoms of the digestive, cardiovascular, and respiratory system (Reizian 1984; Lipson, Reizian, and Meleis 1987). These symptoms can be considered as health indicators for members of the community.

As for psychological complaints presented, they were in the form of hypersensitivity with some degree of feelings of inadequacy, derived from being unable to make adequate social adjustment in their process of acculturation due to language barriers, daily habits, and lifestyle trends (Reizian 1984).

Parents sought care for their children less than 5 years of age for cough, runny nose, fever, diaper rash and eczema, skin infections, burns, earaches, vomiting, diarrhea, allergies, asthma, and accidental injuries. These visits were mostly related to health conditions thus, it could be concluded that the clinics were used mainly for illness or injury rather than preventive care.

Pain and Its Metaphors

When in pain, Arab Americans use words to describe the sensory and affective qualities of their pain. They qualify pain as "something pulling and hard as a stone" (Haga be tched zie el Hagar), "frightening" (A frightening pain in the lower part of my back), a piece of iron (Haga Mou Khifa) ("the pain under my right breast and in my stomach feels like a piece of iron"), a burning fire and the flame of fire (Heta min hadid) ("the pain was like a burning fire, coming out of my chest," "I had this pain in my stomach which was like a flame of fire"). They do not welcome painful experiences or those that create suffering. They think that pain is an unpleasant feeling for which an immediate control should be found. They hope for the success of any type of treatment that would lead to a total and a final relief of their pain (Reizian and Meleis 1986).

Effect of Illness and Problems Caused by Illness Situation

Arab Americans look at illness as causing general worry, fear, unhappiness, and depression, or creating discomfort and affecting their appearance. Illness interferes with their activities of daily living and with work activities. They respond to their illness pragmatically. They view their illness as interrupting routine tasks. Terminally ill patients, despite their deteriorating condition, show a strong faith in God and accept the end willingly.

Diagnosis Processes and Social Networks
Action Taken and Help-Received

Most Arab Americans will wait at least a few days before deciding to go to a health-care facility for professional help. The reasons why they decide to seek professional help or are encouraged to do so are because, most of the time, they suffer severe or sudden symptoms involving the heart, have injuries associated with pain and bleeding, or have symptoms that persist and are not alleviated by home remedies or time. The most important trigger in the decision to take action is the symptom, its progression, its seriousness to the point requiring action, its site, and its association with pain, as well as the subsequent disruption of normal role performance. The presence of lay consultants and type of advice given also influences the action taken.

Helpful Persons
The role of family is predominant in relation to health-care seeking. Arab Americans in need of health help contact their spouse (usually the wife), son or daughter, and parents. The spouse is the primary person most helpful to the subjects, followed by parents (mother and/or father), then the son or daughter. Lay consultation is always initiated at home and rarely reaches out of the family circle. This is rooted in family loyalty and a sense of obligation to take care of the sick or needy.

It is worth noting that the women in the family (the spouse or the mother) are always responsible for nurturing tasks and are usually the ones who are consulted within the family for the health protection of all its members.

Arab-American women have influential roles in relation to health and illness in the family. They discuss and validate symptoms and suggest home remedies. Based on the type, severity, and location of symptoms presented, advice or help offered to the sufferer ranges from consulting a physician, going to the hospital, or resting and practicing home remedies.

Treatment Options and Decisions
Home Remedies and Over-the-Counter Medication Used for Self-Treatment
A wide variety of home remedies and over-the-counter medications are used for treating some health problems. Aspirin is the most popular over-the-counter

medicine reported, together with Tylenol, Anacin, and Robitussin. These medicines are generally taken to treat colds, aches, and pains. Home remedies practiced include rest, rubbing, gargling, hot showers, and other simple procedures.

Olive oil is used in many ways: rubbing chest for colds, earaches, covering skin lesions, and massaging painful body parts. It is believed to have a warming and soothing effect. The use of lemon juice is also common in the Arab-American population to overcome fever and break up colds. The following home remedies are practiced for some conditions:

> "For coughing and chest pain, it is useful to drink every morning on an empty stomach a glass of warm milk mixed with two raw eggs. It's good for the chest; it brings all the black secretions out."

> "For skin problems or boils a poultice made of boiled onions is applied. It helps ripen the boil and all the dirt comes out."

> "For chest congestion and coughing, small cups are applied on the back and chest. A very light incision is made with a razor blade on the skin to let some of the accumulated blood out. This is believed to suck out all the inflammation."

These home treatments are used to remedy some of the symptoms presented before seeking professional health care (Reizian 1984).

Socioeconomic Differences in Health-Seeking Behavior

Socioeconomic background is a major factor that affects illness and health-seeking behavior. According to Reizian (1984), individual relationships exist between age, religion, patient status (inpatient or outpatient), level of education, type of occupation, country of origin, and symptom perception. Moreover, there is a relationship between symptom perception and type of occupation and action taken (advice and help from significant other and/or professional health care).

As an example, a professional would seek professional health care directly instead of seeking advice and/or practicing self-care or home remedies. Furthermore, there is an inverse correlation between level of education and symptom perception. Those who are highly educated do not express their symptoms and do not complain as much as people who are less educated. Those who are poorly educated express and report a higher number of symptoms, but they also delay health seeking. They seek help from their lay consultants for approval and validation.

In addition, country of origin is another variable related to perception of symptoms. Palestinians and Jordanians were found to report higher scores of symptom perception when compared to Lebanese, Iraqis, and Egyptian patients.

Access To and Use of Health-Care System

Health-care providers from both university and county hospitals, with associated clinics in a West Coast city and an urban Midwestern area of the United States, (Lipson, Reizian, and Meleis 1987; Kulwicki, Miller, and Schim 2000) have mentioned the following:

> "Arab Americans misuse the health care system. They overuse the emergency room or go to the wrong clinics. This is due to its complexity and their difficulty to learn how to access and move through the health-care system."

> "Arab Americans are noncompliant, e.g., 'They stop taking their meds when the symptoms disappear' and 'They agree with everything you suggest but then won't do it.'"

> "They present confusing diagnostic pictures and they present problems in care, e.g., 'Their friends and their relatives are always there.'"

> "They create a noise problem and they are demanding and overanxious."

Many Arab Americans refuse to consult mental health professionals. A strong stigma is attached to mental illness and it is common to protect the family name from shame by avoiding mental health services. This can be illustrated through the following examples: Three patients had significant needs for psychotherapeutic care but were not interested in being referred to counselors or therapists. In contrast, a family brought a patient to the emergency room because of agitation and bizarre behavior and stated that they could no longer cope with his behavior.

These opinions may stem from frustration when health providers and patients differ in their expectations of each other; when family and cultural transition stressors complicate patients' health problems; and when health providers lack knowledge of the cultural context within which health problems occur (Nobles and Sciarra 2000). On the other hand, according to Lipson, Reizian, and Meleis (1978), hospitalized patients were described as "pleasant" and "cooperative," even with significant language barriers. One patient showed gratitude following delivery of her infant by kissing her doctor's hand. Moreover, it was reported that patients were enjoying the attention they received during hospitalization. Another patient who had a kidney transplant thanked the nurse before discharge and gave her one of the gold rings she was wearing. This was a sign of appreciation for the supportive and nurturing care she received during her stay in the hospital.

Arab patients consider continuity important and would rather be assigned to the same caregiver; this helps them establish a rapport and develop trust. Their cooperative and apparently compliant behavior noted during hospitalization illustrates the large amount of trust and respect accorded to health-care professional in the United States.

The following example further illustrates some of the misunderstanding, which may arise in the health-care setting:

A family nurse practitioner requested help with a Yemeni family who came to the clinic for well-baby checkups and presumably for family planning. She stated, "I think I know what they need. But I have a sense that I am not reaching them. They don't comply with what I suggest. Yet, they keep coming back. The mother speaks no English, and I sense her frustration, but I can't find out what she thinks."

This family had recently emigrated from rural Yemen, and included the father, mother, her 7-year-old son from a previous marriage, and a new baby. The mother had left her other three children in Yemen. She had thus born five children, but the baby was the father's first. The mother complained of pains all over her body and of being exhausted all the time. The nurse practitioner thought that she did not want any more children. But her opinions were being interpreted differently by her husband and the male interpreter. The consultant [one of the researchers] spoke with the husband in Arabic and obtained a picture of the situation. She explained to the nurse practitioner the significance of bearing many male children, and because the father had one son of his own he was not likely to go along with birth control. In fact, he stated to both the NP and consultant that "She is OK. She gave me a boy. I will keep her." The mother, on the other hand, was grieving over leaving her other children in Yemen and could not express her grief directly because it was at her husband's insistence that she had done so. She was not only recovering from a cesarean, but was expressing her grief somatically. The consultant met family and continued to work with the nurse practitioner.

The following illustrates the interaction between immigration, family stressors, and physical symptoms, which are a culturally acceptable way of expressing distress.

Miss A. is a single 45-year-old Palestinian woman who immigrated to the United States three years ago. She is from a rural background, illiterate and does not speak English. She lives with her brother, his wife, and their four children. She is in and out of the health care system continually because she "hurts all over" and the pain keeps shifting to different locations. After thorough physical assessments in two clinics, the consultant (the researcher), who attributed the intensity of her pain to her family situation, evaluated her. She indeed had pain, but the family tension combined with her feelings of powerlessness and loneliness seriously aggravated it. She has very low status because she is unmarried; her brother supports her, and is her guardian. Because she feels obligated to him, she must do all the housework. She remains at home except for visits to the doctor. When the consultant encouraged her to get out and begin ESL classes, she stated, "I am unmarried woman, I can't go anywhere." In the old country, she depended on a large extended family for socializing but had no such outlets here. She seemed to want the health care system to legitimize her suffering so that she would have sympathy and care, and not be expected to work so hard.

The presence of family members of Arab-American patients was a constant in clinics and hospitals. Patients were brought to the clinics by at least one family member or friend who spoke English—in many cases, by two or more. This provides support and help to the ill family member. When hospitalized, the absence of family members during visiting hours was rare enough to be noted.

In addition to visiting, however, family relationships must be considered in other aspects of care. The following example shows how roles can complicate matters:

Two brothers came to the United States from Lebanon for a kidney transplant. Recognizing the strong family orientation of Middle Easterners and that they only spoke Arabic, the staff put them in a double room together. However, the staff did not know about family status and that a younger brother is expected to tend to all of an older brother's needs. The older brother [the recipient of the kidney] perceived himself as the sicker person, and expected the younger brother [the kidney donor] to help him at all times. The younger brother was unable to recover until the two were separated.

Moreover, there are problems related to differences in cultural styles of interaction and family values. The following example illustrates the kind of complex problem that often occurs in health-care settings and is rarely recognized:

A 6-year-old Palestinian boy from an urban educated family was dying in a tertiary care center. During the three months of hospitalizations, the team had been unable to find a satisfactory diagnosis. Because they were used to dealing with the nuclear family, the staff kept attempting to involve the parents in all decisions for the boy's care and shunned his grandparents, aunts and uncles who were constantly present. The family was obviously dissatisfied with the care and kept demanding to see a more senior physician and threatened to take the very ill child to a near by prestigious tertiary care center. Consultation revealed that the staff had offended the family by negotiating with the parents, who had little authority to make decisions. The consultant [one of the researchers] identified the key spokesperson [the oldest brother, the child's uncle] and suggested that the staff designate one physician to deal with him at all times. The family stopped making unreasonable demands and became much more cooperative until the child finally died.

Frequency and Patterns of Visits
Arab-Americans patients misuse the health-care system. They overuse the emergency room or go to the wrong clinics. Nevertheless, Arab-American patients' use of the health care center's facilities differ. This observation could reflect differences in patient income, education, social, or immigration status.

Understanding of Illness and Compliance

"Patients demonstrate poor understanding of diagnosis or treatment regimen." It was implied that patients overreacted or under reacted to the seriousness of a condition. For example, a couple whose newborn infant was in the nursery because of hyper-bilirubinemia insisted on taking the baby home because "the baby should be with its mother."

Noncompliance with treatment regimens was also reported. For example, a woman with "low back pain" was "taught exercises for her back, but didn't do them." It must be emphasized that to do exercises by an adult woman is not an acceptable dignified behavior.

Failure to return for follow-up appointments was another form of noncompliance in Arab-American patients. It could be attributed to either the patient's feeling better or was not able to reach the health-care facility easily.

A major cause that could be attributed to the problems previously presented and encountered in the health-care settings is language. This is in addition to the cultural context of the illness situation. Varying levels of understanding of the importance of symptoms, as well as noncompliance, may be aggravated by the language barrier. Vague symptoms could also be related to patients' lack of English or inability to express themselves clearly to clinicians. In such a situation, assessment of the patient for abnormal findings is continued and the patient's interpretation of his complaints, as well as his perception of the situation, is underestimated and considered irrelevant. In this case, presenting complaints or subjective data described become distorted and are more often in the language of the health-care provider or the interpreter than in the patient's own words, thus creating a situation where psychosocial and cultural data are lost. The result can be misconceptions, frustrations, and the inability of health-care providers to deliver culturally based competent care.

Conclusion

Arab Americans form a heterogeneous group representing many Arab countries and three major religions. Despite their increasing number, they are still not included in the ethnic group categorization of the United States. Arab Americans are strongly attached to their ethnic identity and keep contact with their cultural heritage. Arab Americans' definitions of health and illness are shaped by their cultural background and values. These beliefs in turn, affect their action and reaction to different health problems, greatly influence their health-seeking behavior, and consequently their use of health-care systems in the United States.

Increased knowledge and awareness of the cultural beliefs and the cultural context within which symptoms of disease are perceived by health-care professionals will help providers to better understand, respect, and resolve cultural barriers that cause misconceptions. Implementing culturally relevant care will contribute to the best use of health-care services by Arab-American patients.

N.B. Much of the information presented in this chapter is derived from research conducted by Reizian (1984) and Lipson, Reizian, and Meleis (1987).

REFERENCES

Abraham N. 1981. Arabs in America: An overview. In *The Arab world and Arab Americans: Understanding a neglected minority*, ed. S. Y. Abraham and N Abraham. Detroit, MI: Wayne State University Center for Urban Studies

Abraham, S. Y., and Abraham, N., eds. *Arabs in the new world: Studies on Arab-American communities*. Detroit, MI: Wayne State University Center for Urban Studies

Abu-Laban, B. 1980. *An olive branch on the family tree: The Arabs in Canada.* McClelland and Stewart. Ottawa; Multiculturalism Directorate.

Arab American Institute. 2000. *Arab Americans Demographics*. Retrieved from http://www.aaiusa.org (June2002).

[Detroit] Free Press. 2001. *100 Questions and answers about Arab Americans: A Journalist's Guide*. Retrieved at http://www.freep.com/jobspage/arabs.html (June 2002).

DeVos, G. 1975. Ethnic pluralism: conflict and accommodation. In *Ethnic Identity, Cultural Continuities, and Change*, ed. G. DeVos and L. Romanucci-Ross. Palo Alto. CA: Mayfield publishing Co..

Djait, H. 1974. *La Personnalite Et Le Devenir Arabo-Islamique*. Paris: Seuil.

Gadalla, T. 1962. Some cultural implications in medical and public health associations. *Journal of the Egyptian Health Association* 37(3): 63–76.

Gold, S. J. 2001. *Arab Americans in Detroit*. Retrieved www.commurb.org/features/sgold/detroit.html.(March 2002).

Kulwicki, A. D., J. Miller, and S. M. Schim. 2000. Collaborative partnership for culture care: enhancing self services for the Arab community. *Journal Of Transcultural Nursing*11(1): 31–39.

Lipson, J. G., A. E. Reizian, and A. I. Meleis. 1987. Arab American patients: a medical record review. *Social Science and Medicine* 24 (2): 101–107.

Lipson, J.G., and A. I. Meleis. 1983. Issues in health care of middle-eastern patients. *Western Journal of Medicine* 139(6): 854.

Maloof, P. S. 1979. Medical beliefs and practice of Palestinian Americans. Ph.D. diss., Catholic University of America, Washington, DC.

Meleis, A. I. 1981. The Arab American clients in the western health care system. *American Journal of Nursing* 81(6): 1180.

Naff, A. 1980. The Arabs. In *Harvard Encyclopedia of American Ethnic Groups*, ed. S. Thernstrom, A. Orlow, and O. Handlin. Cambridge, MA: Harvard University Press.

Nobles, A. Y., and D. T. Sciarra. 2000. Culture determinants in the treatment of Arab Americans: A primer for mainstream therapists. *American Journal of Orthopsychiatry*

Orfalea, G .2005. *The Arab Americans: A history*. Northhampton, Massachussets: Interlink Publishing Group, Inc.

Pillsbury, B. L. 1978. Traditional health care in the near east. A report prepared for the U.S. Agency for International Development, Washington, D.C. U.S Agency for International Development.

Racy, J. 1970. Psychiatry in the Arab East. *Acta Psychiatrica Scandinavica Supplement* 211:160-171.

Reizian, A. 1981. Some folk beliefs and practices in Egyptian communities. unpublished paper. University of California, San Francisco.

Reizian, A. 1984. Illness behavior and help-seeking behavior among Arab-Americans. Ph.D. diss., University of California, San Francisco.

Reizian A., and A. I. Meleis. 1986. Arab Americans' perceptions of and responses to pain. *Critical Care Nurse* 6(6):30–37.

Rodinson, M. 1981. *The Arabs*. Trans. A. Goldhammer. Chicago: University of Chicago Press.

Seattle Times. 2002. Arab Americans: Dispelling myths. Retrieved at http://www.seattletimes.nwsource.com/html/localnews/134342376_arabs1 6m(July 2002)

Shiloh, A. 1968. The interaction between the middle-eastern and western system of medicine. *Social Science and Medicine* 2(3): 235–45.

U.S. Census Bureau. 2000. Census supplementary survey. Retrieved at http://www.ameristat.org (June 2000).

Zogby, J. 2000. Arab American demographics report. Retrieved at www.aaiusa.org (February 2002).

7

Native Hawaiians

Lisa Henry, PhD. Assistant Professor, Department of Anthropology, University of North Texas, Denton, Texas.

Ethnic Identity and Definition

The term "Hawaiian" has no single definition, which can make it difficult to discuss numbers of Hawaiians living in the United States or Hawai'i. The Office of Hawaiian Affairs and other state agencies use the term "Native Hawaiian" to refer to all persons of Hawaiian ancestry regardless of blood quantum. They use the term "native Hawaiian" with a lower case "n" to refer to those with at least 50 percent Hawaiian blood. Some agencies leave it up to the individual to self-identify as Native Hawaiian, whereas other agencies or programs examine the ethnic background of the parents to make a racial classification. In general, "Hawaiian American" or "Native Hawaiian" refers to some degree of ancestral heritage to the original inhabitants of the Hawaiian Islands.

Foreign invasion and U.S. colonization have had a significant impact on the Hawaiian people since the eighteenth century. Foreigners brought devastating diseases that decimated the native population. Americans imported laborers from Asia to work on sugar plantations as the Hawaiian population continued to decline. U.S. businessmen held high political positions in the government during the reign of the Hawaiian monarchy, and eventually overthrew Queen Lili'uokalani and the Hawaiian monarchy in 1893 in favor of annexation by the U.S. government. The decline of Hawaiian culture continued in the twentieth century as Westernization became a driving force of culture change.

The Hawaiian cultural revitalization movement began in the 1960s with the University of Hawai'i's creation of a Hawaiian Studies program. The program offered courses in the Hawaiian language, as well as the performing arts (chanting, weaving, and dancing). The resurgence of Hawaiian culture spread throughout the islands, but was particularly supported by urban Hawaiian youth who felt disconnected with their ancestral language, traditions, and lifestyle (Linnekin 1983). Since the mid-1990s, the politically active Hawaiian sovereignty movement has become increasingly stronger with an emphasis on asserting indigenous rights to land, legislative bodies, and the courts. Although there is not complete agreement on what form Hawaiian sovereignty will take, the process is well underway with the establishment of the Hawaiian Sovereignty Advisory Commission in which Native Hawaiians are appointed to advise the legislature on how to proceed with the issue.

Hawai'i is a diverse state with no one ethnic group holding the majority of the population. As of the year 2000, Hawaiians represent 22 percent of the state population, Caucasians 21 percent, Japanese 22 percent, Filipino 16 percent, and Chinese 6 percent. Although Hawai'i embraces its diversity, ethnic tensions do exist (Office of Hawaiian Affairs 2002). Perhaps the most prominent is between Native Hawaiians and Caucasians; however, these are generally politically and economically motivated tensions and are not considered serious in relation to violence. Native Hawaiians have gained much political power in recent decades, but they lag behind in socioeconomic status. The U.S. Census Bureau reports that the per capita income for Native Hawaiians in 1990 was $11,446, whereas the per capita income for the United States as a whole was $14,143. Native Hawaiians have the lowest attainment of education of any other ethnic group in Hawai'i and are much more likely to be in service, manufacturing, and laboring positions than managerial and professional specialties (Casken 1999).

Although the majority of Native Hawaiians in the United States live in Hawai'i, the state's sagging economy and increasing unemployment is being blamed for Native Hawaiian out-migration to the mainland. What is interesting about Hawaiians living outside of Hawai'i is that they become increasingly more acculturated to an U.S. lifestyle, which can influence health-seeking behavior. Native Hawaiians remaining in Hawai'i have greater exposure to the cultural revitalization and sovereignty movements within Hawai'i and also have greater access to participate in Hawaiian culture on a daily basis.

Demographics
Although many Pacific Island populations were considered healthy and thriving before European contact, the Kingdom of Hawai'i was the largest and most complex. Most estimates put the Hawaiian population around 800,000 at the time of Captain Cook's "discovery." Over the next hundred years, the Hawaiians were exposed to an array of infectious diseases to which they had no natural immunity. Epidemics of tuberculosis and smallpox decimated the population, and reduced their numbers to less than 10,000 by the time the monarchy was overthrown in 1893 (Mau and Beddow 1998; Mills 1981).

Hawaiian Americans make up the largest population of Pacific Islanders in the United States, with a population of 401,162. The majority of Hawaiians live in the State of Hawai'i (60%). On the mainland, there are 161,507 Hawaiians, with the highest concentration living in the West Coast state of California (37%) (U.S. Census Bureau 2002). The ratio of males to females among all Hawaiians living in the United States is 50.1:49.9. Table 7-1 represents the age distribution of Hawaiians in the United States, the continental United States, and the State of Hawai'i for 1990.[1] It is interesting to note that the State of Hawai'i has a higher percentage of both children (0–19 years) and elders (65+ years) than both the

---

[1] The 2000 U.S. Census changed the classification of Native Hawaiian. Respondents could have chosen Native Hawaiian (one race or pure Hawaiian) or Native Hawaiian (two or more races). However, all Pacific Islanders who chose two or more races were lumped together in the summary tables so it is difficult to know the true number of people who claim Native Hawaiian ethnicity other than those who are pure-blooded Hawaiian. For this reason I use the 1990 U.S. Census data to discuss the age distribution of Native Hawaiians.

continental United States and the total population of Hawaiians in the United States (U.S. Bureau 1992).

Table 7-1. Age Distribution of Native Hawaiians for 1990

Age	All United States		Continental United States		Hawai'i	
0–19 years	80,938	38 percent	24,524	34 percent	56,414	41 percent
20–64 years	119,843	57 percent	45,568	63 percent	74,275	53 percent
65+ years	10,233	5 percent	2180	3 percent	8053	6 percent

Major Diseases and Health "Disparities" Compared with Population

Hawai'i is actually considered one of the healthiest states, with the highest longevity in the United States and health status indicators well above average (Mokuau, Hughes, and Tsark 1995; Wood and Hughes 1999). However, since the mid-1980s, much public attention has focused on health issues for Native Hawaiians. It is becoming clear that Hawaiians are suffering at higher rates than the rest of the population. Native Hawaiians have the poorest health of any ethnic group in the state (Blaisdell 1996), and one of the poorest health profiles of any ethnic group in the United States (Curb et al. 1991; Mokuau, Hughes, and Tsark 1995). Although Hawai'i boasts the highest longevity in the United States, Native Hawaiians live about five to ten years less than the state's population as a whole (Hammond 1988; Johnson 1989). Infectious diseases are no longer the major cause of mortality and morbidity. Native Hawaiians' disease pattern is similar to the general disease pattern of the United States in that the major causes of mortality and morbidity are chronic and degenerative diseases. The mortality rates for the top five leading causes of death in Hawai'i (heart disease, cancer, stroke, accidents, and diabetes) are higher for full- and partial-blooded Hawaiians than any other ethnicity (Kieffer, Mor, and Alexander 1994; Blaisdell 1996). The age-adjusted mortality rate of heart disease for Native Hawaiians is 273 per 100,000, whereas the rate for the entire U.S. population is 190 per 100,000 (Mokuau, Hughes, and Tsark 1995).

Obesity and diabetes are major concerns for Native Hawaiian health, as these metabolic conditions are risk factors leading to vascular disease. It is estimated that 64 percent of Native Hawaiians are overweight and 45 percent are severely overweight, whereas the rates for the total U.S. population is 26 percent and 9 percent respectively (Curb et al. 1991; Mokuau, Hughes, and Tsark 1995). The prevalence of diabetes escalates 20.5 percent for Native Hawaiians compared to the rest of the state's population (Mau and Beddow 1998). "Diabetes has increased among Native Hawaiian males by 28 percent, compared to a 15 percent increase for the U.S. population overall. For women, however, there has been a decline of 10 percent among Native Hawaiians, compared to an increase of 21 percent among the U.S. female populations overall" (Casken 1999). Although Hawaiians (similar to other Native-American groups) may have a genetic predisposition to developing Type II diabetes, research shows that acculturation to a Western lifestyle and diet contributes extensively to its prevalence (Mau and Beddow 1998; Wood and Hughes 1999[2]).

There are many other conditions that are of great concern for the Native Hawaiians. The rate of asthma among Native Hawaiians is 139.5 per 1,000, whereas the rate for the state population is 86.5 per 1,000 (Office of Hawaiian Affairs 2002). A 1998 health and behavioral risks update shows that accidental falls have increased 119 percent and firearm accidents have increased 300 percent. These figures can be compared to the general U.S. population whose accidental falls rate has decreased 73 percent and firearm accidents have increased 100 percent (Johnson, Oyama, and LeMarchand 1996, cited in Casken

---

[2] As noted in Wood and Hughes (1999), see also Blaisdell (1989, 1993; Flegal et al. (1991); Howard, Abbot, and Swinburn (1991); Reed, Labarthe, and Stallones (1970); Ringrose and Zimmet (1979); Shintani and Hughes (1994);); Sloan (1963); Taylor et al. (1992); Taylor and Zimmet (1981).

1999). The Hawai'i Department of Health reports that Hawaiians have the highest rate of risk behaviors for obesity, smoking, acute drinking, and drinking and driving of any ethnic group in the state (Hawai'i Department of Health 1993). Young adult and elderly males have the highest rate of suicide in the state. In addition, Native Hawaiians have higher rates of residence in correctional facilities, assaults, and antisocial behaviors (Takeuchi et al. 1987).

Health-Seeking Behavior
When discussing health-seeking behavior, one must consider the behavioral and ideological variation that exists among Native Hawaiians. Many urban Hawaiians have completed acculturated to a Western lifestyle, including diet, concepts of health and illness, and ideas on appropriate health-care providers. Others are more traditional in their lifestyles—living in rural areas on family land, eating more traditional foods, and influenced by Hawaiian cultural beliefs and behaviors. Nevertheless, others live in the urban areas of Hawai'i, yet fully participate in the Hawaiian cultural revitalization (including the revitalization of Hawaiian healing), which influences their behaviors and guides their ideologies of life and wellness. Although not every contemporary Native Hawaiian subscribes to traditional beliefs, the revitalization of Hawaiian healing is affecting contemporary health-seeking behaviors. Thus, it is necessary to discuss indigenous concepts of health and illness prior to foreign contact in order to understand their relevance to contemporary health issues and behaviors.

The Hawaiian word for health is *ola*, which also means "life, health, well-being, livelihood, salvation, curable, healed, saved, to save, and to heal" (Loos 1999:426). The experience of health or wellness was dependent on oneness and harmony with the self, others, and the community. Harmony persisted when thoughts, feelings, and actions toward the spiritual and material world were positive and good. Illness occurred when there was disharmony in relationships with the family, the community, or the supernatural (Blaisdell 1997; Casken 1999). The concept of *mana* (life force or energy) was also central to Native

Hawaiians' concept of health and success. When someone broke a societal norm, or taboo, tension and disharmony led to the loss of *mana*, which could lead to illness. Good things happen to those with lots of *mana* and when one has *mana*, illness is rarely present.

Significant emphasis was placed on a patient's effort to heal oneself through discovery of the cause of tension and disharmony. If the patient was not successful, an elder family member was called upon for assistance. Many elder family members knew remedies for small illnesses, in addition to commanding respect and truthfulness when investigating the cause of the illness with the family. The elder would talk to the patient and family at great length about any disturbances they might be carrying. If the illness was still not healed, a healing priest (*kahuna*) was called upon from the nearest healing temple, where healers were trained in specialties, including surgery, bone setting, clyster enema, medicine plants, childbirth, massage, and engaging spiritual forces (Blaisdell 1997).

Traditional medicine suffered a severe blow with the two major events in Hawaiian history: the arrival of the first major epidemic in 1804, and the collapse of the Hawaiian religious system in 1819. Until then, diagnosis of illness was predominately spiritual—based on the notion that disharmony and tension created illness within the body. But Hawaiian remedies could do little for the devastating epidemics that killed hundreds of thousands of indigenous Hawaiians. Polynesian gods were abandoned for a new Christian God, and the spiritual foundation for Hawaiian healing began to fade. Hawaiian medical knowledge and practice managed to persevere and survive the decline of Hawaiian culture from 1870 to 1950, but it was largely in the form of herbal remedies. In fact, most herbal remedies used today for both precontact and foreign illnesses were probably discovered after European contact, as islanders were constantly experimenting with ways to cure deadly epidemics (Whistler 1992).

Today, illnesses can be divided into two major categories: indigenous illness and foreign illness. Indigenous illnesses can then be subdivided into physical ailments (natural illnesses) and supernatural ailments ("ghost sickness").

"Ghost sickness" is common among Polynesian Islanders and is believed to be caused by spirits of ancestors who are displeased. It is generally diagnosed by a Hawaiian healer who recognizes the illness is not responding to normal treatment, takes on shifting symptoms, or suddenly becomes severe. There are two treatment options for this illness. The first is to take the patient to someone who has a reputation for conversing with the ancestral spirits. The medium will attempt to communicate with the spirits to find out the source of disharmony so the persons involved may solve their conflict. The second treatment is called a *ho'oponopono* (family gathering), intended to discover the source of contention within the family and to correct it (Whistler 1992).

> In the treatment, all family members who may be part of the problem or solution meet and choose a leader, usually an older member of the family, a minister, or healer. Next, repentance is randomly selected and read in hopes that it will shed some light on the problem. The leader then asks all the family members to admit to any grudge in their heart against the ill person. Admissions are made, often only in general terms, and forgiveness is asked. Once all the transgressions and grudges are brought to light and forgiven, the ceremony is finished with a closing prayer (*pani*) (Heighton 1971, cited in Whistler 1992).

In addition to its importance during a *ho'oponopono*, the family continues to be a central component to the coping and healing of physical ailments as well. The cohesiveness of the kinship unit (which could be several related nuclear families) and the reliance members have on each other contributes significantly to the health and well-being of individuals. An individual never faces a health crisis alone, but rather relies on family members (especially elders) for advice, guidance, support, and advocacy, if necessary (Loos 1999). A study by Kakai et al. (2003) highlights Native Hawaiians' reliance on interpersonal communication.

Kakai and others studied the relationship between ethnicity and choices of health information sources for cancer patients using complementary and alternative medicine. Native Hawaiians and other Pacific Islanders tended to rely on interpersonal communication from their physicians and their social groups for information about their cancer and related health issues, whereas Caucasians preferred scientific information sources, and Japanese preferred media and commercial information.

Healers and Practitioners

As noted, Hawaiian healing did not completely vanish during the 1900s, but because of the stigma associated with some aspects of healing (sorcery, communicating with spirits), the practice remained largely a private matter. Healers, who are both men and women, do not advertise, but rather are known for their abilities to heal and are sought after by patients. More often than not the healer is either someone the patient knows or someone who has been recommended by a friend or relative (Whistler 1992). The relationship between healer and patient is one of compassion and trust. Healers give the patient all the time she or he needs without the economic constraints and federal requirements to which biomedical doctors are subjected (Blaisdell 1997). Hawaiian healers generally specialize in herbal treatments, massage therapy, midwifery, and faith healing, but there are other areas of healing as well (Pinkney 1990). Healers consider their abilities to be a gift from the Christian God and would never demand payment for their services. Most patients offer food and gifts as a token of their appreciation. Payment is generally whatever people offer, but it is never asked for or demanded (Pinkney 1990; Whistler 1992). Healers also do not take credit for curing any of their patients. Rather, they contend that God is responsible for the cure because the plants, knowledge, and ability come from Him (Pinkney 1990).

Native Hawaiian approaches to health care have been given a boost from the Native Hawaiian Health Care Act of 1988. This act was established after

Senator Inouye of Hawai'i commissioned the *E Ola Mau: The Native Hawaiian Health Needs Study Medical Task Force Report* to assess the poor health of Native Hawaiians. Its goal is to promote health, prevent disease, and provide primary care services to person of Hawaiian ancestry (Casken 1999). The Act also provides official recognition of local healers by the government, entitles them to practice in the public view, and encourages the integration of Hawaiian healers into the health-care system (Pinkney 1990; Casken 1999). As of 1990, the state had located about sixty to eighty Hawaiian healers, yet only about ten would be considered professionals; the others mainly treat family members and have other jobs and/or tasks that occupy their time. Although healers are historically secretive about their treatments, some have decided to reveal their knowledge for fear that it will be lost if they do not pass it on to future generations. This agreement to reveal their knowledge is not without hesitation, however. Most worry about others' ability to learn the practice in a relatively short period of time, as it takes many years of apprenticeship to become a skilled healer. Others worry that individuals without proper training will set up shop and claim abilities to cure that do not exist (Pinkney 1990). These "quacks" could damage the reputation of legitimate healers who have extensive knowledge of Hawaiian medicine.

Encouraged by E Ola Mau (an organization of Hawaiian health-care providers in both Western and Hawaiian medicine) and the 1988 Native Hawaiian Health Care Act, Hawaiian healers are beginning to become more organized (Blaisdell 1997). E Ola Mau encourages healers to determine the criteria to be use to recognize qualified healers, and to think about ways in which Hawaiian healing can be best integrated with biomedicine to ensure the health-care needs of Hawaiians. Healers have conducted many community education workshops to familiarize the public (Hawaiians and non-Hawaiians) with Hawaiian medicine. In addition, they are meeting with physicians to collaborate on setting up a formal referral network between the new Hawaiian healing clinics and biomedical clinics (Pinkney 1990).

Access To and Use of Health-Care System

Western medicine does, however, play a significant role in Native Hawaiian health care today. Native Hawaiians are pragmatic in their health-seeking behavior and use Western medicine for many illnesses, especially those they know can be cured quickly. Nearly all Hawaiians have seen a biomedical doctor at some point in their lives. The State of Hawai'i has had near universal health-care coverage for about the past twenty-five years and, according to the Office of Health Status Monitoring (2001), 94 percent of the state and 94 percent of Native Hawaiians were insured in 2000. Hawai'i is the only state with an employer mandate, which requires employers to pay 50 percent of full-time employees' premiums and employees to pay the other 50 percent. Yet, despite the praise Hawai'i's health-care system has received by some politicians, the mandate does little to provide coverage for part-time employees and the unemployed. Most of these state residents are enrolled in the State Health Insurance Program (SHIP), which provides subsidized insurance for low-income families; however, the program only provides minimal coverage. In 1994, 17 percent of the state's residents reportedly put off medical care because of high costs (Matthews 1994). Issues of insurance, particularly underinsurance, are important for Native Hawaiian health in Hawai'i because the majority have the low incomes, low attainment of education, and are more likely to be in service, manufacturing and laboring positions—positions that are frequently part-time (Casken 1999).

The lack of accessibility poses a serious deterrent for Native Hawaiians' use of Western medicine. The two major issues regarding the inability to receive biomedical services are cost and geographic location. Many Native Hawaiians wait until an illness becomes severe before they visit a Western doctor, thus further increasing the cost of biomedical treatments. Others cannot afford the medication that is prescribed, even with insurance. Rural Native Hawaiians have difficulty affording and accessing transportation to urban areas with more sophisticated medical technology that can help prevent, detect, and treat illnesses with timely intervention (Mokuau 1990; Mokuau, Hughes, and Tsark 1995).

Although linguistic barriers are not as much of a problem for Hawaiians as they are for other minority populations in the United States, cultural barriers to health-care acceptability and compliance continue to affect Native Hawaiian health. As noted, harmony with the self, others, and the community is essential to Native Hawaiian well-being. In addition, Hawaiians are raised in close-knit communities where the cohesiveness of kinship units contributes significantly to the health and well-being of individuals. These cultural characteristics are often in contrast to the larger societies' emphasis on individuality and the role of individual responsibility of health and wellness (Mokuau, Hughes, and Tsark 1995; Casken 1999). Hawaiians prefer the familiarity of local healers, who they often call "papa" or "uncle" (Pinkney 1990). Hawaiian healers are less constrained by time and money, and they take the time to develop relationships with patients, which is considered an important aspect of healing. The impersonal and hurried environment of Western hospitals and clinics is oftentimes intimidating to Native Hawaiians (Pinkney 1990; Whistler 1992). In addition, there are compliance issues between Hawaiians and biomedical treatment/prevention procedures because Hawaiians are unlikely to respond well to non-Hawaiians telling them how to live their lives (Mokuau, Hughes, and Tsark 1995). Suggestions on improving the acceptability of biomedicine include integrating Hawaiian healers into the system to break down barriers.

Public health programs are now recognizing the need to address the cultural needs of Hawaiians in order to successfully improve health. Clinics are being placed in community settings that offer both nurse practitioners and Hawaiian healers to uninsured and underinsured residents. Broad and Allison (2002) conducted a pilot study to examine the use and acceptance of the clinics. They concluded that 75 percent of the respondents were satisfied with the care received from both nurse practitioners and Hawaiian healers. In addition, they reported that patients generally sought treatment from healers for neck and back problems (chronic conditions) and sought treatment from Western practitioners for most acute conditions and those chronic conditions that required medication (e.g., diabetes, hypertension).

Cultural Strategies to Improve Health

As noted, many of the illnesses experienced by Native Hawaiians are attributed to the fast-paced, stressful lifestyle that Hawaiians have adapted to in the past several decades. Mokuau notes,

> The physical death of native Hawaiians has often been linked with the psychological and emotional death of the people. When westerns arrived, they began to plant within the native Hawaiian consciousness a perception of inferiority. . . . This type of erosion of self-pride and cultural pride and confidence has been manifested in the last 200 years by the suppression of native Hawaiian language, religion, values, economic traditions, and general way of life (Mokuau 1990, 238).

Mokuau discusses guidelines to implementing culturally appropriate strategies to improve Hawaiian health.

> If it is believed that in times of transition and modernization cultural suppression has occurred and that this suppression has contributed to poor quality of life, then it would follow that restoration of holistic health for native Hawaiians would involve cultural promotion. Models for delivering services to native Hawaiians must be developed and implemented in context of their worldviews, values, and practices (Mokuau 1990, 238)

One successful example of a culturally appropriate strategy is the ability to reduce obesity, lower the risk of heart disease, and manage diabetes with the consumption of a traditional Hawaiian diet. The traditional Native Hawaiian diet consisted of foods that are low in fat and cholesterol and high in fiber and complex carbohydrates, such as fish, taro, sweet potato, breadfruit, bananas, and taro leaves. Diet programs, which are sponsored by a variety of agencies and schools, encourage Native Hawaiian participants to consume traditional foods (ad libitum) and promote Hawaiian values such as spirituality, community bonding, and outreach to others. Carefully monitored programs show a reduction in weight, blood pressure, and blood sugar (Shintani et al. 1991; Blaisdell 1996; Wood and Hughes 1999).

Health professionals recognize that using culturally appropriate strategies can improve Native Hawaiian health. An increasing number of Native Hawaiians are attending medical and other health-care professional schools, and are embracing a more holistic approach to medicine. They recognize the family's role in health-care decisions, understand the role spiritually plays in healing, and understand the need to establish bonding relationships with patients (Mokuau 1990).

149

REFERENCES
Blaisdell, R. K. 1989. Historical and cultural aspects of Hawaiian health. In *Social Process in Hawai'i, The Health of Native Hawaiians: A Selective Report on Health Status and Health Care in the 1980s*, ed. EL Wegner, 32: 1-21., Honolulu: University of Hawai'i Press.

————.1993. The health status of Kanaka Maoli (indigenous Hawaiians). *Asian American and Pacific Islander Journal of Health* 1(2): 117–62.

————. 1996. 1995 update on Kanaka Maoli (indigenous Hawaiians') health. *Asian American and Pacific Islanders Journal of Health* 4(1–3): 160–65.

————. 1997. Historical and philosophical aspects of Lapa'au traditional Kanaka Maoli healing practices. In-*Motion Magazine*, November 16: 1-7.

Broad, L., and D. Allison. 2002. Nurse practitioners and traditional healers: An alliance of mutual respect in the art and science of health practices. *Holistic Nursing Practice* 16(2): 50–57.

Casken, J. 1999. Pacific Islander health and disease. In *Promoting health in multicultural populations: A handbook for practitioners,* 397–417. eds. Robert M. Huff, Michael V. Kline. Thousand Oaks, CA: Sage.

Curb, J. D., N. E. Aluli, J. A. Kautz, H Petrovitch, SF Knutsen, R Knutsen, et al. 1991. Cardiovascular risk factor levels in ethnic Hawaiians. *American Journal of Public Health* 81(2): 164–67.

Flegal, K., T. Ezzati, M. Harris, SG Haynes, RZ Juarez, WC Knowler, et al. 1991. Prevalence of diabetes in Mexican Americans, Cubans, and Puerto Ricans from the Hispanic health and nutrition examination survey, 1982–84. *Diabetes Care* 14: 628–38.

Hammond, O. 1988. Needs assessment and policy development: Native Hawaiians as Native America. *American Psychologist* 43(5): 383–87.

Hawai'i Department of Health. 1993. Hawai'i's health risk behaviors. In *Behavioral risk factor survey*. Honolulu, HI: Author.

Heighton, R. H. 1971. Hawaiian supernatural and natural strategies for goal attainment. Ph.D. diss., Univ. Hawaii. 170 pp.

Howard, B., W. Abbot, and B. Swinburn. 1991. Evaluation of metabolic effects of substitution of complex carbohydrates for saturated fat in individuals with obesity and NIDDM. *Diabetes Care* 14: 786–95.

Johnson, D. 1989. An overview of ethnicity and health in Hawaii. *Social Process in Hawaii* 32: 67–86.

Johnson, D., N. Oyama, and L. LeMarchand. 1996. Papa Ola Lokahi Hawaiian health update: Mortality, morbidity, morbidity outcomes, and behavioral risks. Report presented to Papa Ola Lokahi, MEDTEP Research Center, Honolulu, HI.

Kakai, H., G. Maskarinec, D. Shumay, Tatsumura Y, and Tasaki K. 2003.Ethnic differences in choices of health Information by cancer patients using complementary and alternative: An exploratory study with correspondence analysis. *Social Science and Medicine.* 56(4):851-62.

Kieffer, E., J. Mor, and G. Alexander. 1994. The perinatal and infant health status of Native Hawaiians. *American Journal of Public Health* 84(9): 1501–1504.

Linnekin, J. 1983. Defining tradition: Variations on the Hawaiian identity. *American Ethnologist* 10(2): 241–52.

Loos, G. 1999. Health promotion planning in Pacific Islander population groups. In *Promoting health in multicultural populations: A handbook for practitioners*, 419–47. eds. Robert M. Huff, Michael V. Kline. Thousand Oaks, CA: Sage.

Matthews, M. 1994. Hawaii offers no model for health reform. *Human Events* 50(35): 12–15.

Mau, M. K., and R. M. Beddow. 1998. Paradise lost. *Diabetes Forecast* 51(6): 44–45.

Mills, G. 1981. Hawaiians and medicine. *Hawaii Medical Journal* 40(10): 272–76.

Mokuau, N. 1990. The impoverishment of Native Hawaiians and the social work challenge. *Health and Social Work* 15(3): 235–42.

Mokuau, N., C. Hughes, and J. Tsark. 1995. Heart disease and associated risk factors among Hawaiians: Cultural responsive strategies. *Health and Social Work* 20(1): 46–51.

Office of Hawaiian Affairs. 2002. Native Hawaiian data book. Honolulu, HI: Author.

Office of Health Status Monitoring. 2001. Health insurance status by counties, year 2000. Honolulu, HI: Hawai'i State Department of Health.

Pinkney, D. S. 1990. Native healers: sharing the cares and hopes of traditional Hawai'ian medicine. *American Medicinal News* 33(4):9-11.

Reed, D., D. Labarthe, and R. Stallones. 1970. Health effects of westernization and migration among Chamorros. *American Journal of Epidemiology* 92: 94–112.

Ringrose, H., and P. Zimmet. 1979. Nutrient intakes in an urbanized Micronesian population with a high diabetes prevalence. *American Journal of Clinical Nutrition* 32: 1334–41.

Shintani, T., C. Hughes, S. Beckham et al. 1991. Obesity and cardiovascular risk intervention through the ad libitum feeding of traditional Hawaiian diet. *American Journal of Clinical Nutrition* 53(6): 1647–51.

Shintani, T., and C. Hughes. 1994. Traditional diets of the Pacific and coronary heart disease. *Journal of Cardiovascular Risk* 1: 16–20.

Sloan, N. 1963. Ethnic distribution of Diabetes Mellitus in Hawai'i. *Journal of the American Medical Association* 183: 419–24.

Takeuchi, D., N. Higginbotham, A. Marsella, K. Gomes, L. Kwan Jr, B. Ostrowski, et al. 1987. Native Hawaiian mental health. In *Contemporary issues in mental health research in the Pacific Islands*, ed. A. Robillard and A. Marsella. Honolulu: University of Hawai'i Social Science Research Institute.

Taylor, R., J. Badcock, H. King, K. Pargeter, P. Zimmet, T. Fred, et al. 1992. Dietary intake, exercise, obesity and noncommunicable disease in rural and urban populations of three Pacific island countries. *Journal of the American College of Nutrition* 11: 283–93.

Taylor, R., and P. Zimmet. 1981. Obesity and diabetes in western Samoa. *International Journal of Obesity* 5: 367–76.

U.S. Census Bureau. 2002. 2000 census of population, general population characteristics. Washington, DC: Government Printing Office.

———. 1992. 1990 Census of population, general population characteristics. Washington DC: Government Printing Office.

Whistler, W. A. 1992. *Polynesian herbal medicine*. Hong Kong: Everbest Printing.

Wood, D. W., and C. K. Hughes. 1999. Promoting health in the Pacific Islander populations: Case studies. In *Promoting health in multicultural populations: A handbook for practitioners*. eds. Robert M. Huff, Michael V. Kline. Thousand Oaks, CA: Sage

8

Resettled Refugees of Southeast Asian Ethnicities: Health-Seeking Behavior

Lance A. Rasbridge, PhD. Coordinator, Refugee Outreach Program, Parkland Hospital, Dallas, Texas

Charles Kemp, FNP, FAAN, Senior Lecturer in Community Health, Louise Herrington School of Nursing, Baylor University

Introduction to Southeast Asian Refugees in the United States

The United States is a mosaic of immigrants, each ethnic group with its own set of belief systems, customs, and practices: i.e., culture. How people view and define sickness and well-being and what actions they take to maintain or restore health are cultural phenomena. The efficacy of care provided to diverse populations by the medical community is predicated on an understanding of that cultural diversity (cf. Kemp and Rasbridge 2004). This chapter explores the cultural aspects of health in refugee communities from Southeast Asia that we see in the United States: Vietnam, Cambodia, and Laos, while also gaining an understanding of refugees in general.

Of course, there is great intracultural heterogeneity within these groups, so not all Southeast Asian refugees resettled to the United States adhere to the principals discussed below. Level of education, residence in rural versus urban areas in the homeland, and length of time in the United States are just a few of the variables that affect health-seeking beliefs and practices. Nonetheless, most of the ideas discussed here are so fundamental to people from Southeast Asia that they may be considered to represent traditional cultural values. Indeed, many of these concepts have emerged over centuries from Chinese and Indian traditions; hence this chapter provides at least a generalized insight into pan-Asian health beliefs and practices. Moreover, certain concepts discussed below, such as humoral balance and mind-body holism, are found in indigenous cultures in many regions of the world. Thus the goal here is to demonstrate a few of the avenues where culture and ethnicity influence health-seeking behavior, an understanding that can ultimately be used not only to improve the care provided to this growing population, but to other immigrant communities as well.

Definitions and Background

By definition, a refugee is someone outside of his or her country of origin and unable to return "because of a well-founded fear of persecution on the basis of race, religion, ethnicity, membership in a political party or social group" (U.S. Department of State 2001). Tens of millions of people fall within that definition the world over, but less than 1 percent is resettled in the West on an annual basis. Overall, between 1975 and 2000 the United States admitted 2,284,956 refugees (Department of State 2001). Although the decision-making process is complex and beyond the scope of this chapter, it is fair to say that politics in addition to humanitarianism play a large role. Upon acceptance, a refugee is sponsored by a national resettlement agency in a public/private cooperative partnership known as the U.S. Resettlement Program (USRP). Through the resettlement agency and its subsponsors the immediate needs of the refugee, such as food, clothing, housing and medical care, are arranged. In time, the agencies also assist with other activities such as employment, school enrollment, and English instruction, for a specific, albeit limited, period of time mandated under the USRP.

Refugees in the United States are hence a type of immigrant, but they differ in an important aspect from other kinds of immigrants, especially economic immigrants. The critical difference is that refugees are nearly always *forced* from their homes and countries, often leaving all or most possessions (and even family) behind to come to countries with unfamiliar cultures. Physical, psychological, social, and spiritual trauma is common among refugees, and the term "dose-effect relationships of trauma" (to mental health problems) is found in the literature on refugees. War, killing, torture, suffering, and grief are central to the refugee experience in most cases. Trauma, changes in socioeconomic status, and other factors commonly result in a long and difficult acculturation process.

Since 1975, nearly 1.5 million refugees from Vietnam, Cambodia, and Laos and their families now live in the United States (Southeast Asia Resource Action Center [SEARAC] 2002). Although they share certain similarities, there are also many differences between each group and even within each ethnicity, to be discussed next.

Vietnamese Americans

Although the language and culture of Vietnam have been strongly influenced by China for centuries, France as a colonial power dominated the country politically from the late 1800s to independence in 1954. The country has seen warfare for much of the twentieth century. The struggle for independence resulted in the division of the country through the Geneva Convention of 1954. Soon thereafter began the war between communist North Vietnam, with its southern allies, the Viet Minh (later called Viet Cong) on the one hand and the Republic of South Vietnam on the other. U.S. intervention began in the mid-1950s, escalated first in the early 1960s, and peaked in the late 1960s and early 1970s. The last U.S. troops were withdrawn March 29, 1973, and the war ended with the fall of Saigon in South Vietnam on April 30, 1975, resulting in the installation of the present communist regime. Although wholesale killing did not ensue, many thousands of (formerly) South Vietnamese officials, military, and others were sent to brutal "re-education" camps for periods of time ranging from a few years to more than twenty years (Dutt 1985; Fall 1966; Karnow 1983).

Vietnamese comprise the largest group of Southeast Asian refugees in the United States; the population of refugees, together with their American-born children, numbers nearly 1 million (SEARAC 2002). The largest Vietnamese communities are in Orange County (California), Los Angeles, Houston, Dallas, and Washington, D.C.; the states of Washington, Pennsylvania, Minnesota, Massachusetts, New York, and Illinois all have sizeable populations (SEARAC 2002). Although there are many shared cultural traits among all the Vietnamese Americans, such as the Vietnamese language, strong emphasis on the extended family, and opposition to the communist government, there are also marked differences. This heterogeneity is represented largely by the refugee "wave" in which the individual or family arrived, as well as differences among individuals, families, and socioeconomic groups.

The first group of refugees to come to the United States in 1975 were educated and urban professionals (and their families) who were airlifted directly from Saigon or nearby ships. They were closely associated with U.S. interests in Vietnam; many spoke English and were familiar with U.S. culture. This group has for the most part gone on to resume their professional lives and relative social statuses in the United States, including serving as staff members of social service agencies that assist more recently arrived Vietnamese. In contrast, the second wave of Vietnamese refugees, arriving from the late 1970s through the mid 1980s, included a much higher proportion of merchants, farmers, and other rural Vietnamese who escaped communist Vietnam in small boats. These "boat people" suffered extreme hardship and loss through the refugee process, often remaining in harsh refugee camps in other Southeast Asian countries for years. Many who came from rural origins or limited educational backgrounds have had a more difficult time adapting to urban U.S. life, whereas others from rural backgrounds found that intelligence and persistence are stronger than 100 generations of rural deprivation.

Finally, the third wave, continuing to arrive through the present, comes to the United States under more "orderly" programs, typically on the basis of their statuses as political prisoners in Vietnam or offspring of Vietnamese women and American fathers ("Amerasians")—two groups that faced serious discrimination in Vietnam. They come with their families, except that in the case of Amerasians, more often than not the father is unknown or otherwise out of the picture. And among the more recent arrivals are numbers accepted for residence through refugee and immigration programs, because of their immediate family relationships with Vietnamese refugees already here.

Cambodian Americans

The present Kingdom of Cambodia has long been influenced by Indian culture, and the ancient Angkor civilization was once the dominant military and economic force of all Southeast Asia. However, with the empire long-declined by the late 1800s, Cambodia became a part of French Indochina (as were Vietnam and Laos). From the beginning of colonial rule, there was resistance to the French. The Geneva Convention of 1954 resulted in independence, and Prince Norodom Sihanouk took power. Communism and other dissident activities were repressed from that point until the late 1960s when the Khmer Rouge, led by Maoist extremists, in particular a cadre known as Pol Pot, became active. A brutal and complex armed struggle ensued, resulting in many deaths. In 1970, a *coup d'état* replaced Prince Sihanouk with right-wing military rulers. Fighting escalated and on April 17, 1975, a deeply divided Cambodia fell to the Khmer Rouge.

Within days of victory, the Khmer Rouge initiated a radical restructuring of Cambodian society. Liquidation of all noncommunist leaders began immediately and eventually encompassed not only military and political leaders, but also monks, teachers, people who wore glasses, and anyone else judged to be a "new person" or corrupted by capitalism and the West. The cities were totally emptied of residents, who then were put to work on agricultural communes, reminiscent of the Angkor civilization a thousand years earlier. Families were separated according to the needs of working units and a deliberate effort was made to replace traditional relationships and structures such as family, village, and Buddhism with absolute obedience to the communist party or *Angka*. Under this tyrannical regime, estimates as high as 2 million Cambodians (of a total population of 7 million at the time) perished either from direct execution or starvation and illness. In late 1978, the Vietnamese army invaded Cambodia and routed the Khmer Rouge; a guerilla war ensued for the next two decades.

Beginning in late 1978, Cambodian refugees began fleeing to the relative safety of Thailand; eventually the refugee camps held nearly 1 million individuals. Of these, approximately 175,000 were resettled in the United States, mostly between 1981 and 1985 (SEARAC 2002). The largest communities are found in Long Beach, California, and Lowell, Massachusetts, with populations in other urban areas as well.

Once in the United States, the Cambodians have tended to follow one of several paths. Some have enjoyed financial success (usually through salaried jobs rather than entrepreneurship) and have become homeowners in mixed middle-class neighborhoods. Others have scattered to suburban apartments. Still others have stayed in the urban neighborhoods in which they were originally resettled and have become a generally hidden part of inner-city life. In many cases, there has been little assimilation. In an extraordinarily high number of cases, regardless of external appearances, there is great pain related to past trauma and current difficulties (Blair 2000; Carlson and Rosser-Hogan 1994).

Laotian Americans
Laos shares many cultural similarities with Cambodia (and India), but though the languages are similar, they are not mutually intelligible. Laos is a landlocked country surrounded by China, Vietnam, Cambodia, and Thailand. From its beginnings in the sixth century C.E., Laos has been ruled by competing kings and foreign powers, including Thailand, Japan, and France. Full independence was achieved in 1954 with the end of France's colonial rule of Indochina. Years of conflict ensued and in 1975, the communist Pathet Lao emerged in control of the country. Both lowland Lao and Hmong refugees began fleeing to Thailand. (Although this work focuses on lowland Lao [*Lao Lum*], readers should note that there are other ethnic and cultural groups from Laos living in the United States, including the Hmong, Mien, Tai Dam, and ethnic Chinese from Laos). Most of

the resettlement in the United States occurred between 1975 and 1985, primarily in California, Iowa, Minnesota, Texas, and Washington. Today the largest populations of the approximately 135,000 Lao-born Americans live in the San Diego and the San Francisco Bay areas of California (SEARAC 2002).

Laotians have tended to live in tightly knit communities to a greater extent than most other refugees from Southeast Asia. In several states there are now rural or semi-rural communities in which Laotians live in a traditional mutually assisting social structure. Many of the adults work in nearby towns or cities, whereas elders live more or less traditional lives. As with other first generation refugees or immigrants, assimilation has been especially difficult for many older Laotians.

Southeast-Asian Refugee Health

Although there is considerable ethnic diversity among the different groups of refugees from Southeast Asia, there are certain common denominators in their health profiles. Upon arrival to the United States, many had diseases (e.g., hepatitis B, tuberculosis, malaria, Hansen's disease) that are endemic in Southeast Asia (Erickson and Hoang 1980). Virtually all refugees from Southeast Asia experienced tremendous social disruption through the war years and its aftermath, including perilous journeys over land and sea, life in concentration camps, and overcrowded refugee camps. Consequently, the incidences of war and violence-related trauma, nutritional deficiencies, and parasitism were high in new arrivals. Concomitantly, the psychological effects of this period, resulting in Post Traumatic Stress Disorder (PTSD), depression, and other mental health problems were profound and continue to manifest to the present day in a large proportion of these refugees. Adjustment difficulties in attempting to retain traditional values in the face of the dominant U.S. culture also play an important role in mental health (Becker, Beyene, and Ken 2000).

Over time, the epidemiological profile has shifted from these more acute problems, typical to all refugees initially, to a more chronic disease picture (e.g., diabetes, hypertension, cancer). Problems of illness are compounded by under- or sporadic treatment resulting from accessibility barriers, including limited English skills, transportation difficulties, and cultural misunderstandings between the health-care system and the refugees (cf. Kemp and Rasbridge 1999).

Mental health problems are common, especially among Cambodian survivors of the Khmer Rouge holocaust and Vietnamese and Laotians whose cumulative trauma dose is high or severe. PTSD and depression are the most common diagnoses recognized in the literature (Kleijn, Hovens, and Rodenburg 2001; Mollica et al. 1998). The authors of this chapter have observed high levels of alcoholism, though this is not widely recognized in the literature.

Although the majority of the population of Southeast Asians living in the United States have adapted at least minimally to life here, there are segments, especially the elderly and the childless, who have yet to learn English and continue to interact almost exclusively with their own ethnic communities. As with all refugees, the emotional and even economic ties to the homeland can remain strong, even decades later; although many former refugees become U.S. citizens, some with the means do return to their homelands as conditions there improve; others remain "caught" between two worlds.

Buddhism and Health

Although there are substantial numbers (~10%) of Vietnamese refugees who have practiced Catholicism since Vietnam, and other Southeast Asian refugees who have converted to other branches of Christianity, Buddhism is the predominant faith throughout most of Southeast Asia. Among Southeast Asian communities in the United States, there are many temples reflective of the numerous sects of Buddhism adhered to in Asia, but the fundamental tenets are universal. Buddhism teaches that life is a cycle of suffering and rebirth: if one lives life in adherence to the moral Buddhist path, one can expect less suffering in this and future existences. Buddhism stresses disconnection to the present, especially materialism and self-aggrandizement. Hence, pain and illness are sometimes endured and health-seeking remedies delayed because of this belief in fate. Similarly, preventive health care has little meaning in this philosophy. However, despite assertions to the contrary (often by hostile interpreters from non-Buddhist religions), Buddhism does offer hope to its followers. Hope is leavened with acceptance or passivity, but hope for a better life now, a better next life, and hope for a better life for one's children is strong.

Buddhism on the whole is best understood not as a religion in the Western sense but more a philosophy of life and guide for living well. For example, Buddhists profess profound respect for elders and those in authority. This means that Asians in this country will rarely be confrontational with their U.S. counterparts; in disagreement, a "face-saving" measure of avoidance or superficial acceptance is preferred to questioning or defiance, especially of those in positions of superiority, such as doctors and teachers. Even direct eye contact or physical positioning of elevation over one's superior is considered forward and impolite by some traditional Southeast Asians.

Another tenet of Buddhism holds that the family unit is more important than the individual, with less emphasis on the "self." Accordingly, health-care decision making is frequently a family matter, and the family would typically be involved in treatment. Extended families living together or in close proximity are the cultural ideal, but nuclear families are common. Men are the heads of the household, but increasing numbers of households are headed by widowed or divorced or separated women. Extended families usually are headed by an older parent or grandparent. Because of the inevitable adjustments and changes resulting from living in a foreign land, decision making may fall to younger family members. However, even when it is clear to health-care staff that a younger son or daughter is making important decisions, it will benefit all concerned to go out of the way to show respect to the older family members.

Respect for and veneration of ancestors is fundamental to Buddhism and is highly ritualized. The prospect of burial away from ancestral burial sites is a source of significant distress to older refugees. Difficulty visiting burial sites in the homeland is also distressful.

Health-Seeking Behavior

The diagnosis and treatment of illness is frequently understood in three different, although overlapping, models of health and illness: spiritual, balance, and Western concepts (Kemp and Rasbridge 2004; Kemp 1985; Buchwald, Panwala, and Hooton 1992; Muecke 1983; Sargent and Marcucci 1984).

Spiritual

The first model of health (and illness) could be considered supernatural or spiritual, where illness can be brought on by a curse or sorcery, nonobservance of a religious ethic, or loss of the spirit or soul through fear or trauma. Traditional medical practitioners are common in Southeast Asian cultures, both here and in the homeland; some are specialists in the more magico-religious realm. For example, a specialist may be called upon to exorcise a bad spirit via chanting, a magical potion, or consultation from and recitation of ancient Chinese or Indian texts.

Amulets, such as Buddha images and other forms of spiritual protection, are ubiquitous. Though some are made of gold or jade, their true worth is found in their spiritual qualities, sometimes determined by their origin or source of blessing. Commonly, children, even newborns, wear *bua* (in Vietnamese) or *katha* (in Cambodian), a talisman of cloth or a strip of precious metal containing a Buddhist verse, sometimes blessed by a monk, worn on a string around the wrist, ankle, or neck. It is important for health-care staff to respect that these items are not decorative jewelry in the Western sense and should only be removed when absolutely necessary, and then only with permission. Similarly, Buddhist and other folk symbols may be found in tattoos and sacred cloths that are believed to provide bodily and spiritual protection. For spiritual illness of a more Buddhist etiology, religious practices may be intensified, such as significant offerings at a temple, measures to appease ancestors, or consultation with a Buddhist monk.

Asians in general traditionally do not have a concept of mental illness as discrete from somatic illness, and hence are unlikely to utilize Western-based psychological and psychiatric services. Instead, most mental health issues (e.g., depression, anxiety) fall into this spiritual health realm and are treated accordingly. Similarly, physical expression of spiritually-based illnesses (known as somatization) is common, and treatments overlap with the other realms of health understanding discussed below.

Balance

A widespread and fundamental belief throughout Asia (and other areas of world) is that the universe is composed of opposing elements held in balance. Consequently, health is a state of balance between these forces, known as *am* and *duong* in Vietnamese, based on the more familiar concepts of *yin* and *yang*. Specific to health, these forces are frequently translated as "hot" and "cold," although it is important to understand that because of the limitations of the English language, these concepts are not necessarily referring to inherent temperature but rather perceived effect on the body. Illness results when there is an imbalance of these "vital" forces. The imbalance can be a result of physiological state, such as pregnancy or fatigue, or it can be brought on by extrinsic factors like diet or overexposure to "wind," one of the body forces or "humors." Balance can be restored by a number of means, including diet changes to compensate for the excess of "hot" or "cold," Western medicines and injections, traditional medicines, herbs, and medical practices. The traditional practices and medications include:

- *Coining* (*cao gio* in Vietnamese, *kaw kchall* in Cambodian): Coining is used to treat a variety of ailments, including fever, upper respiratory infection, nausea, weak heart, and malaise. An edge of a coin is dipped in mentholated oil (e.g., Tiger Balm) and vigorously rubbed across the skin of the arms or torso, in a prescribed manner, causing a mild linear dermabrasion. This common practice is believed to release the excess force or "wind" from the body and hence restore balance.

- *Cupping:* A wad of cotton or kapok soaked in alcohol (or sometimes a small candle) is briefly ignited and extinguished under a small glass. This heated glass, in multiple series, is immediately placed on the skin, usually the back or forehead, forming a momentary vacuum that leaves a red circular mark, drawing out the bad force.

- *Pinching:* Similar to coining and cupping, the bruising formed by pinching the skin in prescribed locations (e.g., the bridge of the nose) allows the force to leave the body. (It should be noted that many of these practices are performed on young children, even infants, and the temporary marks they produce should not be confused with abuse or injury).

- *Moxibustion:* A small wad of kapok is burned directly on the abdomen, in treating gastrointestinal and other disorders. Moxibustion is seldom performed in the United States, but the abdomens of many adults will have four to six 1–2 cm round scars resulting from the procedure.

- *Steaming:* A mixture of medicinal herbs is boiled, the steam is inhaled, and the body bathed.

- *Balm:* Various medicated oils or balms, like Tiger balm, are rubbed over the skin.

- *Acupuncture:* Specialized practitioners insert thin steel needles into specific locations known as vital-energy points. Each of these points has specific therapeutic effects on the corresponding organs.

- *Acupressure or massage:* Fingers are pressed at the same points as with acupuncture, and together with massage, stimulate these points to maximize their therapeutic effects.

- *Herbs:* Various medicinal herbs are eaten directly or more frequently boiled in water in specific proportions or mixed with "wine" and consumed to restore balance.

- *Patent medicines:* These powdered medicines come packaged usually from Thailand or China and are mixed or boiled with water in specified proportions and taken for prescribed ailments.

Pregnancy and the postpartum are particularly significant within the humoral balance system found in all the Southeast Asian cultures, so a more detailed analysis may be illustrative here. The pregnancy is understood to be associated with tissue and blood development in the fetus, as well as the absence of blood loss through menses, all factors associated with "heat" or energy retention in the body. Dietary prescriptions favor foods perceived to be humorally neutral or "cold" during pregnancy to provide balance. Proscriptions against perceived humorally "hot" foods (e.g., ginger, black pepper) are observed in pregnancy lest a miscarriage result from excessive "heat." Indeed, a common abortifacient is a patent medicine of powdered tiger bone, considered to be one of the most powerful energy and virility enhancing "hot" medicines (Sargent, Marcucci, and Elliston 1983).

At parturition, the woman is seriously vulnerable to "cold" imbalance as a result of delivery and blood loss. Long-term negative health consequences such as arthritis and neuralgia are believed to result from inadequate restoration of humoral balance in the postpartum. Consumption of medicinal herbs steeped in wine and other traditional medicines, steaming, heated towels (and sometimes bricks) on the abdomen, consumption of "hot" foods, and avoidance of "cold" foods are all common restorative practices. Other taboo activities may include showering, heavy labor, and even sex for prescribed periods to prevent vulnerability to "cold" or "wind."

Western
Virtually all Southeast Asian refugees also recognize the more "Western" concepts of disease causation (e.g., germ theory) at least at a rudimentary level. There is widespread understanding, for example, that disease can come from contaminants in the environment, even if full concepts of microbiology or

virology are not grasped by all. Concomitantly, through decades of French occupation and more recently the U.S. influence in Southeast Asia, even the most rural have come to know the life-saving power of antibiotics.

When Southeast Asians enter the U.S. health-care setting, they do so mainly with the goal to relieve symptoms. In general, the patient expects a medicine to cure the illness quickly. When a medication is not prescribed initially, the patient is likely to seek care elsewhere. In addition to the myriad of traditional healers and other traditional medicines and practices available to resettled Asians, Western pharmaceuticals, especially vitamins and even antibiotics, are obtainable, either through specialized "injectionists" or from relatives in other countries such as France where some of these medicines are available without prescriptions. When refugees first began coming to the United States, Asian stores often had antibiotics and other prescription medications for sale under the counter. This is less common now, and the primary source of such medications is usually Mexican flea markets.

Southeast Asian patients frequently discontinue medicines after their symptoms disappear. Similarly, if symptoms are not perceived, many believe there is no illness. Thus, preventive, long-term medications such as antihypertensives must be prescribed with culturally sensitive education and on-going reinforcement. It is common for Vietnamese patients, for example, to amass large quantities of half-used prescription drugs, even antibiotics, many of which are shared with friends and even make their way back to family in Vietnam.

Western medicines, especially oral medications, are held in general to be "hot" medicines, in their effect on the balance of the body. For example, when medicines are prescribed for a skin irritation, which is understood traditionally as a "hot" illness, where the excess force "erupts" through the skin, a compliance issue may result. In this case, alternatives like a balm or poultice may better meet the patient's understanding of balance. Similarly, Asians commonly believe that Western pharmaceuticals are developed and dosed for Americans and Europeans, and hence dosages are too strong for their more slight builds, resulting in self-adjustment of dosages.

As mentioned above, Southeast Asians hold great respect for those with education, especially physicians. The doctor is considered the expert on health; therefore, the expectation is that diagnosis and treatment should happen at the first visit, with little examination or personally invasive laboratory or other diagnostic tests. In fact, a doctor who probes a great deal into symptoms may be held incompetent by some traditional refugees for not being able to diagnose readily. Trying to teach self-management of illness (e.g., a low sodium diet) is difficult. Of course, communication is a major issue in assessment and all other phases of care.

Communication barriers may be due to language or cultural issues. The latter include attempting to use a translator who, because of gender, age, social status, or past relationship incompatibilities, may be rejected or not listened to. Assessment is complicated: First, by a reluctance to complain or express negative feelings. It is common for patients to not report or even to deny symptoms or problems. This may be a cultural issue or may be due to past difficulties in obtaining health care. In other cases, symptoms or problems may be reported to several sources or to one source and not another.

Commonly, laboratory procedures involving the drawing of blood are feared and even resisted by some Southeast Asian patients, who believe the blood loss will make them sicker and that the body cannot replace what was lost. Surgery is particularly feared for this reason. Overall, as health is believed to be a function of balance, surgery would be considered an option only of last resort, as the removal of an organ would irreparably alter the internal balance.

Noncompliance with treatment regimens is frequent and may be due to several factors. The patient may not believe that he or she has communicated the problem and thus has little faith in the solution. A common Asian orientation to symptoms (vs. cause) of illness may result in discontinuation of treatment as soon as symptoms are resolved. Treatment through dietary measures is complicated by difficulty in food substitutions, differences in perceptions of foods, and in some cases, financial issues. Often there is an erroneous assumption on the part of health providers that the patient will be able to independently obtain refills or reappointments. Many Asian refugees (and others) have great difficulty negotiating the business aspects of the health-care system. Upon receiving a large bill, some will react by simply not going back and thus be noncompliant. Some patients, rather than report a less than efficacious response to treatment, will report "no problem" or "its okay."

Prevention

In general, as mentioned, Southeast Asians are oriented more to illness than prevention of illness. Childhood immunizations are accepted by nearly all, but adult immunizations such as influenza and pneumonia are resisted by many Cambodians until they become ill. However, we have noted that many Vietnamese eagerly seek influenza immunization.

Prevention of heart disease through diet and exercise is a major challenge. Traditional diets tend to be high in sodium and in the United States, high in saturated fats. Fast foods are also popular. Exercise among middle to older age is usually limited to leisurely strolling or Tai Chi type activities that have little cardiovascular benefit. Cancer screening is also a difficult concept to promote. Southeast Asian women are typically the lowest utilizers of breast and cervical cancer screening measures in the United States (Carey-Jackson et al. 2000; Tu et al. 2000).

End of Life

In every culture, the rites of passage surrounding dying and death are multifaceted and profound, but for Southeast Asians and other refugees, the confrontation with the end of life may be especially troubling (Rasbridge, Dinh, and Kemp 2000; Langford 2000). The old personal issues that may resurface in any human being are compounded by the immense losses and trauma common to refugees.

Geographic and spiritual distance from the homeland may also be painful. The most common responses we have seen are acceptance or resignation and withdrawal.

Family involvement with health-related decision making usually intensifies in a terminal situation. Most families strongly prefer that discussion of end-of-life issues be with the family and not the patient. Discussion of a poor prognosis with the patient is unthinkable to many families and patients. Withdrawal of treatment generally calls for several extended discussions with the entire family (except the patient) present.

The most common response to pain and other symptoms is stoicism. It is thus essential that pain and other symptoms be assessed frequently and in several different ways. The use of the "faces" pain assessment scale (a picture series of five round cartoon faces with expressions ranging from distressed to happy to indicate degree of pain) is usually met with complete—but polite— incomprehension. Equanimity in the face of death is a cultural and spiritual ideal and thus highly valued.

Conclusion

In sum, Southeast Asian refugees view health and illness from a variety of different perspectives, sometimes simultaneously. In other words, it is not uncommon for a sick person to interpret an illness as an interaction of spiritual factors, internal balance inequities, and even an infective process. Accordingly, there may be a combining of diagnostic and treatment elements from all three realms to obtain maximum health benefits. This broad perspective suggests an understanding of mind-body interactions and predisposing factors to illness that Western medicine is only beginning to fully understand.

REFERENCES

Becker, G., Y. Beyene, and P. Ken. 2000. Health, welfare reform, and narratives of uncertainty among Cambodian refugees. *Cultural and Medical Psychiatry* 24(2): 139–63.

Blair, R. G. 2000. Risk factors associated with PTSD and major depression among Cambodian refugees in Utah. *Health and Social Work* 25(1): 23–30.

Buchwald, D., S. Panwala, and T. Hooton. 1992. Use of traditional health practices by Southeast Asian refugees in a primary clinic. *Western Journal of Medicine* 156: 507–11.

Carey-Jackson, J., V. M. Taylor, K. Chitnarong, J. Mahloch, M. Fischer, R. Sam, et al. 2000. Development of a cervical cancer control intervention program for Cambodian American women. *Journal of Community Health* 25(5): 359–75.

Carlson, E. B., and R. Rosser-Hogan. 1994. Cross-cultural response to trauma: A study of traumatic experiences and post-traumatic symptoms in Cambodian refugees. *Journal of Trauma and Stress* 7(1): 43–58.

Dutt, Ashok K. 1985. *Southeast Asia: Realm of contrasts.* Boulder, CO: Westview Press.

Erickson, R., and G. N. Hoang. 1980. Health problems among Indochinese refugees. *American Journal of Public Health* 70(9):1003–1006.

Fall, B. 1966. *Vietnam witness, 1953–1966.* New York: Frederick Praeger.

Karnow, S. 1983. *Vietnam: A history.* New York: Viking Press.

Kemp, C. 1985. Cambodian refugee health care beliefs and practices. *Journal of Community Health Nursing* 2(1): 41–52.

Kemp, C. and L. A. Rasbridge. 2004. *Refugee and immigrant health: A handbook for health professionals.* Cambridge: Cambridge University Press.

Kemp, C., and L. A. Rasbridge. 1999. Refugee health immigrant health. Accessed January 12, 2002 at http://www.baylor.edu/~Charles_Kemp/refugee_health.htm.

Kleijn, W. C., J. E. Hovens, and J. A. Rodenburg. 2001. Posttraumatic stress symptoms in refugees: Assessments with the Harvard Trauma Questionnaire and the Hopkins Symptom Checklist-25 in different languages. *Psychological Reports* 88(2): 527–32.

Langford, J. M. 2000. Death and dying in ethnic America: Findings in Lao Lum, Khmu, Hmong, Khmer, and Cham communities. In *Death and dying in ethnic America,* ed. N. R. Z. Solomon and J. M. Langford. Seattle, WA: Cross Cultural Health Care Program.

Mollica, R. F., K. McInnes, C. Poole, and S. Tor. 1998. Dose-effect relationships of trauma to symptoms of depression and post-traumatic stress disorder among Cambodian survivors of mass violence. *British Journal of Psychiatry* 173: 482–88.

Muecke, M. 1983. In search of healers: Southeast Asian refugees in the American health care system. *Western Journal of Medicine* 139: 835–40.

Rasbridge, L., A. Dinh, and C. Kemp. 2000. Vietnamese health beliefs and practices related to the end of life. *Journal of Hospice and Palliative Nursing* 2(3): 109–17.

Sargent, C., J. Marcucci, and E. Elliston. 1983. Tiger bones, fire and wine: Maternity care in a Kampuchean refugee community. *Medical Anthropology* 7(4): 67–80.

Sargent, C., and J. Marcucci. 1984. Aspects of Khmer medicine among refugees in Dallas. *Medical Anthropology Quarterly* 16(1): 7–9.

Southeast Asia Resource Action Center [SEARAC]. 2002. Southeast Asian Communities. Accessed January 29, 2002, at http://www.searac.org/commun.html.

Tu, S. P., Y. Yasui, A. Kuniyuki, B. Thompson, S. M. Schwartz, J. C. Jackson, et al. 2000. Breast cancer screening among Cambodian American women. *Cancer Detection and Prevention* 24(6): 549–63.

U.S. Department of State. 2001. U.S. Refugee Admissions for FY 2000. Accessed January 13, 2002, at http://www.state.gov./www/global/prm/fy2000_budget.pdf

Ethnicity and Health-Seeking Behavior in India

Vijayan Pillai, PhD. Professor, School of Social Work, University of Texas-Arlington, Arlington, Texas

Hector Luis Diaz,Ph.D. Professor, College of Health Sciences & Human Services, University of Texas at Pan American, Edinburg, Texas.

This chapter presents an overview of the health-care system in India. We attempt to identify a select number of cultural, social, and economic components that influence health behavior in the Indian subcontinent. The selected components are ethnic identities, existing disease patterns, and cultural definitions of illness; identification and diagnosis process, approach to treatment following the diagnosis, access to health-care system, and, finally, dealing with end of life issues usually resulting from long term chronic illness.

Ethnic Groups

India has a total land mass of 2,973,190 square kilometers and is divided into three main geological regions: the Indo-Gangetic Plain, the Himalayas, and the Peninsula region. India has twenty-nine states and seven union territories. India is physiographically divided into ten regions: the Indo-Gangetic Plain, the northern mountains of the Himalayas, the Central Highlands, the Deccan or Peninsular Plateau, the East Coast, the West Coast, the Great Indian Desert and the Rann of Kutch; the valley of the Brahmaputra in Assam, the northeastern hill ranges surrounding the Assam Valley, and the islands of the Arabian Sea and the Bay of Bengal. Several major rivers, including the Ganges, Brahmaputra, and Indus, flow through India.

The Indian Union is composed of twenty-nine states and six centrally administered union territories. The States are Andhra Pradesh, Arunachal Pradesh, Assam, Bihar, Chhatisgarh, Delhi, Goa, Gujarat, Haryana, Himachal Pradesh, Jammu and Kashmir, Jharakhand, Karnataka, Kerala, Madhya Pradesh, Maharashtra, Manipur, Meghalaya, Mizoram, Nagaland, Orissa, Punjab, Rajasthan, Sikkim, Tamil Nadu, Tripura, Uttaranchal, Uttar Pradesh and West Bengal. The centrally administered territories are the Andaman and Nicobar Islands, Chandigarh, Daman and Diu, Dadra and Nagar Haveli, Lakshadweep, and Pondicherry.

There are fifteen official languages and many dialects. The official languages are Assamese, Bengali, Gujarati, Hindi, Kannada, Kashmiri, Malayalam, Marathi, Oriya, Punjabi, Sanskrit, Sindhi, Tamil, Telugu, and Urdu. English is recognized as an official language along with Hindi, the national language. English is widely used among educated Hindi and non-Hindi–speaking populations.

The 2000 census of India counted more than 1 billion people. The sex ratio is 927 females per 1,000 males. The annual population growth rate is about 2 percent. Birth rate is 28.7 per 1,000 population and the death rate is 9.3 per 1,000 population. About 25 percent of the population is urban and the rest rural. The literacy rate is 64 percent for males and 39 percent for females. Many religions are well represented in the population; Hinduism easily predominates, claiming 82 percent of the population. There are more than 75 million Muslims; 18 million Christian, 14 million Sikhs, 5 million Buddhists, 3.5 million Jains, and about 100,000 Parsis.

There have been three waves of South Asian immigration to the United States (Weinstein and Pillai 2001). The first wave was a small stream of migration from Punjab, which lasted over two decades, beginning in the early part of the twentieth century. Most Punjabis worked as manual laborers, first in Canada (Chandrasekhar 1982). A second wave of immigration of highly educated and skilled personnel began after 1965. A large increase in South Asian immigration took place in the 1960s with the passing of the Immigration Reform Act of 1965. The provisions of this reform enabled highly qualified individuals (e.g., physicians, engineers) from developing nations to immigrate to the United States. A high proportion of the educated immigrants originate from South Asia. Consequently, South Asians immigrants constitute a high income group. The parents and relatives of these immigrants were among the third wave of South Asian immigrants under the Family Reunification Act. The top states of intended residence for new immigrants in 1996 were California, New York, Florida, Texas, New Jersey, and Illinois. The state of Texas in particular attracts a large number of Latino/a as well as Asian immigrants. South Asian families are more likely to contain first generation elders than nonimmigrant native populations (Gupta and Pillai 2002)

Major Diseases and Health Disparities

There is widespread prevalence of infectious diseases in India. Infectious diseases account for about 57 percent and noncommunicable diseases for about 30 percent, respectively, of the disability adjusted life years (DALY) lost (Naylor et al. 1999). Pulmonary disease (e.g., tuberculosis, pneumonia), gastrointestinal disorders, and water-borne diseases are common. In addition, the incidence of malaria remains high even today. Filariasis is prevalent in coastal areas. In rural areas, the incidence of respiratory diseases increases during monsoon season. In urban areas, the high level of pollution, as well as overcrowding, contributes to marked increases in respiratory infections. Dental and periodontal disease occurs among most of the adult population. Sickle-cell disease is also prevalent, with the gene detected in about 16.5 percent of selected populations.

Occurrence of diseases is influenced by dietary habits. In rice-eating areas of the south, thiamine deficiency is widespread. Several other diseases that are caused by nutrition deficiency (e.g., pellagra, beriberi, lathyrism) are common in India (Edmundson, Sukhatme, and Edmundson 1992). Lack of minerals in the diet is also common. Mineral deficiencies result in diseases such as goitre. The prevalence of goitre is high in the Himalayan regions. The presence of high fluoride content in water in the states of Karnataka and Andhra Pradesh have contributed to widespread occurrence of fluorosis.

Economic development during the last half of the century has contributed to increases in the incidence of cardiovascular diseases. With economic development, sanitation and nutrition have improved. However, life-cycle changes involving high-calorie intake, in the form of fat and carbohydrates, in addition to increases in stress, have contributed to high levels of cardiovascular diseases. Enas,Garg and Davidson, et al. (1996) note that the heart-disease–related death rate stood at approximately 97 per 1,000 adults in the 1990s.

In addition to the risk of infections and cardiovascular diseases, women suffer from risk of death from childbirth. In India, nearly 300,000 women die from pregnancy-related causes. Nearly 27 percent of the entire world=s births occur in the South Asian region. However, the South Asian region accounts for more than half of all maternal deaths. The maternal mortality being approximately 42 per 10,000 births (Bandyopadhyay 1998).

Since the 1990s the Indian subcontinent has been ravaged by the AIDS epidemic. Within the next ten years, it is believed that India will become the epicenter of the world=s AIDS epidemic, resulting in extremely high rates of adult mortality. The crisis is generated by the widespread lack of acceptance and willingness to discuss individual sexuality at the family level. As a result, the incidence of sexually transmitted diseases [STD] is on the rise. It is estimated that one-third of the population is infected with an STD (Kapur 1993).

Perhaps one of the most notable intergroup disparities in health is indicated by the fact that since 1950 the Indian sex ratio has been masculine. Mortality among children under 5 is characterized by disproportionately high levels of mortality among females than males. In addition, female mortality rates surpassed male mortality rates at all ages below 35–39 (Dyson 1987). The excess mortality risk that females face in India stem from cultural values that favor males and therefore allocate scarce resources, such as food and health care, to males at the cost of female children (Basu 1992). Low female status is an important component of mortality risk. The 1991 census indicates an improvement in male-female sex ratio owing to a decrease in maternal mortality rate. These improvements may be attributed to the consequences of fertility decline more than they are due to an improvement in female status. As fertility declines, the risk of dying from pregnancy-related causes result in decreases in maternal mortality. Indian families are patrilineal. Women are expected to be submissive and acquiescent. They are expected to depend upon males all through their lives and the dependency is nurtured through several constraints and limitations imposed on women from developing individually. A number of decisions with regard to women's health care are made by males in the family and this lack of freedom to control one=s own body is a serious threat to women=s health and reproductive health in India.

Another subpopulation that suffers from poor health levels as compared to the rest in India is the tribal population. The scheduled tribes are tribal groups that have been recognized by the Indian government for the purpose of affirmative action. No other group suffers from poorer health as indicated by scores on indicators of quality of life such as life expectancy. The life expectancy for males is about 38 years and 40 years for females among the Bastar tribal groups in Madhya Pradesh (Basu and Kshatriya 1989). One reason for poor health is that tribal groups often live in hilly, mountainous and forest areas poorly served by transportation and other modern facilities. They have poor drinking water, suffer a high level of malnutrition, and live in dilapidated housing under unsanitary conditions. Almost 90 percent of the Bhils, a tribal group in Madhya Pradesh, depend upon water from the stream for drinking. Their dietary intake is low in nutritional value. Infant mortality rate is high owing to hard labor during the course of pregnancy. Availability of prenatal care is poor. The alcohol consumption level is high and the incidence of tetanus infection remains high among the tribal populations.

Cultural Definition of Illness and Health-Seeking Behavior

Any physical or mental condition that constrains day-to-day activities is defined as illness. Feeling ill is often associated with a lack of ability to perform fully in any aspect of physical, mental, or spiritual functioning. Health-seeking behavior is also influenced by beliefs about disease causation. In South Asia, it is believed that diseases are caused by a lack of appropriate attention to a number of social, physical, and spiritual activities. For example, too much sexual activity may be associated with having tuberculosis (Taylor 1976). In most instances, the "trigger for action" to seek medical help is the inability to work and perform daily tasks. A study among sex workers in Calcutta found that most of the women sought help within one to three days for severe incapacitating complaints (Evans and Lambert 1997). For mild complaints women waited at least a week or more before they visited with the doctor. During the waiting period, most women attempted self-medication by obtaining over-the-counter drugs. Self-medication often depended on an understanding of the etiology of the disease. Diseases are often classified into two categories, those stemming from the fact that the body is overheated and the other from the body being too cold. The loss of equilibrium between hot and cold states in the body is believed to be a major reason for illnesses. For illness resulting from the body being dangerously hot, cooling diets are prescribed. Many of the well known self-medications attempt to achieve a balance between the hot and cold state through appropriate diets.

One of the most important health surveys in India currently available is the Rapid Household Survey of Reproductive and Child health (Indian Institute of Population Science 1999). The survey asked a number of questions on conceptions about modes of AIDS transmission. Survey results suggest that even in a highly literate state such as Kerala, nearly 60 percent the respondents had one or more misconceptions about AIDS transmission. Popular misconceptions were that one can get AIDS by sharing clothes, school wash rooms, kitchen utensils, kissing, hugging, and shaking hands. (Raju 2002; Bhattacharya, Cleland, and Holland 2000). Lack of accurate information about the sources of HIV infection is likely to increase the risk of HIV infection.

Not all aspects of physical health are considered important. There is considerable neglect of sexual health. Information about puberty, sex, and sexual diseases is not publicly available and there is secrecy about sexual concerns. Jejeebhoy (1998) reports that awareness among females about menstruation and other puberty related physical changes appear to be poor. There is considerable disparity between young men and women with respect to sexual knowledge. In a study of sexual knowledge in slums, nearly 67 percent of the girls and about 50 percent of the boys possessed adequate knowledge about sex within marriage (Bhende 1994). The restriction on sexual activity also differs across the gender. Modernization and Westernization have increased access to pornography and adult sexual entertainments, whereas the traditional approach to regulating sexual life remain restrictive and resistant to public debate and scrutiny. Owing to this, there is tension between the sexual revolution and conservatism (Abraham 1999).

The cultural definition of a disease may be very different from its biomedical definition. In India, this discrepancy is perhaps best seen in a number of diseases labeled *Gupt Rog* (secret disease). These diseases are often associated with the perceived state of sexual health and sexual performance and considered as either extremely personal or secret. A survey of *Gupt Rog* among slum dwellers in Mumbai found that respondents were more concerned about illnesses related to sexual functioning than those resulting from sexual contact with others. A wide variety of symptoms were termed *Kanjori* (weakness). Consequently, a large number of terms and words are present in the local language to refer to various states of Kanjori. In the Indian tradition, the term *Virya* stands for vigor and semen (Nag 1996). The loss of semen through nocturnal emission or masturbation is believed to be harmful for emotional, physical, and spiritual well being. A large number of traditional healers cater to men who believe that they suffer from *Gupt Rog* (Verma et al. 1998).

Health Concerns

Indian cultural practices and beliefs influence the decision to seek health care as well as the effective utilization of available health-care services. The role of cultural factors on health-care practices is evident in ways people utilize health care during all too common occurrences such as pregnancy and childbirth. Pregnancy brings about changes in dietary habits. Manocha, Manocha, and Vir (1992) in a study of three villages in Haryana found that the consumption of citrus fruits, mango, guava, red chilies, and all kinds of pickles increased during pregnancy. They report that a high proportion of these women craved, and many ate, ash from the hearth (*chullah*), *chullah* mud, and clay. Consumption of milk during pregnancy did not increase in spite of the fact that survey villages had abundant supply of milk produced by local dairy farms owned by most of the villagers. A high proportion of the women surveyed did not believe that it is necessary to increase caloric intake during pregnancy. Purohit, Mathur, and Sharma (1973) observe that a reduction in dietary intake often occurs due to fear of having a large fetus, causing obstruction and pain during delivery.

Prenatal care remains low. Manocha, Manocha, and Vir (1992) report that only 50 percent of women in the study village receive a prenatal check up. Most pregnant women visit the primary health-care center located in the village only if complications arise. Deliveries often take place at home. In most instances, a closed room with poor ventilation is chosen for the delivery, which is attended by either a midwife or a selected elderly woman. During cold season, the room is heated by using either wood charcoal or dried cow-dung cakes. The burning of these materials produces high levels of carbon dioxide and carbon monoxide. Prolonged exposure to these gases is an important cause of infant mortality and maternal death in India (Chandrasekhar 1982).

Diagnostic Process

The diagnostic process practiced by Western medicine is sometime rendered ineffective and inapplicable due to physical and social characteristics. At the biological level, there is high variation in Indian skin color and physical types. In the North, skin color is white; in the Northwest it is yellow; in the South, it is black. There are similar differences in head structure. Due to variations in skin color, physical symptoms associated with hues and tones of skin color may considerably vary from person to person. The yellow discoloration often associated with liver disease is hard to detect in non-White Indian populations. Diagnosis is also hampered by communication patterns. Women seldom make eye contact with other men. Even though men make direct eye contact with each other, they may not do so with other men who are either older or possess more authority. Nonverbal communication is used extensively. Hand gestures and head movements are part of the communication process. Most men and women also avoid hugging and embracing. Physicians will have to become adept at reading nonverbal language extensively used by their clients.

There are fundamental differences between modern and South Asian ideas of causation. Modern medicine places considerable emphasis on relevant events immediately prior to one falling ill. Detailed account of events in the immediate past is relevant for diagnosis. The South Asian measure of time is seldom precise. The past involves a number of events that can be recalled. Events in the present are not of any more importance than the ones that were experienced a long time ago. This view of time emerges from South Asian perspectives on life. They believe that each individual is made up of several metaphysical components such as *Atma* and *Jeevatma*. *Atma* is indestructible. It is the presence of God in a person. The *Jeevatma*, on the other hand, is the sum total of all past experiences that propels one into the future. Righteous actions (*Karma*) lead to positive experiences. Actions that do not contribute to physical, social, and spiritual well being of others result in undesirable consequences to the self. Some of these consequences may be experienced during this life, whereas the rest may be experienced during the course of the next life. Thus, current sufferings and illness have their roots in an inconceivable past composed of several births during which a person accumulated ill effects of bad deeds and actions. The focus is on taking the right actions in the present. The force of the *Jeevatma* can not be changed. Events in the immediate past may not be recollected specifically unless probed and asked about in detail through skilled interviews. In addition, South Asians may not fully realize the importance of keeping an appointment at the precise time scheduled. All these issues may hinder diagnostic procedures followed in modern medicine.

Treatment Options

South Asians have an eclectic approach toward treatment. There are three mainstream systems of medicine: Ayurvedic, Siddha, and Unani. In addition, the Allopathic (Western medicine) and homeopathic system are also widely used. Ayurvedic medicine is deep rooted in Indian traditions. It views illness as an outcome of imbalances in the three fundamental body elements: *Vatha* (wind), *Pitha* (bile), and *Kabha* (phlegm). The imbalances occur due to either inadequate or incorrect intake of foods. Owing to this view, the healing process involves rigid adherence to dietary regulations. Ayurvedic medicine believes that good health results from adequate functioning of mind, body, soul, and senses.

Yet another source of illness emanates from the displeasure of the gods, family deities are ceremoniously worshiped and appeased in order to receive physical, mental, and financial security. Wrongful actions and failure to be mindful of the presence of gods may incur their wrath resulting in ill health, mental illness, and poverty. South Asians often combine ceremonial worship of deities along with receiving treatment.

In spite of widespread knowledge of traditional systems of medicine, the Indian public is not averse to Western medicine. Although, most consumers of Western medicine do not understand the scientific approach toward diagnosis, treatment, and prognosis, Western medicine is seen as an effective system of medicine capable of curing disease symptoms. Given the lack of understanding of the scientific method, when diseases are cured, it is at times attributed to the magical powers of Western medicine. The two systems of medicine, the traditional and the Western, provide two strong choices for people to seek medical assistance. In many instances, they combine the two in desirable amounts. In general, there is widespread trust in the effectiveness of Western medicine. The cure stems from not only the effectiveness of the medicine but also in the special power of the physician. Demand for an instant cure is high and as a result physicians prescribe powerful drugs and large dosages (Evans and Lambert 1997).

Many South Asians will have engaged in self-diagnosis and self-medication before they seek professional medical help. Over-the-counter medications are easily available in India. A study of Antenatal care in rural Karnataka found that a high proportion of women engaged in self-medication (Matthews et al. 2001).

The outbreak of the AIDS epidemic in India has not only strained the existing meager health-care infrastructure but also has given rise to a new group of AIDS healers. This is partly due to the stigma and untouchability attached to the disease (Pandya 1997). Fearing ostracization, the HIV infected seek the private and confidential services of these healers. Indian laws allow individuals, who without formal medical qualifications self-identify themselves as healers, to advertise in the newspapers.

Healing Process

Adherence and compliance to medicinal prescriptions is fundamental to the healing process. South Asians often tend to disregard suggested timings for medicine intake and at times skip the prescribed daily dosages. This is in part due to a lack of appreciation for strict mechanical time regulated activities in day to day life. There is widespread ignorance about the fundamental positivistic assumptions of Western medicine. Lack of understanding of the Western medical system combined with lack of compliance is likely to delay the healing process unless South Asian clients are adequately counseled about the need to comply with prescribed dosages and regimens.

The healing process may also be compromised by various genetic factors that are specific to South Asian populations. For example, South Asians in general have low lactose tolerance. They are also more easily intoxicated from alcohol consumption. It has also been found that South Asians have significantly different rates of metabolism for certain drugs as compared to Western populations. It has been found that in general, South Asians require lower dosages of psychotropic medicines. However, even at these lower dosage levels, they tend to have more side effects than North Americans (Levy 1993).

Social Network and Social Support
South Asians seek out a wide network of friends and relatives for support during health crises. Marriage alliances widen the social network of relatives. Marriages are arranged by the parents of the bridegroom and bride. Potential spouses are selected from same caste groups. Once marriage is consummated, it is considered to be a contract between the spouses, their families, and their kin groups. Events such as the arrival of the first child are attended by a large number of family members. Elder members from the neighborhood and village offer help and counsel the young. Women are entrusted with all aspects of care giving. The responsibility for elder care giving is on the son. However, daughters-in-laws take an active role in elder care giving (Gupta and Pillai 2002). Women=s health tends to be overlooked and ignored as they focus on their care-giving roles. However, due to the close bonds that exist within the joint family system, the sick role (Gupta and Pillai 2001) is accepted without any feeling of guilt. The responsibility for caring for the sick is shared among all family members.

Closure to Chronic Illness
In general, South Asians have a fatalistic attitude toward chronic illness. It is seen as an outcome of bad deeds performed during this life or in past lives. There is

also hope that the next life will be less burdensome and painful as one has already grieved and paid for his or her undesirable activities in the past. The stage in life during which the chronic illness occurs is likely to influence the seriousness which remedies are sought (Gupta and Pillai 2001) . If the person is elderly, he or she is more likely to spend time focusing on spiritual well being and is likely to be less concerned about aggressively curing the disease. Death is therefore not seen as an end in itself. It is more a transition point from one life to another. For this reason, South Asians are less likely to seek aggressive life prolonging treatments involving life-support systems. The passage to the afterlife of the deceased may be less hazardous by undertaking prescribed rituals by grown children and other close relatives designated by the priest. The eldest son has a prominent role in enabling the course of the journey of his parent from this world to the other. The eldest son lights the funeral pyre. His presence is required all through the cremation ceremonies.

Access to Health-Care System
Health-care services are provided by both government and private agencies. The government sector provides health promotion, disease prevention, and curative services free of charge. The health-care system is multilayered. At the bottom is the rural subcenter, serving approximately 5,000 people. Each subcenter provides first aid, health education, and basic health-care services. Cases that cannot be cared for at the subcenter level are referred to the Primary Health Centers (PHC). PHCs mostly treat outpatients. They typically offer a number of public health programs, outpatient clinics, and limited inpatient facilities. For every four PHCs, there is at least one Community Health Center or District Hospital. The district hospitals provide inpatient treatment and a variety of out-patient services at centers throughout the country. The last tier in the health-care system is the tertiary care hospitals associated with medical schools located in large cities. There are about 4,500 government hospitals. However, nearly 70 percent of these hospitals are located in the urban areas where 20 percent of the total Indian

population lives. In rural India, the physician/population ratio is 1 per 7,900, whereas in urban India, the ratio is 1 per 790 (Duggal 1991). Thus, the rural areas are severely underserved (Dreze and Sen 1995). The government services are often used by the poor who cannot afford to purchase private medical care. As a result, a wide range of practitioners and facilities operate either on a nonprofit basis or for those who can afford to pay. The average cost of hospitalization in the private hospitals located in urban areas was nearly 350 percent higher than the hospitalization cost in urban government hospitals (Gumber and Berman 1995). The urban poor spend a disproportionately larger share of their income on health care than the urban middle class. A recent health study conducted in Delhi (Gupta and Dasgupta, 1999) suggests that 2.3 percent of the total annual expenditures incurred by low income household were on health care. This proportion was as low as 0.5 percent among middle and higher income households. The government supports both the traditional and the Western systems of medicine. Current levels of infrastructure development for delivery of Western medical care have not kept pace with the growing demand for Western medicine.

It should be noted that the health-care sector in India has recently experienced enormous growth in infrastructure in the private and volunteer sector. The private sector now has state of the art hospitals staffed by highly skilled medical professionals. Nearly 57 percent of all hospitals and 32 percent of all hospital beds in the country are in private sector hospitals. It is estimated that 75–80 percent of health-care services in India are now provided by the private sector. Contrary to expectations, a higher proportion of poor households (as compared to middle and higher income groups) depend on private clinics (Gupta and Dasgupta 1999). The cost of complex medical procedures performed in these hospitals is only a fraction of the treatment cost for the same procedures in Western countries. As a result, there is considerable medical tourism to India.

Conclusion

The Indian population will exceed China=s within the next two decades. Even though life expectancy has increased steadily since the mid-1980s, a large proportion of deaths still occur due to infectious disease and malnutrition. Economic development has created a large middle class. Owing to changes in life styles as well as consumption, there has been an increase in cardiovascular and chronic diseases among members of the middle class. Women suffer from greater health risks than men. Cultural definitions play a crucial role in health maintenance. Cultural practices and beliefs influence the decision to seek health care as well as effective utilization of available health-care services. Several cultural practices restrain access to health-related knowledge as well as create disparities between men and women with respect to health-related information. Yet, another group that suffers disproportionately from health disadvantages when compared with the rest of the population is scheduled tribes.

The South Asian belief systems on disease causation influence the ways in which symptoms are manifested. South Asians are less likely to seek treatment. They are likely to either delay or refuse treatment. Many South Asians engage in self-diagnosis and self-medication before they seek professional medical help. Lack of understanding of the Western medical system combined with lack of compliance delays the healing process. Over-the-counter medications are plentiful and readily available in India. Family members and extended family members are often involved in the caring of the sick. The Government of India provides free medical health care; however, the facilities are often dilapidated. There is widespread practice of traditional systems of medicine such as Ayurveda and Unani. The government promotes the traditional systems along with modern medicine.

Health-care needs of the Indian subcontinent present a challenge for the Indian government as well as the people of India. It is impossible to ignore the health-care needs of one-fifth the world population. Programs for promoting gender equality as well as eliminating the discrimination against women can go a long way in reducing health disparities among subpopulations such as women and scheduled tribes. Given the strong cultural influences on health-care practices, it is essential to train social workers who are culturally sensitive.

REFERENCES

Abraham, L. 1999. Where to draw the Lakshman Rekha? Gender dimensions of youth sexuality in urban India. Paper Presented at the Conference on Sexualities, Masculinities and Culture in South Asia: Knowledge, Practices, Popular Culture, and the State. Melbourne, Australia, July 6–8.

Bandyopadhyay, M. 1998. *Women and health: Tradition and culture in rural India*. Aldershot, UK: Ashgate.

Basu, A. 1992. *Culture, the status of women and demographic behavior*. Oxford: Clarendon Press.

Basu, S. K, and G. Kshatriya. 1989. Fertility and mortality in tribal populations of Bastar, District, Madhya Pradesh, India. *Biology and Society* 6:100–12.

Bhattacharya, G., C. Cleland, and S. Holland. 2000. Knowledge about HIV/AIDS, the perceived risks of infection and sources of information of Asian-Indian adolescents born in the USA. *AIDS Care* 12(2): 203–210.

Bhende, A. 1994. A study of sexuality of adolescent girls and boys in underprivileged groups in Bombay. *Indian Journal of Social Work* (4): 557–71.

Chandrasekhar, S., ed. 1982. *From India to America: A brief history of immigration, problems of discrimination, admission, and assimilation*. La Jolla, CA: Population Review.

Dreze, J., and K. Sen. 1995. *India: Economic development and social opportunity*. Oxford: Clarendon Press.

Duggal, R. 1991. Private health expenditure. *MFC Bulletin* 173/174:14–16.

Dyson, T. 1987. Excess Female Mortality in India: Uncertain Evidence on a Narrowing Differential. In *Dynamics of population and family welfare*, ed. K. Srinivasan and S. Mukerji. Bombay, India: Himalaya Publishing House.

Edmundson, W. C., P. V. Sukhatme, and S. A. Edmundson. 1992. Diet, disease and development. New Delhi, India: Macmillan India.

Enas EA, Garg A, Davidson MA, Nair VM, Huet BA, Yusuf S: Coronary heart disease and its risk factors in first generation immigrant Asian Indians to the United States of America. Indian Heart J 1996 Jul-Aug; 48(4):343-53.

Evans, C., and H. Lambert. 1997. Health-seeking strategies and sexual health among female sex workers in urban India: Implications for research and service provisions. *Social Science and Medicine* 44(12): 1791–1803.

Gumber, A., and P. Berman. 1995. Measurement and pattern of morbidity and utilization of health services. Working Paper No.65. Ahmedabad, India: Gujarat Institute of Development Research.

Gupta, I., and P. Dasgupta. 1999. Health-seeking behavior in urban Delhi: An exploratory study. *Journal of Health and Population in Developing Countries* 3(2): 80–95.

Gupta, R., and V. K. Pillai. 2002. Eldercare giving in south Asian families: Implication for social service. *Journal of Comparative Family Studies* 33(4): 565–77.

———. 2001. Eldercare giver burden in south Asian families in the Dallas-Fort Worth metropolitan area. *International Journal of Aging* 2(2): 93–104.

Indian Institute of Population Science. 1999. Rapid household survey, 1998–1999. Mumbai, India: Indian Institute of Population Science.

Jejeebhoy, S. J. 1998. Adolescent sexual and reproductive behavior: A review of the evidence from India. *Social Science and Medicine* 46(10): 1275–90.

Kapur L.T,R.1993. Pattern of Sexually Transmitted Diseases in India. *Indian Journal of Dermatology, Venereology and Leprology* 49(1): 23--34

Levy, R. A. 1993. Ethnic and racial differences in responses to medicines: Preventing individualized therapy in managed pharmaceutical programs. *Pharmaceutical Medicines* 7: 139–65.

Manocha, S., A. Manocha, and D. Vir. 1992. Cultural beliefs and practices affecting the utilization of health services during pregnancy. *Journal of Indian Anthropological Society* 27(2): 181–85.

Matthews, Z., S. Mahendra, A. Kilaru, and S. Ganapathy. 2001. Antenatal care, care-seeking and morbidity in rural Karnataka, India: Results of a prospective study. *Asia-Pacific Population Journal* 16(2): 11–28.

Nag, M. 1996. *Sexual behavior and AIDS in India.* New Delhi, India: Vikas Publishing.

Naylor, D. C, P. Jha, J. Woods, and A. Shariff. 1999. *A fine balance: Some options for private and public health care in urban India.* Washington, DC: World Bank.

Pandya, S. 1997. Patients testing positive for HIV: Ethical dilemmas in India. *Issues in Medical Ethics* 5(2): 49–55.

Purohit, C. K., R. M. Mathur, and R. Sharma. 1973. Study of social customs and child birth. *Indian Journal of Preventive Social Medicine* 4: 86–89.

Raju, K. N. M. 2002. Awareness, knowledge and misconception about HIV/AIDS: A comparison of two states in southern India. A paper presented at the International conference on Issues of Population Stabilization and Development; Cuttack, India, February 8–10, 2002.

Taylor, C. E. 1976. The place of indigenous medical practitioners in modernization of medical services. In *Asian Medical System*, ed. C. Leslie. Berkeley: University of California Press.

Verma, R. K., G. Rangaiyan, S. Narkhede, M. Aggarwal, R. Singh, and P. J. Pelto. 1998. cultural perceptions and categorization of male sexual health problems by practitioners and men in a Mumbai slum population. *Times of India*, Bangalore edition.

Weinstein, J and V.K. Pilllai. 2001. *Demography: The science of population.* Massachussetts:Allyn and Bacon

10

Big and Little Moon Peyotism as Health-Care Delivery Systems

Dennis Wiedman, PhD. Associate Professor, Department of Sociology and Anthropology. Florida International University, Miami, Florida

Introduction

The use of peyote for health-care purposes was noted by the Spaniards, who recorded its use among the Aztec (Slotkin 1955, 1956), but few scholars have focused on health care as an explanation for the acceptance and persistence of Peyotism, the largest intertribal religion practiced by more than 125,000 North American Indians. Ethnographic fieldwork among the Delaware in northeast Oklahoma indicates that the majority of Peyote meetings were specifically for health-care purposes.

From 1885 to the 1920s, when Peyotism and traditional Delaware ceremonies were practiced simultaneously, Peyotism added an important aspect to Delaware life that the traditional religion did not. During these years U.S. Indian Agents and Christian missionaries actively denounced traditional Indian religions, dances, languages, and customs. U.S. government policy promoted Western medicine through Indian hospitals and physicians, although not recognizing the activities of medicine men and other traditional healers. This transition also mirrored the changes that had occurred throughout the United States, where the medical care system had been transformed from a home-oriented, family-centered system into a stratified system associated with the new social and economic urban centers (Duffy 1979; Knox, Bohland, and Shumsky 1983).

Peyotism as an organized intertribal religion, with Christian elements and a legal charter as a church, was a direct response to this development and federal policy. Even though traditional Delaware ceremonies continued to take place until the 1920s, they followed the traditional ritual cycle, with the major Big House ceremony held only for twelve days each fall. An annual healing ceremony, the Doll Dance, ceased to be held in the 1930s (Weslager 1973; Prewitt 1981). Peyote meetings, however, could be called at any time an individual had an immediate social, spiritual, or health need. From this perspective, Peyotism became the most prevalent religious and healing system among the Delaware because the traditional religious system and healers did not meet Delaware health needs

The primary purpose of this paper is to present Peyotism as a religious system, which provides moral and spiritual needs, while also functioning as a health-care system providing for its members' physical and mental well-being. This chapter will also highlight the importance of the health-care aspects of Peyotism in the acceptance and persistence of two major ritual forms among the Delaware: Big Moon and Little Moon Peyotism.

History of Peyotism as a Religion
Legally recognized in Oklahoma since 1918 as the Native American Church, the Peyote religion is based upon the sacramental use of peyote, a small spineless cactus. Peyotists believe God placed this cactus on earth for use by Indians, and they consider it a teacher of the correct way of life, a helper in times of need, and a medicine in times of sickness (Wiedman 1985).

After the forced settlement of many tribes to Indian and Oklahoma Territory in the late 1800s, the use of peyote was formalized into a structured ritual incorporating Native American and Christian concepts. Two major variations, or Peyote Ways, developed in southwestern Oklahoma by 1885: the Kiowa, Comanche, and Apache developed the Little Moon ritual, and the Delaware-Caddo developed Big Moon Peyotism (La Barre 1967[1938]).

Compared with Little Moon Peyotism, Big Moon Peyotism incorporated additional ritual roles, material items, and symbols. Big and Little Moon Peyotism, as developed in Oklahoma, form the basis of the two major variations of this religion as practiced by Indian tribes throughout North America. Among the northern tribes Little Moon Peyotism is known as "Half Moon" or the "Tipi Way." In Oklahoma, Big Moon is also known as "Wilson Moon," whereas the northern and western tribes know it as the "Cross Fire" because of lines drawn on the altar forming a cross (Petrullo 1975[1934], 79; Stewart 1987). Stewart (1987, 209) noted that both versions "remained dedicated to curing, to sobriety, and to Christian ideals."

Although the Cross Fire ritual of the northern tribes derived from the Wilson Moon, this form of Peyotism is nowhere practiced in the complexity that developed in northeastern Oklahoma. This chapter focuses upon northeast Oklahoma Delaware Peyotism, which distinguishes most notably between the two variations.

Ritual Structure of Delaware Big Moon and Little Moon Peyotism

When the ritual, social, material, and belief structures of Big and Little Moon Peyotism are compared, there is a common basic structure. In general, the basic structure of Peyotism involves the communal consumption of peyote during an all-night ceremony, in which a participant's attention should be focused on peyote and the purpose of the meeting. A basic belief is that peyote can teach the proper way of life and that it can cure illnesses. During the ceremony, the participants sit around a crescent moon-shaped altar constructed on the ground. A line extends along the moon from point to point, indicating the "peyote road," or the "road of life," and a large peyote is placed on this line midway between its points. All the participants face towards this "grandfather" peyote and are led by a "road-man" or "road chief," who sits closest to it. The roadman is assisted by a drum chief to his right and a fireman, who sits on the opposite side of the moon near the door. The ritual items consist of a staff, fan, rattle, drum, and drumstick (Wiedman 1985).

The ceremony is highlighted by five events: the start, midnight, morning, breakfast, and conclusion. Between these events each man takes his turn singing four songs while shaking the rattle and holding the staff and fan. He is accompanied on the drum by a man to his right. After completing his songs, he passes the ritual items to his left, so that they pass clockwise around the altar throughout the night. Following the ceremony, participants, family, and friends eat a dinner prepared by the women.

Big and Little Moon Peyotism were founded upon this basic structure. Since the standardization of these two variations in the 1880s, only minor additions have been made to accommodate the belief and ritual systems of the various Native communities of North America (Wiedman and Greene 1988). The additions include social, material, and symbolic elements, which primarily concern the construction of the ceremonial altar, the addition of ritual officials, the decoration of the ritual items, etiquette during the ceremony, and distinctions in beliefs about prayer and the individual's relation to the roadman, peyote, and God.

Petrullo (1975[1934]), La Barre (1967[1938]), Stewart (1987), and Wiedman (1988a, 1988b) provide descriptions and illustrations of these two religious traditions. Briefly stated, the major differences between these two variations as practiced by the Delaware are:

Little Moon Peyotism
1. Crescent moon-shaped altar made of earth.
2. Four officials: roadman, drum chief, fireman, and cedarman.
3. Singer accompanied on a drum by man who sits to his right, or another man invited to drum by singer.
4. Water outside of *tipi* can be drunk only after special events.
5. Five events in the ceremony:
    - Start: Statement of purpose; prayer with tobacco smoked by all; Peyote consumed by all; four songs sung by roadman.

- Midnight: Water bucket brought in by fireman; coals from fire spread and cedar incense placed on coals; eagle whistle blown outside of *tipi* in four directions by roadman.

- Morning: Water brought in by woman who says prayer while smoking tobacco.

- Breakfast: Woman brings in water, meat, corn, and fruit.

- Quitting: Four songs sung by roadman shortly after breakfast, or after four complete circles of altar by staff during night.

6. Participants can go outside *tipi* during night, preferably after midnight, by requesting permission from roadman. On return they can go directly to their seats.

7. When not in use, the staff, fan, rattle, and drum are laid on a cloth in front and slightly to the left, of the roadman.

8. The staff is property of roadman, who uses it wherever he leads a meeting.

Big Moon Peyotism

1. Altar is in the form of a large crescent moon with ground recessed between its points. A line runs along edge of recessed area forming "Peyote Road." Two lines form a cross on the altar. A line runs from the grandfather peyote to sun in the shape of a globe on eastern edge of altar, and a line across the altar forms a crossmark.

2. Eight officials: In addition to four major officials, there are two additional firemen and two crossmark men, one sits at each end of the line that forms the cross on the altar.

3. A fireman drums for all singers.

4. Water is inside and is distributed by a fireman on request.

5. Five events in ceremony:

- Start: Purpose stated. Prayer with tobacco smoked only by roadman; Peyote consumed by all; four songs sung by roadman.

- Midnight: Coals from fire are spread; four songs sung by roadman.

- Morning: Person sponsoring meeting or person, who is being healed, stands in recessed area between fire and sun; he or she is fanned with eagle fan; fanning of others, if they so desire.
- Breakfast: Brought in and placed in recessed area of altar; water, meat, corn, and fruit.
- Conclusion: Four songs sung by roadman at noon.

6. The staff, which is ornately decorated with draped ribbons, is never laid down. When not in use it is placed upright before the roadman, its tip placed in a hole in the ground.

7. The staff is passed clockwise throughout the night; however, when there is a second row of persons, the staff is passed from the left of a front-row person to a person in the second row. After blessing themselves by passing their hands over the staff, second-row person returns staff to next person in front row, to left of person who passed it originally.

8. When a person wishes to go outside, they must get attention of a crossmark man, who signals the roadman to allow the person to exit. On return, before they can take a seat, they stand in the recessed area facing the fire and grandfather peyote and is fanned by a fireman with an eagle fan. They then pass to left or right of altar according to side on which they are seated, and walks along edge of recessed area to grandfather peyote. The person touches grandfather peyote and then returns to their seat. (DW: modified this text to be gender neutral)

9. Anyone who desires to say a prayer out loud with tobacco addresses roadman and communicates his or her needs. Roadman then rolls a tobacco cigarette and prays for individual.

10. Sponsor of meeting or person for whom meeting is held takes a sweatbath directed by roadman at noon before meeting.

11. In most cases recessed altar is made of concrete. Osage and Quapaw built large round houses containing permanent altar; Delaware used *tipi*, no houses were built.

12. Staff stays with owners of permanent altar. Although different roadmen are asked to lead meetings, they use staff, which is associated with altar.

History of Delaware Peyotism

The Delaware tribe was originally located in present-day New Jersey, Pennsylvania, and Delaware. After many forced displacements, the largest group (985) settled in northeastern Oklahoma along the Caney River in 1867, and a smaller number (83) settled with the Caddo near Anadarko in southwestern Oklahoma. In northeastern Oklahoma, the Delaware purchased lands from the Cherokee equal to 160 acres for each Delaware man and they became members of the Cherokee Nation with the same rights and immunities as native Cherokees (Weslager 1972, 426–30). In the 1970s, the nearly 8,000 Delaware lived primarily near Dewey and Bartlesville in Washington County (Weslager 1978). By 1990, the Delaware tribal office reported a total of 11,000 members.

The two forms of Peyotism were introduced to the northeastern Delaware within one year of each other: Little Moon in 1884 and Big Moon in 1885. Elk Hair, a prominent Delaware leader, was the primary adherent of the Kiowa-Comanche Little Moon ritual, while at the same time he was a leader in traditional Delaware ceremonies (Speck 1933).

John Wilson, a Delaware-Caddo also known as Moonhead, was the originator of Big Moon Peyotism and the person who introduced this ritual into northeastern Oklahoma. Ethnologist James Mooney interviewed John Wilson in 1891. He reported that Wilson: "assumes the occult powers of authority of a great medicine man, all the powers claimed by him being freely conceded by his people" (Mooney 1965[1896], 161).

From about 1885 until his death in 1902, Moonhead regularly visited the Delaware, Osage, and Quapaw among whom he established many peyote churches; Speck (1907, 171) reports that by 1902 most of the Osage had taken up Big Moon Peyotism and had become devoted to it. In the 1920s and 1930s, ethnologists Vincenzo Petrullo and Frank Speck wrote that the Delaware primarily practiced Big Moon Peyotism (La Barre 1967[1938], 115; Speck 1931, 1937).

George Anderson, the primary Delaware Big Moon leader, related to Speck that Wilson taught his followers: "Sincere devotion to the sacred rites and teachings revealed, along with aadministration of Peyote when taken in the right spirit during the meetings by believers sincere in purpose and observant of the regulations imposed upon them, would result in the curing of disease" (Speck 1933, 543).

Ethnologist Newcomb visited the Delaware in 1955 and recorded that "Most Delaware Peyotists belong to the more liberal and Christianized sect which has been termed Big Moon; a few are adherents to the Little Moon sect" (Newcomb 1955, 1042; 1956).

When I began my fieldwork in 1970, I found that the Delaware continued to have great respect for Moonhead, something that was emphasized by the fact that four families claimed a kinship relationship to him. But it was puzzling to find that the leading Delaware roadman and inheritor of Big Moon Peyotism practiced Little Moon Peyotism.

Delaware Peyotism in the 1970s
In 1970, only the Osage practiced the elaborate Big Moon ritual in large wooden houses with concrete altars. The Quapaw, who at one time had as many as nine permanent Big Moon altars, had no active roadman. The last Delaware Big Moon ceremony had been held in 1969.

This does not mean that Peyotism had completely disappeared among the Delaware. The Little Moon ritual had taken its place. For five years, from 1970 to 1975, I participated in Delaware activities. From August 1972 to August 1973, my wife and I spent a complete year as participant-observers of the daily activities of the leading Delaware peyote families whose homes were the church grounds for Peyote meetings.

Two rented wooden houses separated by about 300 yards of trees, brush, and hilly ravines were the homes of the extended-family households related through brother and sister. Wood burning stoves heated the homes and kept a man in each household busy chopping, hauling, and splitting firewood. Bottled propane gas was used for cooking in the house, wood fires for cooking outside. One house had an indoor toilet; however, residents and visitors used outside toilets. Water was obtained from rain-filled cisterns; piped-in water and a toilet was later installed in one of the houses. Each house had a specially prepared and maintained ground within a hundred feet of the house where the peyote *tipi* was set up. The nearest neighbors could barely distinguish the all-night drumbeats from the clank-clank-clank of the oil wells, which constantly broke the silence of the oak-and-blackjack-covered hillside.

The Delaware roadman had married a Pawnee woman; his sister, who lived in the other house, had married a Comanche roadman. Both households were identified as Delaware even though the non-Delaware spouses were from prominent peyote families in their own tribes. Delaware and other tribal members from throughout northeast Oklahoma came to these households to ask them to have a meeting for their purpose. This intertribal congregation of the Native American Church was known over a wide area and at each Peyote meeting there were persons from tribes throughout Oklahoma. Regular members represented the Delaware, Pawnee, Comanche, Shawnee, Omaha, Quapaw, and Seneca.

Peyote meetings took place throughout the year except for the cold months of December through mid-March. Most of the fifteen meetings were held in a *tipi* except for one house meeting in November and one in March, when cold weather was extreme. The ceremony usually took place on Saturday night, but when needed it was held any night. During a special time of need, as many as four meetings were held in a two-week period.

An average of seventeen participants (between six and twenty-five) was in attendance at each meeting. Participants ranged in age from 25 to 76 years old, not including the small children, who slept through the night behind their parents or joined their parents in the morning. A total of eighty-six different people took part in at least one meeting that year. If we consider that for every participant, two additional people attended the dinner following the service; about 250 people took part in the church activities.

When there was no weekend meeting at these locations, core members traveled to one of the surrounding Peyote churches. On nine occasions the core members of this church traveled by car 30–250 miles, but usually within 50 miles. On most of these occasions, the meetings were planned well in advance, and members were invited as the roadman, other ritual officials, or as special guests. They included meeting places among the Shawnee, Yuchi, Pawnee, Comanche, Ponca, and Cheyenne. The core group did not attend intertribal *pow-wows*, as they considered them to be a different religious way.

Six different roadmen led the fifteen meetings that year, an indication of intertribal participation in this church. Besides the Delaware roadman and his Comanche brother-in-law, these included Comanche and Yuchi roadmen.

Each meeting had a purpose that was specified in the invitation to the participants. This purpose was the focal point of attention during the ceremony. Four types of purposes were given that year: for a holiday, a social problem, rites of passages, and health problems.

More specifically, one meeting was for the holiday of Thanksgiving, one for a social problem relating to children and separated parents, and three meetings were for rites of passage: a wedding, a birthday, and the end of a mourning period. However the majority of meetings, 66 percent, focused upon specific physical health problems.

Meetings planned well in advance were the rites of passage and Thanksgiving. These were attended by a great number of people as compared to those for health purposes. Four meetings are considered necessary to cure a serious ailment. Because the onset of ailments was often abrupt, first meetings were not planned in advance and the following three occurred as needed, sometimes giving only one- or two-day notice to the participants. A small group of participants is considered more effective when a specific cure is desired; thus, everyone can focus on the one purpose.

Peyotism and Health-Care Delivery

Regardless of the primary purpose, at every meeting some participants brought to the roadman's attention their own problems and health-care needs or those of a family member or a friend. The roadman acted upon these requests through one or all of the following methods: including them in the prayers, rolling a tobacco cigarette for a special prayer, preparing peyote for special consumption by the ill person, fanning the person with an eagle feather and cedar incense, or in a few cases, sucking a foreign object from the ill person.

Meetings for health purposes included cases of blindness, a hernia, high blood pressure, and congestive heart failure. In all these major cases the affected person was also being treated by physicians at Claremore Indian Health Service Hospital, a distance of sixty miles by car.

Persons were not only using Peyotism, they used the Indian Health Service, local physicians, and traditional healers. They also readily used patent medicines and home remedies of traditional Delaware and Western origin. Traditional Delaware recognized two types of healing roles: those who used the power within himself to heal and doctor sick people, and the herbal healer. The power of these healers was obtained through visions granted by the large number of spiritual beings who were subordinate to the creator. To understand the visions, to talk to the medicinal plants, to pray, and to heal in the traditional way, one must be a fluent speaker of the Lenape language (Twaddle 1988, 7).

Delaware medicinal plants have been well-documented by Weslager (1973) and Hill (1971). Like pharmaceutical medicines, these plants and the persons familiar with them are specialists in the treatment of specific ailments.

During this study, several Delaware were known for their healing powers and knowledge of a wide variety of plants used as medicines. When a Delaware was not available for the treatment of a person's sickness, members of other tribes were sought out for their expertise. One case was known to have been treated by a Seminole medicine man seventy miles away.

This use of the various health-care systems, Peyotism, traditional medicine, and biomedicine shows that in times of illness many pathways to health care are followed. Although these various health-care systems operate independently of one another within this health culture, seldom is one the exclusive provider of care to an individual. Although it was often stated that peyote could cure most ailments, it was considered ineffective for diseases like cancer and diabetes, which were considered to have been brought by the White man (Wiedman 1987, 1989).

Like health-care systems in general (Rosser and Mossberg 1977, 25), Peyotism was deliberately formed to perform a set of functions, one of which is health-care delivery: "the attainment of optimal physical, mental, and social well-being and not the mere absence of discernible disease" (Weinerman 1971). As detailed in this paper, Peyotism has organizational structures and specific roles that manage the participants' knowledge, facilities, and commodities—the primary characteristics of a health-care delivery system (Roemer 1986).

Many explanations have been proposed in the literature for the acceptance and persistence of Peyotism; however, few have had sufficient participant-observation fieldwork to document the importance of health care as a major factor.

Shonle (1925) explained its appeal as due to diffusion through a culture area with an underlying belief in the supernatural origins of visions. Peyotism has also been analyzed as a revitalization movement or in strictly sociofunctional terms by Barber (1941) and Hurt (1960). Although Weston La Barre did present its psychotherapeutic aspects, he considered the therapeutic possibilities to be unimpressive (La Barre 1967[1938], 147). David Aberle's (1966, 351) study of Navaho Peyotism accounted for the differential acceptance of Peyotism in terms of relative deprivation: It appealed to those deprived of possessions and status through the livestock reduction program of the U.S. government. The pharmacological study by Anderson (1980, 90) notes the medicinal use of Peyote by North and Central American Indians, but he states that the curative nature of the plant is due to its psychoactive properties rather than healing chemical substances (Anderson 1980, 102).

When data collected over the years are reinterpreted from the health-care perspective, they give new meaning to health aspects of Peyotism. Aberle's work is suggestive in this regard. On the basis of interviews with over a hundred Navajo individuals, Aberle found that:

> In the vast majority of cases, initial recourse to Peyotism is for the purpose of being cured, or occurs when a member of one's family of orientation or of procreation is ill and is taken to a peyote ceremony. This is true of both members, former members, and people who tried peyote only once or twice. Curing one's self or a family member accounts for about three-quarters of all instances (Aberle 1966, 183).

> Thereafter, as they become involved in Peyotist activities, they come to see the Native American Church as a combination of cure, ethical code, and inspiration for life (189).

The use of Peyote as a medicine is also reflected in the words of the Comanche medicine woman Sanapia: ". . . some of the Indians call it a sacrament like White peoples who are Christians.. God gave that Peyote to the Indians to help them when they got sickness." She goes on to say: "It's a medicine and that's the way I use it. Peyote gives me power to make people well."(Jones 1972, 23). Additional evidence and support of this view comes from botanist Richard Evans Schultes, who studied Peyote from the botanical, pharmacological, and cultural perspective. He concluded that the "principal appeal of peyote has been and continues to be centered on the therapeutic and stimulating properties of the plant" (Schultes 1938).

Morris Opler, although not proposing health care as a factor in Peyotism's acceptance and persistence, did document its early curing aspects. He claims that in the early 1800s, as peyote was used by the Carrizo and Lipan Apache, curing was not a central motive. However, when later adopted by the Mescalero Apache, it was emphasized as a curative rite (Opler 1936). The Mescalero may have had an influence on the curative use of Peyote by the Kiowa, Comanche, and Kiowa-Apache in the 1870s (see Stewart 1987, 50).

With the forced settlement of the Southern Plains tribes onto reservations in southwestern Oklahoma, their economic, social, political, religious, and healing systems underwent dramatic transformations. As a result of the influences of Christian missionaries, their religious belief in animism (the belief that all things animate and inanimate possess a spirit or power) was transformed into a greater emphasis on a monotheistic belief in a single, all-powerful God. This change is also reflected by the transformation of the broad use of medicinal plants and substances (Jones 1972) into the Peyotists' increased use of a single medicinal plant and source of spiritual power: Peyote. By 1885, the Big Moon and Little Moon ritual had become standardized (Wiedman and Greene 1988), incorporating many new rules that formalized the structure and refined Peyote's use as a medicine for the sick (Opler 1938, 284).

After seventy-five years, many factors affected Big Moon Peyotism's decline in northeast Oklahoma, including Delaware intermarriage with Euro-Americans, acculturation to urban life, and acceptance of Western medical care. With each passing generation, the land upon which the permanent Big Moon altars were built was divided among the heirs who, in many cases, were non-Peyotists. For this same reason, Big Moon staffs, which remain with the altar, also passed to non-Peyotists. Furthermore, Big Moon Peyotism, with its complex ritual and added officials, became increasingly structured as a religious system and less effective as a health-care delivery system.

Petrullo noted this de-emphasis of the medicinal aspects of Peyote by Delaware Big Moon Peyotists (Petrullo 1975[1934], 171). This is clearly stated by Willie Long Bone in the early 1930s:

> I don't use Peyote as a medicine. I use it to follow in the footsteps of Jesus. Were it not for this I wouldn't use it at all. It is difficult to use it. It is not at all pleasant, but we have to suffer anyway, the way Jesus did, if we want to go to our Father. There are many other medicines for sickness, but I don't believe in using Peyote that way (Petrullo 1975[1934], 109).

The leading Delaware roadman during my fieldwork gave several reasons for the decline of Big Moon Peyotism. To him, the Big Moon ceremony was an important occasion with many people involved and it needed to be planned several weeks in advance. Little Moon meetings, on the other hand, could be called whenever there was a purpose, sometimes the same night (Wiedman field notes).

Although Omer Stewart and others have noted the use of tobacco as one of the ritual differences between Big and Little Moon Peyotism, the social and symbolic differences regarding the use of tobacco with prayer has not been clearly presented. In my view, this is a critical issue that requires further examination. As stated in my field notes the Delaware roadman mentioned:

> that he does not like the Big Moon way because they do not allow an individual to pray with tobacco or allow talks to be heard for any duration. They are less personal. He believes that the reason for people to go into a meeting is for them to pray and to say what is on their mind and bothering them. This is the way it should be or he would not even be in there. His father ran meetings Big Moon way and the first meetings he attended were Big Moon. But Little Moon is now his preference (Wiedman field notes 9/8/72).

This difference was succinctly stated by the Comanche roadman:

> No one could pray to that peyote for another and have a cure occur. In order for a person to be cured he has to tell that peyote what he wants (Wiedman field notes 6/20/73).

Cultural interpretation is warranted here. For example, a basic rule applies during both Little Moon and Big Moon Peyote meetings. Whenever a person is about to consume peyote or is eating peyote, no one should pass between the person and the grandfather peyote placed on the altar. This rule is strictly enforced by the ritual leaders, and if broken, often leads to disputes in the meetings. To break it is considered a bad omen.

This ritual procedure reflects Peyotism's basic cultural theme of the individual's power and the belief that no person should come between an individual and God. This belief could be interpreted as being derived from the individualism of Southern Plains Indian religion, in which an individual was to have a personal power experience and his or her own vision. When Peyotism was formulated, the Apache, Kiowa, and Comanche combined this belief with monotheism, limiting power-seeking to one power through peyote as a representation of God or Jesus. The Big Moon ritual elaborated on this common philosophy by maintaining the rule that no one should physically pass between an individual consuming peyote and the grandfather peyote. However, because Big Moon procedures are complex and often attended by greater numbers of people than Little Moon ceremonies, four additional officials are needed to maintain the ritual rules: two crossmark men and two additional firemen. Whenever a person wants a special prayer, he communicates his needs to the roadman, who at the appropriate time rolls a tobacco cigarette and prays. By restricting formal prayer and the smoking of tobacco to the roadman and his officials, the Big Moon ritual incorporated a social stratification that symbolically placed an intermediary between an individual and God. Thus, in the view of the Delaware roadman, this reduced the power of prayer and the curing power of peyote.

This field research among the Delaware affirms that this religious system has a strong emphasis on health and wellness. Not only could the health-care aspects of Peyotism be a major factor in its acceptance and persistence, but conversely, a de-emphasis on health care could also be cause for its decline.

Health-Related Aspects of Peyotism

Although it is not the primary purpose of this chapter to present the basis for the healing efficacy of Peyotism, a review of health-related aspects of Peyotism may further our understanding of the dynamics involved. These can be presented at several levels: psychotherapeutic, social, nutritional, psychochemical, and physical. Psychotherapeutic effects of Peyotism have been well presented by Weston La Barre. Suggestive techniques used by the healer influence the patient to develop new patterns of thought and behavior. La Barre portrayed the open prayers as confession and a form of cathartic therapy (La Barre 1947).

The altered state of consciousness produced by the ritual and peyote may be an effective means of altering the individual's cognitive paradigm. Following Wallace's 1966 concept of mazeway resynthesis, Peyotism may effectively restructure symbolic meanings or cognitive mapping. In this way, maladaptive behaviors can be modified, and the morals and principles of Peyotism reemphasized. In cases when a Western doctor has informed an Indian patient that he is sick because of complex biochemical reactions, the Indian may not understand these terms. But he can undergo symbolic healing by having his ailments and the doctor's words, reinterpreted during the peyote meeting in such a way that they are understandable. Thus, he is better able to respond to the Western medical system's requests for medication use and dietary and behavioral restrictions. During the year of observation, all the major physical diseases were under a physician's care, and the reinterpretation and explanation of the illnesses were taking place in the Peyote meeting. It might be said that the Western physician treats the "disease," the malfunctioning of biological and/or psychological processes, whereas the Peyote healer treats the "illness," the psychosocial experience and meaning of perceived disease (cf. Fabrega 1974; Kleinman 1980, 72). Thus, the two health-care systems are not in conflict or competition with one another; they are complementary and symbiotic.

Prayers spoken in ritual context also serve as information to the participants about social relations and problem solving. During these symbolic transactions, individual, group, and intergroup stress-producing behaviors are brought to the group's attention in prayers spoken out loud. The evening before and the morning after the meetings are times when participants and visitors carry on casual conversations in small groups. These conversations are often interspersed with jokes and stories about incidents in previous meetings, famous characters, and historic individuals. These abstract conversations often directly relate to a personal problem mentioned in the meeting or to the behavior of an individual. These public statements are ways of conveying advice or opinions without directly talking to the person at whom it is aimed.

Social support systems are of great importance to wellness. Church participation and kin-group involvement provide a sense of identity and social solidarity, a setting to meet and make friends, while participating in an important cultural ritual. This type of participation and kin-group involvement has been shown to have a positive effect on physiology, most notably hypertension (Janes 1986, 196; Walsh 1980). Participants in need benefit from renewed social support and the restructuring of social relations, important aspects of symbolic healing (Csordas 1988; Dow 1986).

The sharing of information and social support also results in more efficient resource distribution as well as reduced social and psychological stress. Attendance at Peyote meetings as a participant at the ceremony, as a visitor or as a worker at the home, includes the ritual consumption of a supper the evening of the meeting, and a complete dinner the next afternoon. The remaining food is often taken home by visitors, especially by the elderly. For elderly males who live alone, this may be the only time during the week they eat complete home-cooked meals, and the leftovers provide two or three more meals for them during the week. For the single elderly male and for low-income families, regular attendance at these dinners and the food taken home provide an important nutritional supplement.

Although still speculative, symbolic healing through trance and altered states of consciousness may have an effect on the immunological system by the release of endorphins, which are pain reducers. Research suggests that chronic stress causes the adrenal gland to pump increased amounts of corticosteroids into the bloodstream and these hormones inhibit immune function (Glaser et al. 1987). Stress reduction, on the other hand, has a positive effect on cortisol levels (McGrady et al. 1987). Chemical properties of peyote are structurally similar to the neurohormone epinephrine (Anderson 1980, 126). Further research on how immune molecules affect the physiology and metabolism of the brain and body is needed before it is understood how peyote affects the immune system, which, in turn may prevent disease and repair damaged tissue (see Mandler et al. 1986; McClelland and Jemmott 1980; Antonie 1987).

The taste of peyote is so nauseating that to consume any amount requires enormous self-control and a heightened awareness of bodily functions in order to prevent vomiting. The Peyotist also needs firm self-control to restrict movement in order to remain in a sitting position for nearly twelve hours. Fasting in the form of limited food and water intake during the ceremony also requires control of emotions and behaviors. For the Peyotist who regularly attends meetings, this exercise of concentrated willpower promotes the individual's ability to control his emotions, bodily functions, and possibly his immune system.

Discussion

Because it has had a standardized organization and ritual structure for over a hundred years, Peyotism must be considered successful in meeting its members' needs. Curing and health care, as well as religious concerns are its primary functions, as evidenced by oral testimony, the literature, and an observed annual ritual cycle. Two-thirds of all the meetings had the stated purpose of dealing with physical health-care problems.

The health culture of a society can be broadly defined as a system of ideas, practices, roles, technologies, and organizations that deal with the problems of health and illness (see Lee 1982, 629). Every population has a health culture that incorporates particular ways of meeting its members' health needs. These are a society's repertoire of patterns for cognition, affect, and behavior "which relate specifically to the maintenance of well-being and problems of sickness with which people cope in traditional ways within their own social networks and institutional structures" (Weidman 1988, 263). Throughout human evolution it has been necessary for the health culture of a population to be composed of one or more health-care delivery systems containing specialized knowledge, medicinal substances technological items, explanations about bodily functions, and social roles for the success of the population. A population that lacked a properly functioning health-care delivery system, in which this specialized knowledge was passed from one generation to another, would be at an adaptive disadvantage.

Traditional Native-American health culture was woven into religious beliefs and curing practices. Health-care delivery was often the role of the religious specialist, the medicine man or a group of individuals in a medicine society. When Native-American tribes were forcibly settled on reservations in Oklahoma, their language, social, economic, religious, health culture, and health-care systems were greatly affected. Under these conditions, Peyotism developed as a structured religious and health-care system. As one of the health-care delivery systems available, Peyotism provides its benefits by assisting its members psychologically, socially, physically, and nutritionally, as well as spiritually and morally. Like physicians, the peyote healer focuses on pathophysiological and social problems. With peyote churches dispersed from at least thirty to fifty miles apart in all but southeast Oklahoma and the western Panhandle, it is accessible to most participants within an hour's drive.

Anthony Wallace argued that when a population's needs are not met, these stressful conditions lead to a revitalization movement: a consciously organized attempt to change cultural behaviors and beliefs (Wallace 1966, 158). In his view, this revitalization process explains the development of new religions. Peyotism can also be placed into this theoretical paradigm, especially if it is viewed as a therapeutic movement that reduces stress and physical ailments. Once established, however, a therapeutic movement must maintain its level of effectiveness or it will decline. This change in overall health culture is part of the intricate process by which populations adapt to their environments (Alland 1970).Within this theoretical framework, we would have to argue that, given health care as its major professed and observed purposes, if Peyotism did not succeed in efficiently providing a positive health outcome, it would lose its members and cease to be a recognized church and health-care delivery system. This has not happened. Peyotism continues to be practiced throughout the United States and Canada. In northeastern Oklahoma, however, where two health-care systems based on peyote developed, Big Moon Peyotism became more structured as a religious system and church with less emphasis on providing health care. Consequently, its membership decreased and it ceased to be practiced among the Delaware and Quapaw.

On the basis of this ethnographic and historical analysis, it is clear that Peyotism, like traditional Native-American cultures, combines religion and health care in a cultural whole. Within this cultural context, Peyotism functions as a health-care delivery system by addressing health needs that are not fully met by the biomedical approach of orthodox medicine or other traditional healing systems. Following this, it might be predicted that, as a health-care delivery system, Peyotism will continue to thrive as long as it efficiently and effectively reaches the population, and as long as real or perceived health outcomes result.

Note: this is a republication of a 1990 journal article

214

REFERENCES

Aberle, D. 1966. *The Peyote religion among the Navaho.* Chicago: Aldine.

Alland, A. 1970. *Adaptation in cultural evolution: An approach to medical anthropology.* New York: Columbia University Press.

Anderson, E. 1980. *Peyote: The divine cactus.* Tucson: University of Arizona Press.

Antonie, M. 1987. Neuroendocrine influences in psychoimmunology and neoplasia: A review. *Psychology and Health* 1: 3–24.

Barber, B. 1941. A socio-cultural interpretation of the peyote cult. *American Anthropologist* 43: 673–75.

Csordas, T. 1988. Elements of charismatic healing. *Medical Anthropology Quarterly* (New Series) 2(2): 121–42.

Dow, J. 1986. Universal aspects of symbolic healing: A theoretical synthesis. *American Anthropologist* 88: 56–69.

Duffy, J. 1979. *The healers: A history of American medicine.* Urbana: University of Illinois Press.

Fabrega, H. 1974. Disease and social behavior: An interdisciplinary perspective. Cambridge, MA: MIT Press.

Glaser, R., J. Rice, J. Sheridan, R. Fertel, J. Stout, C. Speicher, et al. 1987. Stress-related immune suppression: Health implications. *Brain, Behavior, and Immunity* 1: 7–20.

Hill, G. 1971. Delaware ethnobotany. *Oklahoma Anthropological Society Newsletter* 19(3): 3–18.

Hurt, W. 1960. Factors for the persistence of Peyote in the Northern Plains. *Plains Anthropologist* 5: 16–27.

Janes, C. 1986. Migration and hypertension: ethnography of disease risk in an urban Samoan community. In *Anthropology and epidemiology: Interdisciplinary approaches to the study of health and disease,* ed. C. Janes, R. Stall, and S. Gifford, 175–211. Boston: D. Reidel.

Jones, D. 1972. *Sanapia: Comanche medicine women.* New York: Holt, Rinehart and Winston.

Kleinman, A. 1980. *Patient and healers in the context of culture: An exploration of the borderland between anthropology, medicine, and psychiatry.* Berkeley: University of California Press.

Knox, P, J. Bohland, and N. Shumsky. 1983. Urban transition and the evaluation of medical care delivery systems in America. *Social Science and Medicine* 17: 37–43.

La Barre, W. 1947. Primitive psychotherapy in Native American cultures: Peyotism and confession. *Journal of Abnormal and Social Psychology* 42(3): 294–309.

———— 1938 *The Peyote cult*. Repr., New Haven, CT: Shoe String Press, 1967.

Lee, R. 1982. Comparative studies of health care systems. *Social Science and Medicine* 16: 629–42.

Mandler, R., W. Biddison, R. Mander, and S. Serrate. 1986. Beta-Endorphin augments the cytolytic activity and interferon production of natural killer cells." *Journal of Immunology* 136: 934–39.

McClelland, D., and J. Jemmott. 1980. Power motivation, stress and physical illness. *Journal of Human Stress* 6: 6–15.

McGrady, A., M. Woerner, G. Bernal, and J. Higgins. 1987. Effect of biofeedback-assisted relaxation on blood pressure and cortisol levels in normotensives and hypertensives. *Journal of Behavioral Medicine* 10: 301–10.

Mooney, J. 1896. *The Ghost-Dance religion and the Sioux outbreak of 1890*. 14th Annual Report of the Bureau of American Ethnology for 1892–1893, Part 2. Rep., Chicago: University of Chicago Press, 1965.

Newcomb, W. W. 1955. A note on Cherokee-Delaware pan Indianism. *American Anthropologist* 57: 1041–45.

————. 1956. The culture and acculturation of the Delaware Indians. *Anthropological Papers* 10: 113–22.

Olper, M. 1936. The influence of aboriginal pattern and white contact on a recently introduced ceremony, the Mescalero peyote rite. *Journal of American Folklore* 191–192: 143–66.

————. 1938. The use of peyote by the Carrizo and Lipan Apache tribes. *American Anthropologist* 40(2): 271–85.

Petrullo, V. 1934. *The diabolic root: A study of Peyotism, the new Indian religion, among the Delaware's*. Repr., New York: Octagon Books, 1975.

Prewitt, T. 1981. *Tradition and culture, change in the Oklahoma Delaware Big House community: 1867–1924*. University of Tulsa Laboratory of Archeology Contributions in Archeology 9.

Roemer, M. 1986. *Introduction to the U.S. health care system*. New York: Springer.

Rosser, J., and H. Mossberg. 1977. *An analysis of health care delivery*, New York: Wiley.

Schulte's, R. E. 1938. The appeal of peyote as a medicine. *American Anthropologist* 40: 698.

Shonle, R. 1925. Peyote: The giver of visions. *American Anthropologist* 27: 53–75.

Slotkin, J. S. 1955. Peyotism, 1521–1891. *American Anthropologist* 57: 202–30.

———. 1956. *The peyote religion: A study in Indian-White relations.* Glencoe, IL: Free Press.

Speck, F. 1937. *Oklahoma Delaware ceremonies, feasts and dances.* Philadelphia: American Philosophical Society.

———. 1933. Notes on the life of John Wilson, the revealer of peyote, as recalled by his nephew, George Anderson. *General Magazine and Historical Chronicle* 35: 539–56.

———. 1931. *A study of the Delaware big house ceremony.* Publications of the Pennsylvania Historical Commission #2. Harrisburg, PA: Pennsylvania Historical Commission.

———. 1907. *Notes on the ethnology of the Osage Indians.* University of Pennsylvania, *Transactions of the University Museum* 2(2):159–71.

Stewart, O. 1987. *Peyote religion: A history.* Norman: University of Oklahoma Press.

Twaddle, A. 1988. Traditional healing practices of the Delaware. Paper presented at the Delaware Indian Cultural Exchange Symposium, June 1988. New Philadelphia, OH: Kent State University

Wallace, A. 1966. *Religion: An anthropological view.* New York: Random House.

Walsh, A. 1980. The prophylactic effect of religion on blood pressure levels among a sample of migrants. *Social Science and Medicine* 14B: 59–64.

Weslager, C. A. *Delaware Indian Westward Migration.* Somerset, NJ: Middle Atlantic Press, 1978.

———. 1973. *Magic medicines of the Indians.* Somerset, NJ: Middle Atlantic Press.

———. 1972. *The Delaware Indians: A history.* New Brunswick, NJ: Rutgers University Press.

Weidman, H. 1988. A transcultural perspective on health behavior. In *Health Behavior: Emerging Research Perspectives,* ed. D. Gochman New York: Plenum.

Weinerman, E. R. 1971. Research on comparative health service systems. *Medical Care* 9: 272–90.

217

Wiedman, D. 1989 Adiposity or longevity: Which factor accounts for the increase in Type II Diabetes Mellitus when populations acculturate to an industrial technology? *Medical Anthropology* 11 (3) (1989): 237–53

————. 1988 a. "Big and Little Moon Peyotism as Health Care Delivery Systems." Paper presented at the Annual Meeting of the American Anthropological Association, Phoenix, Arizona, November 1988.

————. 1988 b .. The history and ethnology of Delaware peyotism. Paper presented at the Delaware Indian Cultural Exchange Symposium, June 1988. New Philadelphia, OH: Kent State University.

————. 1987. Type II Diabetes Mellitus, technological development and Oklahoma Cherokee. In *Encounters with biomedicine: Case studies in medical anthropology,* ed. H. Baer, 43–71. New York: Gordon and Breach.

————. 1985. Staff, fan, rattle, and drum: Spiritual and artistic expressions of Oklahoma peyotists. *American Indian Art Magazine* 10(3): 38–45.

————. 1970-1973 Unpublished fieldnotes of Dennis Wiedman

Wiedman, D., and C. Greene. 1988. Early Kiowa peyote ritual and symbolism: The 1891 drawing books of Silverhorn (Haungooh). *American Indian Art* 13(4)32-41.

11

Culture and Health Behavior in Three Asian Communities in Singapore

Stella R. Quah, PhD. Professor, Department of Sociology, National University of Singapore, Singapore

Introduction

An important research objective in the sociology of health is the identification of differences across ethnic communities in their approach toward health and illness in general and toward specific diseases and health practices. Additional and significant research questions are whether and how cultural values and beliefs on health and illness are influenced by their exposure to formal education, and what part does education play in the connection between culture and health behavior.

This chapter examines these questions based on the differences in preventive health behavior among Chinese, Malays, and Indians, the three main ethnic groups in Singapore. The first phase of the study was completed in 1978 and the second phase of the study in 1993 (Quah 1986, 1993). The salience of cultural differences in preventive health behavior discussed in this chapter represents one aspect of the larger study. Culture and ethnicity are discussed in detail elsewhere (Quah 2001, 2002) but it is relevant to highlight that the concept of ethnicity used in this study is based on King's (1962, 79) definition of an ethnic group as a cultural setting where members share "common backgrounds in language, customs, beliefs, habits, and traditions, frequently in racial stock and country of origin" as well as "a consciousness of kind." The Singapore subpopulations who identify themselves as Chinese, Malays, and Indians, respectively, constitute three ethnic groups as defined by King. The discussion covers three aspects: a succinct review of relevant studies, the pervasiveness of culture, and the relevance of education on preventive health behavior.

Relevant Studies on Preventive Health Behavior

Health and illness are universal human conditions. Thus their physiological manifestations tend to follow the same pattern around the world. This is the "physiological reality" of illness, but illness has a dual nature (Becker 1963). The second dimension of illness is its social reality, manifested in the "cultural variations of illness categorization and incidence" (Gerhardt 1989, 83). Sociological research findings since 1950 support this dual nature of illness theorized by the functionalist theory, symbolic interaction, and conflict theories (Gerhardt, 1989), best known through concepts such as "sick role" (Parsons 1978); "subjective perception of the situation, labeling, and negotiation" (Mead 1964; Lemert 1951; Becker 1963); and "demedicalization" (Conrad and Schneider 1980). Today, therefore, it is commonly assumed that ethnic communities vary in all three types of health-related behavior identified by Kasl and Cobb (1966), that is, preventive behavior (i.e., what people who believe themselves healthy do to prevent illness); illness behavior (i.e., the way people perceive symptoms and seek to understand them); and sick-role behavior (what people do to treat and solve their illness or disease) (Quah 2001).

This discussion focuses on preventive behavior. The pioneers in the construction of an explanatory model of preventive health behavior were Irwin M. Rosenstock (1966, 1969), S. V. Kasl and S. Cobb (1966), and M. H. Becker (1974). The fundamental premises of their "Health Belief Model" involve three sets of factors. The first set is the "psychological state of readiness" to take preventive action against a disease, which includes the person's perception of his or her own susceptibility to that disease and his or her perception of its seriousness. The Health Belief Model proposes that the higher the perceived personal susceptibility and the higher the perceived seriousness of the disease in question, the more likely it would be for the person to take preventive measures. The second set of factors involves the perceived benefits of and perceived barriers to preventive action. The third set of factors was labeled by Rosenstock the "cues to action" referring to "some instigating event" that prompts the person towards taking action, for example, the interaction with another person, the influence of mass media, or encountering relevant information.

The Health Belief Model has been applied extensively and successfully to the analysis of numerous aspects of health-related behavior, including lifestyle and health risks, acceptance of immunization, seeking dental care, dietary compliance, quitting smoking, and practicing self-care, and attendance at medical check-ups (Becker and Rosenstock 1989; Norma and Conner 1993; Cockerham 1995, 103–106). Its frequent testing and mixed results over the years have led to refinements of the model. Of the variables in the Model, perceived barriers, perceived benefits, and perceived susceptibility are, in that order, the strongest predictors of preventive health behavior whereas perceived seriousness has been found to be "far less valuable as a predictor" (Gochman 1988, 22). Gochman suggests that "additional studies" in the 1980s led to the refinement in the "conceptualization of perceived benefits and developed ways of measuring this variable with greater precision" (410). Studies applying the Health Belief Model in Singapore have highlighted the importance of cultural variations (Quah 1986).

Two of the questions explored in this study are: What are the factors affecting preventive health behavior? Do these factors differ from one ethnic group to another? The study tested an expanded version of the Health Belief Model involving four main triggers of preventive health behavior: the knowledge on disease etiology and prognosis, the perception of social sanctions suffered by people affected by the disease, the perceived threat of disruption of normal role activities, and the perception of personal vulnerability. In addition, the impact of the perception of benefits and the perception of barriers to preventive action was examined following the assumptions of the Health Belief Model.

The answer to the second research question was obtained by analyzing the above factors among representative samples of the three main ethnic groups in Singapore namely, Chinese, Malay and Indians. The findings from the first phase of the Singapore study on the ethnic variations in preventive health behavior indicated that the Health Belief Model was, in general, less successful in explaining preventive action against cancer, heart disease, and tuberculosis (the three targeted diseases) than the ethnic differences among Chinese, Malays, and Indians (Quah 1986, 1993). Pursuing the analysis of the cultural or ethnic dimension of preventive health behavior, the second phase of this study explores differences among Singaporean Chinese, Malays, and Indians with regard to general and specific preventive health behavior. General preventive behavior refers to the keeping of medicines at home for eventualities and practicing at least one activity believed to protect one against the onset of illness. The keeping of medications at home is a useful indication of precaution. Previous investigation disclosed that remarks such as "just in case we need it," "it always helps to be prepared for pains or burns," "I feel better having these remedies at home instead of having to rush out to buy them when you need them," are common explanations people in Singapore give of the assortment of medications in their kitchen cabinets and refrigerator (e.g., vitamins and other over-the-counter medications, leftovers of past prescriptions, herbs, roots, and other traditional medications) (Quah, 1989). Specific preventive behavior refers to three activities: smoking abstention, alcohol abstention, and the practice of regular exercise.

Cigarette smoking and alcohol drinking receive a lot of attention as risk behaviors in studies of cancer, heart disease, and other diseases. The association of these risk behaviors with characteristics such as age and gender is commonly explored and documented (Kirscht 1988; Cockerham 1995. However, ethnic differences tend to be limited to White and Black populations in the United States or are overlooked altogether. Interesting exceptions to this trend are the studies on alcohol drinking among women reviewed by Ames and Rebhun (1996). They covered studies involving various ethnic groups in the U.S. population including "European-Americans," "Latinos," "African Americans," "Native-Americans," "Chinese-Americans," "Japanese-Americans," and "Korean-Americans." Ames and Rebhun concluded that ethnicity has not been given due consideration in studies of drinking behavior. They found that concerning "drinking patterns of women in specific ethnic populations, traditional beliefs about the context of drinking and consequences of alcohol abuse do indeed affect women's work-related drinking patterns." Moreover, "it appears that women's drinking in specific ethnic groups increases slightly with level of acculturation and entry into more culturally diversified workplaces" (1996:1660).

The neglect of the ethnic factor mentioned by Ames and Rebhun is illustrated by the study of lifestyle and health risks in three European cities conducted by Uitenbroek, Kerekovska, and Festchieva (1996). They compared four "health lifestyle behaviors": "cigarette smoking, diet, exercise and alcohol use" among a sample of residents from Varna, Bulgaria, and Glasgow and Edinburgh, Scotland. The researchers examined the impact of four independent variables—gender, educational level, employment status, and age—on the four lifestyle behaviors. They found that none of these independent variables provided a satisfactory explanation of the health behaviors but that "the three cities were very different" in all of the four behaviors: "Generally speaking, the differences seem to follow a continuum with Varna at one end and Edinburgh at the other end, Glasgow taking a position in between, but closer to Edinburgh than to Varna" (Uitenbroek, Kerekovska, and Festchieva 1996, 375). It is evident to the reader that the cultural factor "country of origin" explains variations in health behavior better than age, education, employment, or gender. Yet, the authors failed to consider the cultural differences between Bulgaria and Scotland. In sum, although the dual (physiological and social) nature of illness was identified in the

1950s and is addressed theoretically and empirically in sociology, the role of ethnicity is often neglected. More important, the role of ethnicity on specific risk behaviors concerning major causes of death such as cancer and heart disease requires constant scrutiny.

The Sociocultural Context of Health Behavior

Before presenting the findings on the ethnic dimension of the five preventive activities, a reference to relevant features of Singapore, that is, the sociocultural context of health behavior is in order.

A small island (646 km2) of 3.1 million people, Singapore offers a sociocultural landscape that is both unifying and diverse. Among the most relevant unifying features: the national schooling system emphasizing bilingualism (English and the student's mother tongue); compulsory national service for all male citizens; and the public housing program with emphasis on home ownership and neighborliness, suggest the weakening of ethnic differences among the population. Thus, Singapore is an ideal setting to study the pervasiveness of ethnicity and its assumed impact upon health behavior.

The most readily observable diversity is the ethnic composition of the population. The other main source of diversity is religion. Singapore is fundamentally a multicultural country. Chinese, Malays, and Indians form the three major broadly defined ethnic groups, with a wide variety of religious affiliations found mostly among the Chinese majority and the Indian community. Practically all Malays are Muslim. Ethnic and religious differences, however, have not hindered access to formal education and have not created structural distinctions in the distribution of the total population across income levels and occupations (Quah et al. 1991; Quah 1990; Tan and Chiew 1997).

The ethnic composition of the Singapore population has remained relatively stable over the past 30 years. In 1977 Chinese represented 76.7 percent of the total population; 14.6 percent were Malays; 6.5 percent Indians; and 2.0

percent belonged to other ethnic groups. In 1998, the total population was 3,163,500 of which 77 percent were Chinese, 14 percent Malays, 7.6 percent Indians, and 1.4 percent others (Singapore Department of Statistics 1986, 28; Saw 1999).

Table 11-1. Selected Indicators of Socioeconomic Development and Health Care, 1977 and 1993

Indicators	1977	1993
Per capita Indigenous GDP (Singapore $)	$5,979	$24,871
Literacy rate (pop. 10yrs old & above)	80.5	91.6
Tertiary education graduates per 10,000 population[1]	21.1	63.7
Unemployment rate (pop. 15–64 years old)	3.9	2.7
Persons per public bus	427	296
Persons per private car	17	10
Percentage of total population who are owners of their public housing flats	31%	81%
Per capita government health expenditure (in Singapore dollars)	$68	$385
Infant mortality rate per 1,000 live births Malay[2] Indian Chinese	12.4 14.7 13.4 12.0	4.7 6.1 6.6 5.3
Two major causes of death:[2] % of all deaths caused by heart disease % of all deaths caused by cancer	 20.3% 19.5%	 20.4% 24.5%
Persons per doctor	1,259	693
Percentage of doctors in private practice (Total number of practicing doctors)	59.2% (1,847)	49.4% (3,980)
Persons per dentist	7,725	3,868
Percentage of dentists in private practice (Total number of practicing dentists)	55.8% (301)	75.9% (715)
Visits to government dental clinics per 1,000 population	387.1	365.9

Source: Singapore Department of Statistics (1986) and (1994) Yearbook of Statistics Singapore. Singapore: Department of Statistics.
1. Calculated from Singapore Department of Statistics (1986) and (1994).
2. Taken from Registry of Births and Deaths (1978) and (1992). Report on Registration of Births and Deaths. Singapore: National Registration Department. Figures on Malay, Indian, and Chinese mortality rates, and on heart disease and cancer refer to the years 1977 and 1991.

The 1980 and 1990 population censuses indicated that the proportion of Singaporean Malays who are Muslims has remained stable at 99.6 percent. Among the Singapore Indians, in 1980, 21.7 percent were Muslims, 56.5 percent were Hindu, 12.5 percent were Christian, and 8.1 percent professed other religions. In 1990, 27 percent of the Indians were Muslims, 52.6 percent were Hindu, 12.2 percent were Christian, and 7.0 percent were from other religions. Among the Chinese, the religious affiliation figures from the 1980 census were: 34.1 percent Buddhism, 38.4 percent Chinese ancestor worship and Taoism, 10.7 percent Christianity, and 16.6 percent no religion. The corresponding figures from the 1990 census were 39.3 percent Buddhism, 28.4 percent Chinese ancestor worship and Taoism, 14.0 percent Christianity, and 18.0 percent no religion (Singapore Department of Statistics 1994, 3). This overall distribution of the population in terms of ethnicity and religion has remained relatively stable over the years and no significant changes were observed in the past ten years (Singapore Department of Statistics, 2001).

The time span between Phase 1 and Phase 2 of the study was fifteen years. During this time Singapore moved decidedly forward in socioeconomic development. Singaporeans were more affluent and better educated in the 1990s than they were in the 1970s (Table 11-1). In the 1990s they enjoyed better health-care facilities, including a significant increase in the number of physicians and dentists and wider options on medical and dental services as reflected in the larger proportion of practitioners in the private sector.

In contrast to the marked improvement in socioeconomic development, there was been no change in the nature of the two major causes of death (Table 11-1). Cancer and heart disease have been the two main causes of death in Singapore since the mid-1980s. Hence this study focuses on the three preventive activities smoking abstention, alcohol abstention, and the regular practice of exercise.

227

Method

Both phases of this study were based on personal interviews with representative samples of the population of Singapore citizens. The representative stratified sample for the first phase of the study conducted in 1977–78 included 1,271 adults. The same sampling procedure was applied for the representative sample of 660 adult Singaporeans in the second phase of the study conducted from 1992 to 1993. To ensure comparability of data, both phases of the study used the same questionnaire for the structured personal interviews. The target diseases in the first phase of the study were cancer, heart disease, and tuberculosis (Quah 1986). Cancer, heart disease, and AIDS were the target diseases in the second phase of the study. The personal interviews lasted, on average, fifty-five to sixty minutes and included open-ended and closed-ended questions. The interviews were conducted at the home of the respondents and in the language of the respondents' choice (most Singaporeans speak at least two languages). As representative samples of the population in both phases of the study, the respondents covered the full social class spectrum with Malays more likely to be found in the lower and middle categories of education and income and more Chinese in the upper education and income categories.

The level of education of the respondents was recorded in two ways. One was the level of formal schooling indicated by the formal school system. The system currently encompasses six years of primary (or elementary) school; four years of secondary (or high) school culminating in the "Ordinary" Level Certificate; and two years of pre-university to obtain the "A" Level Certificate. The "A" Level Certificate is required for students wishing to enter university. The labels given to these education levels have changed over the years. Consequently, the second and more accurate recording of formal education used in this study is the total number of years of formal schooling completed.

Pervasiveness of Cultural Differences

We may turn now to the comparison of findings on ethnic differences from the two phases of the longitudinal study. Table 11-2 presents the inclination towards the practice of the five preventive health activities by each of the main ethnic groups in Singapore, Chinese, Malays, and Indians. In the first phase of the study, the Malays were found to be the most inclined towards the practice of four of the five preventive activities and the difference among the three groups was statistically significant. In contrast to Chinese and Indians, Malays were more inclined to keep medicines at home for eventualities, to practice at least one activity that in their view prevented illness, to exercise regularly, and to avoid alcoholic drinks. Malays in Singapore are predominantly Muslims. Islam prohibits alcohol drinking and the eating of pork in any form. These rules harmonize with medical advice on the avoidance of alcoholic drinks and oily foods for the prevention of heart disease and cancer. Apart from this positive influence among Malays, religion was not significantly influential in promoting directly any of the other four preventive activities in the population. The only preventive activity that was more common among Chinese and Indians than among Malays was the abstention from smoking. Malays were more inclined to smoke, although the ethnic difference in smoking was not statistically significant.

When these findings are compared to the situation found in the Phase 2 of the study, four important changes are found. First, there is a trend towards better health maintenance in the 1990s among Chinese and Indians. Larger proportions of Chinese and Indians are keeping medicines at home, practicing at least one preventive activity, and exercising regularly, compared to the 1970s. Second, the Indian community appears to have become more aware of the health risks of smoking and alcohol drinking. Although 28 percent of the Indians respondents smoked regularly in 1977, the proportion of smokers dropped to 10.8 percent in 1993. Similarly, 36 percent of the Indians reported drinking alcohol regularly in 1977 but this proportion dropped to 21.5 percent in 1993.

Third, some interesting changes have occurred in the preventive health behavior of Malays. The practice of general preventive behavior and regular exercise among Malays declined from 1977 to 1993. But Malays, particularly Malay women, are now even less inclined than in the 1970s to smoke cigarettes or to drink alcohol and more inclined to the storing of medicines at home for eventualities. One of the most common traditional medicines kept at home has the generic name *Jamu* and it refers to a combination of herbs, roots, oils, and other ingredients for different types of ailments. *Jamu* can be taken in capsules, tablets, or powder dissolved in water, or as a brew, tea or soup made with herbs, leaves, roots and other ingredients. There are different varieties *Jamu* to protect one from illness as well as to treat various health complaints. Keeping medicines at home is also part of daily life among Chinese and Indians in Singapore. The type of traditional herbs, roots, and ointments varies for each ethnic group but traditional remedies are found in the typical household together with modern over-the-counter medications such as painkillers and cough medications. One type of Chinese medication that may be found now in Malay households is *Poh Chai* pills used to treat digestive problems (Faten Hana 1998, 50). This "borrowing" of traditional medications from a different ethnic community is the expected manifestation of pragmatic acculturation (Quah 1989).

In' general, ethnic differences in preventive behavior found in Phase 1 of the study have diminished. As indicated in Table 11-2, there were no longer significant differences in 1993 among the three ethnic groups in the practice of a general preventive activity and in regular exercise. On the other hand, there was no significant ethnic variation in smoking in 1978, but the three ethnic groups showed a difference in smoking in 1993, with the Indian group being the least inclined to smoke and Malays the most inclined.

Another relevant dimension of the trend towards preventive health behavior is offered by the overview of the respondents' preventive activities. The findings from Phase 1 and Phase 2 of the study are presented in Table 11-3 in the form of

an ethnic comparison of the number of general and specific preventive activities
reported.

**Table 11-2. Health-related Activities by Ethnic Group, Phase 1 and Phase 2
(in percentages)**

Percentage of Respondents Answering "Yes"	Phase 1 (1977–78)			Phase 2 (1992–93)		
General Preventive Activities	Malay	Indian	Chin.	Malay	Indian	Chin.
Keep medicines at home[1](N)[2]	62.0 (167)	56.0 (122)	50.0 (963)	81.0 (174)	58.5 (65)	65.6 (418)
Practice at least one activity to prevent illness[3](N)	74.0 (167)	45.0 (125)	44.0 (975)	60.9 (174)	60.0 (65)	52.9 (418)
Preventive						
Exercise regularly[4](N)	59.0 (167)	29.0 (126)	34.0 (974)	48.9 (174)	46.2 (65)	42.3 (418)
Risk Activities						
Smoke regularly[5](N)	35.0 (166)	28.0 (126)	27.0 (972)	29.3 (174)	10.8 (65)	23.2 (418)
Drink alcohol regularly[6](N)	5.0 (166)	36.0 (124)	35.0 (971)	2.3 (174)	21.5 (65)	32.3 (418)

[1] A statistically significant difference was found among the three ethnic groups at
p<.0001 (Chi-square test) both in Phase 1 and Phase 2.
[2] N= total number of interviewees answering each question. Non-respondents were
excluded.
[3] The difference among ethnic groups was significant in Phase 1 (p<.00001) but not in
Phase 2.
[4] The difference among ethnic groups was significant in Phase 1 (p<.00001) but not in
Phase 2.
[5] There was no statistically significant difference in Phase 1 but there was in Phase 2
(p<.01).
[6] Statistically significant difference both in Phase 1 (p<.00001) and Phase 2 (p<.00001).

The findings in Table 11-3 suggest that the overall inclination of the population towards preventive behavior improved between 1978 and 1993. Larger proportions of respondents from all three ethnic groups practiced all the general and specific preventive activities in 1993 compared to 1978. The improvement is most prominent among the Indians followed by the Chinese. However, the ethnic differences in preventive behavior remain, with the Malays still leading general prevention and the Malays and Indians ahead of the Chinese in specific preventive activities. The cultural ethos that supports the health beliefs and practices of the Malay community appears to have remained largely undisturbed by the socioeconomic development of Singapore between 1978 and 1993. Perhaps more important is the trend suggested by the 1993 data whereby all three ethnic communities, and especially the Indian community, may have been positively influenced by the official efforts in public health education of the past decade.

In this respect, the Health Belief Model and numerous studies on health practices have indicated that education is an important determinant of health-related behavior. This has been found also in Singapore in relation to the receptiveness to public health education campaigns (Quah 1988). It is thus important to examine further the apparent pervasiveness of cultural influences by exploring the impact of formal education and public health campaigns upon preventive health behavior in each of the three ethnic groups.

The Relevance of Education
Is the influence of ethnic values equally important among people with different levels of formal education? The three ethnic groups differed in the practice of general preventive behavior both in the first Phase (Phi=.190) and the second Phase (Phi=.166) of the study but the influence of ethnicity was weaker than the influence of education (Phi=.206 in Phase 1 and Phi=.283 in Phase 2).

Table 11-3. Overview of Preventive Health Behavior by Ethnic Group, Phase 1 and Phase 2 (In percentages)

Preventive Activities Observed	Phase 1 (1977–78)			Phase 2 (1992–93)		
	Malay	Indian	Chinese	Malay	Indian	Chinese
(Total respondents)[1]	(167)	(108)	(978)	(174)	(65)	(418)
GENERAL[2]						
None	10.2	26.7	31.2	6.9	20.0	21.1
Only one	44.3	46.5	44.0	44.3	41.5	39.7
Both	45.5	26.7	24.8	48.9	38.5	39.2
Total	100.0	100.0	100.0	100.0	100.0	100.0
SPECIFIC[3]						
None	1.8	8.3	8.2	0.0	0.0	7.2
Only one	12.6	26.9	26.8	14.9	18.5	21.5
Only two	50.3	51.9	50.4	52.9	49.2	48.6
All three	35.3	13.0	14.6	32.2	32.3	22.7
Total	100.0	100.0	100.0	100.0	100.0	100.0

[1] Nonrespondents (20 in Phase 1 and 3 in Phase 2) were excluded from the calculations.

[2] The general activities refer to keeping medicines at home and taking general care of one's health. The association between general preventive behavior and ethnicity was statistically significant (Chi-square test, $p=.001$) in both Phase 1 and Phase 2.

[3] The specific preventive activities were regular exercise, abstention from smoking, and abstention from alcohol. The association between specific preventive behavior and ethnicity was statistically significant (Chi-square test, $p=.0002$) in Phase 1 and Phase 2 of the study.

Ethnicity and education affect the practice of the three specific preventive actions with education being more influential as seen in Table 11-4. This table shows a summary of the main argument explored in this chapter: Values and beliefs of each ethnic group have some influence on individuals' decisions on preventive action. But do the ethnic differences in values and beliefs weaken as people become better educated and thus more exposed to information on health risks and preventive measures?

The findings show that, in combination, both ethnicity and education help to explain better the inclination towards preventive behavior. The differences among ethnic groups in the practice of general and specific preventive activities found among people with less than nine years of formal education in Phase 1 of the study disappear among the best educated population. This impact is sustained across time as it continued in Phase 2.

Nevertheless, two additional features in Table 11-4 require consideration. One feature is the particular inclination towards preventive health behavior among Malays and the stability of this inclination over the years. This inclination may be explained by religion. As described earlier, the overwhelming majority of Malays in Singapore are Muslims. Islam represents a fundamental feature of the cultural landscape of the Malay community, prescribing guidelines of behavior in all aspects of daily life with a stringency not commonly found among followers of other major religions. The case of the Malays and Islam leads me to agree with Levin's (1996) call in his study of how religion influences morbidity and health. Levin suggests that "A closer examination of the role of religion in human life may serve as a radix for the discovery of new constructs that might be studied epidemiologically, whether in conjunction with religion or in and of themselves" (1996: 862).

The second feature is that the ethnic differences in preventive behavior are strongest among people with intermediate levels of education (five to eight years of formal schooling). This "curvilinear" shape of the ethnic influence requires further and careful analysis. It seems to contradict the assumption that exposure to higher levels of formal education provides more objective information and thus serves as an equalizer across ethnic communities by correcting "negative" traditional beliefs and practices.

Table 11-4. Relative Influence of Ethnicity and Education upon Preventive Health Behavior

Years of Formal Education and Ethnicity	Preventive Health Behavior			
	General[1]		Specific[2]	
	Phase 1	Phase 2	Phase 1	Phase 2
4 or less years of formal education				
Malays	38.7 (62)	39.3 (28)	77.4 (62)	92.9 (28)
Indian	28.0 (28)	27.3 (11)	71.4 (28)	81.8 (11)
Chinese	19.3 (410)	20.8 (77)	62.7 (416)	68.8 (77)
All three ethnic groups	22.1 (497)	25.9 (116)	65.0 (506)	75.9 (116)
[Phi coefficient; level of significance p][3]	[.222; .0001]	[nss]	[nss]	[.240; .035]
5—8 years of formal education				
Malays	45.5 (55)	41.3 (63)	89.1 (55)	79.4 (63)
Indian	20.6 (34)	35.3 (17)	48.6 (37)	82.4 (17)
Chinese	20.6 (243)	27.3 (110)	57.3 (246)	55.5 (110)
All three ethnic groups	24.7 (332)	32.6 (190)	61.5 (338)	65.8 (190)
[Phi coefficient; level of significance p]	[.233; .001]	[.296; .002]	[.256; .0001]	[.256; .002]
9—12 years of formal education				
Malays	53.3 (45)	58.3 (72)	91.1 (45)	87.5 (72)
Indian	36.1 (36)	36.7 (30)	72.2 (36)	86.7 (30)
Chinese	31.7 (259)	48.5 167)	73.6 (265)	76.0 (167)
All three ethnic groups	35.0 (340)	49.8 (269)	75.7 346)	80.3 (269)
[Phi coefficient; level of significance p]	[nss]	[nss]	[.139; .035]	[nss]
13 or more years of formal education				
Malays	60.0 (5)	54.5 (11)	100.0 5)	81.8 (11)
Indian	0.0 (6)	71.4 (7)	85.7 (2)	57.1 (7)
Chinese	56.0 (50)	57.8 (64)	76.5 (51)	89.1 (64)
All three ethnic groups	50.8 (61)	58.5 (82)	79.4 (63)	85.4 (82)
[Phi coefficient; level of significance p]	[nss]	[nss]	[nss]	[nss]

[1] The two general preventive activities are keeping medicines at home for eventualities and engaging in at least one activity believed to prevent illness. The figures in this table are the percentage of Malay, Indian and Chinese respondents in each educational category that undertook both activities. The figures in brackets show the total number of respondents in each ethnic category. To illustrate: 38.7 of the 62 Malays with 4 or less years of formal education in Phase 1 reported taking both general preventive activities.

[2] The three specific preventive activities are: smoking abstention, alcohol abstention, and the practice of regular exercise. The figures in this table are the percentage of Malay, Indian, and Chinese respondents in each educational category that undertook two or three activities. The figures in brackets are the total number of respondents in each educational category.

[3] The association of ethnicity with the preventive activity in each educational category is indicated by the level of significance p and the statistical test of association Phi, suitable for nominal variables. When the significance level p is less than .05, the link between the two variables is deemed to be not statistically significant [nss].

The latter assumption is partially clarified by examining what happens to the correlation between preventive behavior and education among people in each ethnic group. Malays are inclined to practice general and specific preventive activities and this inclination does not vary significantly with their level of formal education (the correlation between preventive behavior and education found in the total sample disappears among the Malays). The same occurs among the Indians with respect to the practice of the three specific preventive activities. This is in line with the stronger inclination towards specific preventive behavior among Indians in Phase 2, as shown in Tables 11-2 and 11-3. However, the impact of education upon the practice of general preventive activities is stronger among the Indians (Sp=.325) and the Chinese (Sp=.316) compared to that in the total sample (Sp=.274). Thus, the basic finding is that although education is important in promoting preventive health behavior, the influence of the cultural beliefs and practices of each ethnic group cannot be overlooked. Each ethnic group may respond differently to health information received through formal schooling. People integrate factual health information from modern medicine with the array of traditional health beliefs and practices typical of their ethnic community. This is part of pragmatic acculturation, the general tendency to make use of as many options as possible including those from other cultures, to deal with a health problem and to obtain protection from illness.

This brings us to the final aspect of this discussion, the role of public health campaigns. As expected, the better educated respondents tend to be more aware of health campaigns (the correlation between education and health campaign awareness is Sp=.349). There are two or more national health campaigns every year in Singapore dealing with various issues, including the promotion of healthy lifestyles, AIDS prevention, and the harmful effects of cigarette smoking. Television and newspapers are the main mass media used for these campaigns by the Ministry of Health.

During the personal interviews, respondents were asked if they had heard of any health campaign during the previous twelve months and, if so, could they recall what diseases were mentioned in those campaigns and what advice was given. Exposure to the campaigns did not have a significant influence upon the practice of the three specific preventive activities (regular exercise, abstention from smoking, and abstention from alcohol). A significant correlation (Sp=.207) between health campaigns exposure and the practice of general preventive activities—keeping medicines at home and taking general care of one's health—was found only among people with middle-school education. People with very low or very high formal education do not appear to be influenced by health campaigns. People with no formal education or only few years of schooling may not be interested or knowledgeable enough to follow the campaign messages. On the other hand, formal education has a positive influence or, as explained by Ross and Van Willigen, "Education is the root cause of individual well-being" shaping many aspects of people's life including "their social psychological resources" (1997, 292). Thus, it is expected that highly educated people usually have access to a wider and more sophisticated range of health information sources than people with lower or no formal education.

Conclusion

How important is ethnicity as a social determinant of preventive health behavior in Asian communities? Three related aspects were investigated: the factors affecting preventive health behavior; the variations in those factors across ethnic groups; and the role of education. The variables in the Health Belief Model are useful in the analysis but the findings indicate that in the three Asian communities studied, ethnicity—represented by the array of cultural values and beliefs on health and illness—explains variations in preventive health behavior better than the factors proposed by the Health Belief Model. Moreover, the role played by formal education in promoting preventive health behavior is important but not absolute or isolated. The influence of education is concomitant with the influence of ethnicity on preventive health behavior. The findings suggests that programs involving public health education, immunization and other health-related activities should be designed taking into consideration the cultural and educational characteristics of the target population. Better still, programs designed for specific ethnic and educational groups are likely to be more effective than those addressed to the general population in a multiethnic society.

238

REFERENCES

Ames, G. M., and L. A. Rebhun. 1996. Women, alcohol and work: Interactions of gender, ethnicity and occupational culture. *Social Science and Medicine* 43(11): 1649–63.

Becker, M. H. 1963. *Outsiders: Studies in the sociology of deviance.* New York: Free Press.

Becker, M. H., ed. 1974. *The health belief model and preventive health behavior.* Thorofare, NJ: Charles B. Slack.

Becker, M. H., and I. M. Rosenstock. 1989. Health promotion, disease prevention and program retention. In *Handbook of medical sociology,* 4th ed., ed. H. E. Freeman and S. Levine, 284–305. Englewood Cliffs, N.J.: Prentice-Hall.

Cockerham, W. 1995. *Medical sociology.* 6th ed. Englewood Cliffs, NJ: Prentice-Hall.

Conrad, P., and W. Schneider. 1980. *Deviance and medicalization: From badness to sickness.* St Louis, MO: Mosby.

Faten Hana, B. M. 1998. The practice of self-medication among the Malays on Singapore. Unpublished B.Soc.Sc. Thesis. Singapore: National University of Singapore.

Gerhardt, U. 1989. *Ideas about illness: An intellectual and political history of medical sociology.* New York: New York University Press.

Gochman, D. S., ed. 1988. *Health behavior: Emerging research perspectives.* New York: Plenum.

Kasl, S. V., and S. Cobb. 1966. Health behavior, illness behavior, and sick-role behavior. *Archives of Environmental Health,* 12 (February): 246–66.

Kasl, S. V., and S. Cobb. 1966. Health behavior, illness behavior, and sick-role behavior. *Archives of Environmental Health,* 12 (April): 531–41.

King, S. H. 1962. *Perception of illness and medical practice.* New York: Russell Sage Foundation.

Kirscht, J. P. 1988. The health belief model and predictions of health actions. In *Health behavior:Emerging research perspectives,* ed. D. S. Gochman, 27–41. New York: Plenum.

Lemert, E. 1951. *Social pathology.* New York: McGraw-Hill.

Levin, J. S. 1996. How religion influences morbidity and health: Reflections on national history, salutogenesis and host resistance. *Social Science and Medicine* 43(5): 849–64.

Mead, G. H. 1964. *Selected writings.* Indianapolis, Ind.: Bobbs-Merrill.

Norma, P., and Conner, M. 1993. The role of social cognition models in predicting attendance at health checks. *Psychology and Health* 8(6): 447–62.

Parsons, T. 1978. *Action theory and the human condition*. New York: Free Press.

Quah, J. S. T., ed. 1990. *In search of Singapore national values*. Singapore: Institute of Policy Studies.

Quah, S. R. 2002. Cognitive innovations and the conceptualization of ethnicity. In *Advances in sociological knowledge over half a century*, ed. N. Genov, 248–311. Paris: International Social Science Council.

———. 2001. Health and culture. In *The Blackwell companion to medical sociology*, ed. W. C. Cockerham, 23–42. Oxford: Blackwell.

———. 1993. Ethnicity, health behavior and modernization: The case of Singapore. In *Health and health care in developing countries: Sociological perspectives*, ed. P. Conrad and E. B. Gallagher, 78–107. Philadelphia: Temple University Press.

———. 1989. *The triumph of practicality: Tradition and modernity in health care utilization in selected Asian countries*. Singapore: Institute of Southeast Asian Studies.

———. 1988. Private choices and public health: A case of policy intervention in Singapore. *Asian Journal of Public Administration* 10: 207–24.

———. 1986. Social science and illness prevention: An overview of the health belief model. *Journal of Social and Economic Studies* 3(4): 345–57.

Quah, S. R., S. K. Chiew, Y.C. Ko, and M. C. Lee. 1991. *Social class in Singapore*. Singapore: Times Academic Press.

Rosenstock, I. M. 1969. Prevention of illness and maintenance of health. In *Poverty and health: A sociological analysis*, ed. J. Kosa, A. Antonovsky, and I. K. Zola, 168–80. Cambridge, Mass.: Harvard University Press.

———. 1966. Why people use health services. *Milbank Memorial Fund Quarterly* 44(3): 94–124.

Ross, C., and M. van Willigen. 1997. Education and the subjective quality of life. *Journal of Health and Social Behavior* 38: 275–97.

Saw, S. H. 1999. *The population of Singapore*. Singapore: ISEAS.

Singapore Department of Statistics. 2001. *Singapore census of population: Advanced data release*. Singapore: Author.

———. 1994. *Singapore census of population. Release 6: Religion, childcare and leisure activities*. Singapore: Author.

———. 1986. *Yearbook of statistics Singapore*. Singapore: Author.

Singapore National Registration Department (1978) *Report on the Registration of Births and Deaths*. Singapore: NRD.

Singapore National Registration Department (1992) *Report on Registration of Births and Deaths*. Singapore: NRD.

Tan, E. S., and S. K. Chiew. 1997. Citizen orientation towards political participation in Singapore. In *Understanding Singapore society*, ed. J. H. Ong, C. K. Tong, and E. S. Tan, 328–52. Singapore: Times Academic Press.

Uitenbroek, D. G., A. Kerekovska, and N. Festchieva. 1996. Health lifestyle behavior and socio-demographic characteristics: A Study of Varna, Glasgow and Edinburgh. *Social Science and Medicine* 43(3): 367–77.

12

Telemedicine: Health-Seeking Behavior in the Information Age Among Affluent Americans

Arushi Sinha, PhD. President, Big Think Media, Inc.

Introduction

Over the years, high-dollar technology has become one of the major defining features of U.S. biomedicine. Biomedicine is enamored with the latest technology. The current emphasis includes new telecommunications and information technologies. The application of telecommunications and information technology in the health sector has produced telemedicine, telehealth, and medical informatics. The Internet, the telecommunications and information revolution, and its impact on our everyday lives has been documented by anthropologists (Appadurai 1991; Hakken 1999; Jones 1997).

A report by the Department of Commerce estimates that over 40 percent of U.S. households own a home computer. A quarter of all U.S. households have Internet access (U.S. Department of Commerce [DOC] 1999). The technology boom has also created the "digital divide," referring to the gap between those who have access to the digital world and those who do not. The number one predictor of Internet use, according to the DOC, is income. Families earning over $75,000 per year are almost universally Internet savvy, regardless of other variables (DOC 1999). Another aspect of the digital divide is racial. It is estimated that Whites are twice as likely to have access to the Internet as African Americans (DOC 1999). Features such as these have definite implications for who will be included and who will be excluded from our digital communities. In order to be effective social researchers, anthropologists must understand this social phenomenon, its causes, and its ramifications.

It can therefore be argued that those with access to information technologies are the affluent members of U.S. society. Although this means largely White America, it also includes Asian Americans, whose household income and technology consumption is on par with, if not above, the median (DOC 1999). By extension, these are the same individuals who access health information on the Internet. Although government statistics examine the distribution of the technology, they do not examine the functionality of it. What sorts of applications do people use it for?

One of the most common uses of the Internet is accessing health information. It is estimated that as much as two-thirds of all Internet use is for health information research. In addition, two-thirds of physicians report that their patients have researched their condition on the Internet (Hafner 1998). Cognizant of this trend, biomedicine has a large presence on the Internet. Hospitals, biomedical health portals, physician groups, insurance companies, medical organizations, and health vendors all have a Web presence. The Internet has changed both the nature and the provision of health care for those who have access to the cyber realm. Unlike television programming, which is unilaterally transmitted, the Internet is a dialogue, providing advertisers direct access to the viewing behaviors of Internet patrons. "Thousands" of patients reportedly now receive their routine medical monitoring over the Internet (Fischman 1999a). They dial up to a hospital or HMO network where a nurse monitors the relevant vital statistics, such as blood pressure, in the case of heart disease. According to the estimates, such monitoring costs a fraction of what a home health visit or hospitalization would cost for such patients. Because the feedback is immediate, the program helps patients take more responsibility and exercise more control over their own treatment. Physicians utilize on-line services to provide individualized information. And thanks to on-line pharmacies, patients can now order and receive prescriptions without leaving home.

Because there are so many different kinds of people online in large numbers, there is also some effort at market segmentation of various cyber communities. For instance, senior citizens, particularly as they grow in proportion to the rest of the population, are gaining a significant political voice. This has prompted some interest in catering specifically to their needs. For instance, there are some "senior-friendly" sites that do things such as provide "email alerts to take medication or reminders about a doctor's appointment" (Cable News Network [CNN] 2000. Another potential market is the growing fascination with "alternative" medicine. "Etailers" (electronic retailers) are appealing to "dissatisfied patients, who don't want to spend time and money dealing with doctors face to face" (Fischman 1999b). According to the earliest comprehensive survey, it estimated that one-third of all people in the United States use alternative therapies. The landmark study by Eisenberg and others (1993) defines "alternative" or "unconventional" therapies as "medical interventions not taught widely at U.S. hospitals" (246). Eisenberg's article concludes that because "use of unconventional therapy in the United States is far higher than previously reported, physicians should ask their patients about the 'use of unconventional therapy whenever they obtain a medical history'" (246).

It can be inferred that the popularity of unconventional therapies and people's willingness to try such practices—to the tune of $10.3 billion, about one-half of the amount spent on all physicians' services—is fostered by the ability to exchange such information in forum such as the Internet. Significantly, those using unconventional therapies most frequently are White, college-educated, higher-income, individuals between the ages of 25 and 49: exactly the type of person who is also likely to have the benefits of private health insurance as well as access to the information technologies and the Internet. The biomedical community is competing for exactly the same target audience already interested in these same unconventional therapies. The Internet, however, is only one aspect of a much larger aspect of biomedicine that combines health information with telecommunication technologies, collectively known as telehealth or telemedicine.

Telemedicine: A Working Definition
Though there are many definitions of telemedicine, they all agree that telemedicine involves the movement of health information across a distance among geographically separated individuals. Unlike audio-based telephone communication, telemedicine makes use of visual cues using videoconferencing and Internet technologies. Although telemedicine includes patients searching the Internet for health information, it also includes the many different types of programming transmitted over telephone and video lines within the health industry. Telemedicine involves Continuing Medical Education (CME) programming and administrative meetings for health-care providers, along with, but not limited to, the clinical diagnosis aspect of medicine. Though "telemedicine" and "telehealth" are used interchangeably, telehealth is considered to have a broader view. Telehealth encompasses educational and administrative activities such as distance learning and administrative videoconferencing. Because telemedicine is the more widely used term, for the purposes of this discussion, telemedicine will refer to both telemedicine and telehealth.

Over the past few years, the government has made over $20 million available, specifically for the advancement of telehealth technologies (Office for the Advancement of Telehealth [OAT] 2000). Telemedicine is a medicine of the present and of the future, and there is not one of us who will go untouched by this new technology. One physician said that he does not foresee telemedicine as the only type of medicine in the future, but as an important supplement to "traditional" biomedicine (personal communication). Telemedicine replaces both physician and patient with television monitors. It is also an environment in which the doctor-patient relationship is dependent upon nontactile cues for

245

communication, where vision and hearing are paramount in the absence of touch, smell, and presence. In such an environment, the success of this type of health-care delivery system depends upon the strength of the relationship that is established between the patient and health-care "provider," in other words, the physician. To date, the research suggests that patients are extremely satisfied with and receptive of the convenience that telemedicine offers.

The future of medicine is likely to follow the trend that has happened in other business and service providers. For instance, we can now conduct commerce at any time of the day or night. The Internet and the telecommunications and information revolution (Appadurai 1991) have affected everyday life in some detail (Hakken 1999; Jones 1997), but the critiques have only now begun to address their impact on the health sector (Sinha 2000). The current emphasis has shifted to include the new telecommunications and information technologies. Their applications in the health sector have produced telemedicine, telehealth, and medical informatics.

Each medical specialty has sprouted its own "tele-" prefix, engendering such subfields as teleradiology, teleoncology, and teledermatology. Though telemedicine technology has been around since the 1970s, it is only now that the virtual (Foucault 1963) has become feasible, precisely because of the current political and economic climate in which there is the desire to reform the system and constrain health-care costs (Bashshur 1997). Telemedicine is being touted as the medicine of the future combining high tech and low cost. In addition to its clinical applications, many other health support functions are also employing and developing the technology.

How do patients respond to telemedicine technology? Though the popularity of the Internet is well documented, what is less well-known is how telecommunications technology is changing the clinical environment. The following section relies on data gathered at one suburban spine specialty clinic.

Gauging Suburban Patient Response to Telehealth Technologies: A Case Study

A survey instrument sought to answer the question, "How receptive are patients to the idea of using telecommunications in health care?" A one-page survey was developed in order to answer this basic question. The survey instrument was kept brief for three reasons: 1) that it should be a self-survey; 2) that it would not add significantly to the rather large bulk of paperwork that patients already complete; and 3) that it should be quick and easy. Patients were asked to complete the survey while they filled out other paperwork or waited for their doctor. The purpose of the survey was described to patients as "to determine patient familiarity with information technology." Telemedicine was not specifically mentioned or described on the survey because it might have led to uncontrolled anxiety among patients. The survey was pre-tested and administered at a suburban spine specialty clinic located in a town I will call Center City. Center City (pop. 236,539) is a suburban town located on the northern edge of a large southwestern metropolitan area. It is a bedroom commuter community. Local industry consists of white-collar offices and non-manufacturing jobs. Many young, well-educated professionals live in Center City. As a result, several large national computer and retail corporations have their headquarters in Center City. Statistics from Center City reveals that the town is affluent (median household income: $63,000) and mainly White (85.8%). Southwest Spine Group is located in the newest, fastest growing region of the city, where neighborhoods are filled with large houses, and an even wealthier and more homogenous population than the Center City as a whole reside (median household income of the neighborhood: $74,000; 87% White) (Sinha 2000).

The ethnic composition of Southwest Spine Group patients reflects the ethnic composition of Center City area. The most commonly treated ailments at Southwest Spine Group include degenerative diseases of the spine, often age-related, motor vehicle injuries, and workers' compensation claims.

247

Table 12-1. Patient Respondent Characteristics (N = 143)
Female 61 (43%)

Male 82 (57%)

Age (median) 45 years

When asked, "Do you have a computer at home?" participants demonstrated that home computer use is radically different between the largely urban and the largely rural areas. Among Center City patients, 71 percent answered in the affirmative. Responses to the question: "Do you have or use email?" indicated that Center City patients have a high rate of email use (about 43%). Of those who use the Internet, about half the patients surveyed reported using it to find health information. About 10 percent of patients used the Internet to access information specifically about the clinic.

Results indicate that patients are willing consumers of electronic information. Upon learning that the clinic had a Web page, a patient remarked, "Oh, I didn't know they had a Web page; I'll go home and take a look at it."

The data also shows some other trends. The highest frequency of use was among the middle-age cohort of 41–60. Among the patient population of the clinic, there were a few elderly patients (over age 60), and almost no one below the age of 21; other than scoliosis (curvature of the spine), children are not represented among back patients.

Data indicate that members of the largest cohort (age 41–60) are more technologically savvy than those in the younger 21–40 cohort. This is reflected in similar rates of email, Internet, and health-directed Internet use. Only those in the oldest age cohort (age 61–80) exhibited significantly less prowess with reference to the use of information technologies. This finding is consistent with national trends that report that the middle-age cohort is the most common consumer of Internet technology in the United States (DOC 1999).

With reference to gender, women had similar rates of telecommunications usage to that of the men in this sample. Women were as likely to use email, Internet, and health-directed Web pages as men. This finding mimics a trend in the United States in general, which finds little statistical difference in Internet use rates between men and women (DOC 1999). More recent studies have indicated that the small gap between men and women may be narrowing and that women may have even surpassed men in their use of Internet technologies.

Although gender differences were not a significant variable in this sample, language use did present some special cases. Literacy and language use became an issue more than once during the course of the survey. Two respondents (both Caucasian) encountered during the course of the survey were functionally illiterate, though native speakers of English. One of the two respondents agreed to orally respond to the survey. This particular respondent sold paint for a living, an occupation at which has significant exposure to computers. Though he said that he did not understand computers, he still felt that they were quite useful, especially at his job where he used them to mix colors of paint. The second respondent said that she "didn't know nothin' about computers" and therefore did not feel compelled to complete the survey. These two individuals raise many questions about the universality of the information age and about individuals' ability to adapt technology to fulfill their own needs.

Qualitative Responses

The last item on the survey was open ended. The item asked for the patient's comments on the role of information technology in the provision of health care. Their comments can be broken down into one of three categories: 1) skepticism, 2) enthusiasm, and 3) suggestions for innovation. Skeptical respondents did not dismiss the technology out of hand. Only one patient admitted to outright distrust of communications technology, citing the importance of face-to-face contact: "This so called technology will never replace the trust in your doctor made by face-to-face consultation." Another respondent cited the poor ergonomics of technological interaction; a common reason for back pain is a sedentary lifestyle. One patient replied, after finding out about the clinic's Web site, "I will also check out your Web site. I was unaware of one, but also have not spent any time on the PC [due to] back problems." Similarly, another patient who did not like an extended wait in the doctor's waiting room due to her back pain, expressed similar concerns with prolonged sitting.

Telemedicine even appealed to those patients who seem most opposed to it. The two functionally illiterate patients commented upon the importance of "looking the physician in the eye." The paint salesman rather eloquently stated his position, saying a face-to-face consultation with the physician is preferable because it affords him an opportunity to judge if the physician is "an asshole." For patients who are unable to read, judging character—hence, the validity of information—take on heightened importance. The paint salesman also thought that although computers do have some value, they cannot replace human relationships. If a patient is unable to confirm the doctor's opinions by reading the latest medical literature or accessing health information because they are unable to read, then visual cues and body language during interpersonal interaction become of paramount importance. The other functionally illiterate patient also indicated that she likes to "look the doctor in the eye to make sure they're telling the truth." By providing face-to-face interaction, telemedicine can fulfill the needs of even these patients who might otherwise be hesitant about computers. A second theme in patients' responses was a desire for a timely response to their queries and concerns. One patient said, "I prefer minor questions done over the telephone and I would expect an answer within twenty-four hours." Another, himself a physician, noted, it is "very important to contact your personal physician when an important problem occurs (not an on-call fellow); however, being a M.D. myself I do realize the logistics of such an arrangement." Patients, even those with limited communication skills, are intrigued by the idea of using technology to access the latest information. One patient wrote, "I think it is a good idea, so people can get more information on their condition."

The most intriguing suggestions came from patients who were not only enthusiastic about technology and its potential, but were also eager to suggest new uses for it. For instance, one patient suggested an alternative to the intake forms completed by new patients, which often take over half an hour, detailing medical history, insurance, and personal information. He suggested, "It might be nice to be able to fill out the patient information by computer at home and then verify and sign it once you arrive." Another said, "When I have to call scheduling, I wait an average of 10 minutes. I think this is terrible. Many times I don't have 10 minutes to wait." One patient said that a tracking system detailing how late the clinic was running would save her waiting time at the physician's office. The delay is not unusual, as physicians have been known to run several hours behind schedule, therefore, suggesting that she would like a phone call for an appointment delay or when the doctor is running more than half an hour behind schedule. She pointed out that in the past she had waited over an hour and a half, and indicated that she was sure she was not "the only patient who can't sit for very long due to pain." In a sense, patients have foretold the future of a decentralized clinic. Being able to communicate rapidly and easily with patients, updating them on appointments, and reminders regarding medication are some of the services being suggested for telehealth programs. In addition, physicians can correspond with patients via email. Some physicians prefer this system because it can be done at their leisure, and from any location, including home. As one patient wrote, "I prefer to correspond via email or telephone as long as responses are timely and the person is willing to take the time to answer my questions." Instead of being "beeped" on a pager, a physician can respond to an email alert. These are the kinds of services that can be easily provided by a well-connected clinic.

For spine patients, sitting for extended periods of time with severe back pain is problematic (which is why long drives are also unpalatable to these patients). A tracking system, one which would update the queue and let patients know scheduling delays, would allow patients to adjust their own schedules accordingly, making the whole system more "user friendly." As one patient said upon finding out that the clinic supported its own Web page, "I'll visit the Web page in the future. Can you check appointments?" In a similar vein, another patient said, "Seeing a doctor is good for the initial visit or two but follow-ups by phone or email would be a great time-saver when appropriate." Although, currently the clinic's Web site is largely informational and promotional in nature, the patients point to a feasible future use of the Web site. From an administrative perspective, Internet updates would provide a good tracking system for evaluating clinical efficiency and making it more streamlined.

In these examples, patients express a preference for timely response rather than face-to-face interaction. A main selling point of telemedicine is that it has the potential to combine both of these characteristics: the promise of personalized service, as well as, ease of access. This convenience reduces travel time and cost, and discomfort for patients who may otherwise travel long distances to visit their specialists. In this survey, 87 percent of respondents indicated that they would prefer a "face-to-face" encounter with the physician to any other type of encounter, including telephone conversations.

For patients, a decentralized clinic might mean reduced waiting times, prompt response, and most important, establishing face-to-face rapport with the physician. Patients associate biomedical technology as a key component of superior health care, along with an acceptance of spinal implants and spinal stimulators, and pain relief modalities of both invasive and noninvasive types.

Although this represents the views of only one small set of patients within one clinical environment, some of the themes expressed by these respondents do have relevance within the larger universe of patients across the country. The next section addresses how patients responded to well-established telemedicine programs in a nationwide sample. Although the following discussion does not make reference to ethnicity of patients, it does provide context for the patients' responses discussed above in the suburban clinical setting.

252

Responses from Programs across the Country

The Office for the Advancement of Telehealth (OAT) lists approximately 200 federally funded programs. Another database, the Telemedicine Information Exchange (TIE) catalogs over 160 distinct telemedicine programs in the United States alone, as well as several abroad. Taking into account the significant overlap in the two directories and eliminating multiple sites that form part of the same network, there are about 280 unique projects.

Table 12-2. Majority of Patient Responses as Given by Telemedicine Program Managers

31 Positive to extremely positive

7 Qualified positive

2 In progress

2 No concrete information available

1 Negative response

43 Total

Of the total number of programs nationwide, only forty-three had any measure of patient response. And only twenty-nine out of forty-four programs (66%) formally measured patient responses to their program. The remainder relied on anecdotal evidence from patients as indicators of their performance. Table 12-2 shows that the majority of the programs find patients to have high opinions of the technology.

According to the statistics reported by telemedicine providers, high satisfaction rates were common. Of course, program managers have a vested interest in putting a positive gloss on patient acceptance of their programs, so their encouraging perspective on patients' responses is not surprising. Comments such as "anecdotally positive," "highly positive," and "well received" are to be expected as program managers' perceptions of patient response.

What was surprising was not that the program managers reported positive patient responses, but that they reported overwhelmingly, almost unanimous, positive patient responses. Two large studies commissioned by OAT have found patient response to be "highly positive," exceeding "98.3 percent" in one case (Thompson 2001). One program manager said, "The satisfaction was overwhelming; it was like 99 percent." Another example: "No patient has declined the opportunity to participate," and, "No patient has ever refused a second encounter." Another phrased the same thought by stating that at their facility the "refusal rate from patients not wanting to do telemedicine is about 1 percent." Patient acceptance of telemedicine technology might occur for a number of reasons. The most common reason given is that it affords immediacy of physician access and saves travel time. One provider, echoing the sentiments of the patients in the clinic case study cited above, said "most of the patients prefer earlier treatments with telemedicine to later treatments with face-to-face consultations." Another said, "Patients responded favorably due to the fact they did not have to travel and they were able to be scheduled for a telemedicine consultation sooner than a traditional office visit." Published studies on the issue of patient satisfaction are consistent with the comments elicited by this research. These studies find patient satisfaction derives from the "substantial level of comfort and satisfaction among families" (Dick, Filler, and Pavan 1999). In another study, researchers note that out of a survey of 1,500 patients, satisfaction was found to be rated at 6.61 out of a possible 7 scale, which translates to a 94 percent approval rating (Romeo-Wolff et al. 2000, raw data).

In Arizona, patients were excited to see the telemedicine program featured in the local paper, and proud that they were part of the project. One telemedicine specialist indicated that patients are attracted to it because it is a "novelty for them." Adding, "in rural family practice for four years, nobody has turned it down." The problem with novelty, of course, is that after a while, it wears off. As one physician stated: "Euphoria, however, had been relatively short lived and after a while people lost interest." Therefore, telemedicine programs cannot depend on novelty to be a draw for a sustainable, long-term program. They must establish "value" for their clientele, with ease and quality of service rather than just newness.

It is not surprising that patients should like the ability to stay near home and simultaneously consult with otherwise removed medical experts. It means decreased travel and expense. As one program coordinator put it, by not having to make a "400–500 mile drive saves time, money, and risk." Another program coordinator described it as being of benefit due to "decreased unnecessary travel for health reasons and for remotely located or elderly patients." In other words, it enabled those who had physical difficulty getting to see the physician, such as the elderly and those who were located far away. This is also the case in some pediatric specialties where handicapped or otherwise impaired children, such as those who require an oxygen tank, must be transported. As one physician put it, "They didn't have a waiting time. They didn't have to travel to the clinic." Another said, "patients are very appreciative when it saves them a trip to the specialist." "Love" was a common adjective used to describe patient responses to telemedicine by the telemedicine providers. One physician said that family members "loved the fact that they didn't have to take off work to take grandma or take mom or dad to the doctor," and that they did not "miss half a day or more from their own productivity." In addition, he said, "What we've found out is that the families of the elderly really love telemedicine." Family members, according to this physician seem to be great supporters of telemedicine. As he put it, "What really made a difference to the family members was that they did not have to take off work. The cost savings we found were broken down to lost wages to family members." And, "the average saving in visits of all those patients turned out to be more than $122," realized mostly in transportation and associated costs. Cost saving was one of the more mundane reasons that patients like telemedicine.

Reasons for patient resistance cited by two telepsychiatry programs were the fear of invasive procedures. Some psychiatric patients refused teleconsultations fearing that it was subversively invasive. The telemedicine coordinators attributed this response to the patients' delusional state that brought them for treatment in the first place. These findings demonstrate that patients support the technology that dispenses biomedicine from the "depersonalized nowhere." In locations where patients do not have timely access to biomedical specialist, telemedicine clearly provides a viable option. The force of patient response indicates support for the health-care provider efforts.

What Does the Future Hold for Telemedicine?
Several conclusions can be inferred from the preceding discussion. The first is that telemedicine is here to stay. It is the medicine of the future, at least in some form. In many institutions (e.g., prisons) telemedicine will become the primary mode of biomedical service, and other places physicians are reluctant to go and where the provision of medical care faces special obstacles. The second conclusion is that telemedicine has transformed health care in fundamental ways. For example, today there are patients who have never shaken hands with their physician. A third aspect of medicine is that telemedicine is in the health-care business and as such, there are aspects of this that impinge on the new "attention" economy (Dyson 1999). The health-care industry is primed to enter this type of economy because it is already in the service business. A fourth conclusion is that the health-care industry has transcended geographical boundaries with the implementation of telemedicine. Patients and physicians are no longer constrained by space, time, and distance in the health interaction. New relationships are being forged within the health-care sector as a result of this technology. This includes the inclusion of telecommunication experts and technology specialists who work as program specialists, advisors, and policy planners.

There is also the danger that the digital divide will continue to exacerbate the lack of communication between the haves and the have-nots. As demonstrated above, the digital divide has real implications for health status and health-seeking behavior.

With shrinking health-care dollars and rising insurance costs for employers, there is an increased reliance on patients to fund their own health care in the practical and cognitive sense. This means that patients must become knowledgeable negotiators in the health-care process (Furin 1997). Tools such as the Internet provide some measure of control to patients who are able to access and utilize communications technologies. At least a few doctors take their patients Internet search efforts seriously, taking the time to discuss their findings (personal communication 3/7/99).

The contemporary world is captivated by the virtual world. It is the current imaginative frontier, employing our best and brightest minds from medicine to banking to merchandising. It affects daily life through imagined communities comprised of individuals not within the geographic space, but outside of it. Hence, community formation, commerce, health care, and many other facets of individual experience are now occurring outside of geographical boundaries.

This has definite impact for community formation and maintenance (Appadurai 1991). However, not all things can be delocalized. Personal crime, food and water consumption, housing, and public health are all still local concerns, having definite geographic components. In the coming years, society will decide which institutions and community functions are definitely bounded by geographical constraints and that can transcend them. At its core, biomedical technology obviates the urban-specialist/rural-generalist divide at the logistical level. However, a greater impact will be on a second, cognitive level to decentralization—a decentralization of the individual's cognitive map of health opportunities. This shift in worldview is important to telemedicine and will take much longer to fully effect.

Telemedicine is the further exportation of the biomedical system of the world's only superpower. With regard to health as a means of conditioning behavior—hygiene, nutrition, mental health, child development—and is exported across global networks, a concurrent backlash will develop in response to this attempt at forced homogeneity (Brewis, Schmidt, and Meyer 2000). It is at our own peril that we dismiss telecommunications technologies and the cyber reality that they create as mere fantasy. Anthropologists have a unique, global perspective on social change and social process. Insofar as telemedicine will change the health landscape, it presents an intellectual challenge as well as a practical exercise (Escobar 1994). Anthropologists will have to devise new methodological and theoretical tools to assess the role of these imagined communities (Anderson 1983). As Goldschmidt (2000) reminds us, it is a mistake to think of material reality as having more impact than the social confines within which we function: "social constructs have as much influence on us as physical ones and in a practical sense are as real."

258

REFERENCES

Appadurai, A. 1991. Global ethnoscapes: Notes and queries for a transnational anthropology. In *Recapturing anthropology: Working in the present,* ed. R. Fox, 191–210. Santa Fe, NM: School of American Research.

Bashshur, R. . Telemedicine and the health care system. In *Telemedicine: Theory and practice,* ed. R. Bashshur, J, H. Sanders, and G. Shannon, 5–26. Springfield, IL

Brewis Al., 2000. Research report: ADHD-type behavior and harmful dysfunction in childhood: A cross-cultural model. *American* 102(6): 823–28.

Cable News Network [CNN]. 2000. Growing old in cyberspace. CNN Online News Network. February 2.

Dyson, E. 1999. Thoughts on the millennium: Esther Dyson. Interview by Susan Stamberg. *NPR Morning Edition.* National Public Radio. December 15, 1999.

Eisenberg, D. M., R. C. Kessler, C. Foster 1993. Unconventional medicine in the United States: Prevalence, costs, and patterns of use. *New England Journal of Medicine* 328(4): 246–52.

Fischman, J. 1999. A logon a day keeps the doctor away. *U.S. News and World Report,* October 25.

———. 1999. Drug bazaar. *U.S. News and World Report,* June 21, 58.

Foucault, M. 1963. *The birth of the clinic: An archaeology of medical perception.* Translated by A. M. S. Smith. New York: Vintage Books.

Furin, J. 1997. You have to be your own doctor: Sociocultural influences on alternative therapy use among gay men with AIDS in West Hollywood. *Medical Anthropology Quarterly* 11(4): 498–807.

Goldschmidt, W. 2000. Historical essay: A perspective on anthropology. *American Anthropologist* 102(4): 789–807.

Hafner, K. 1998. Can the Internet cure the common cold? *The New York Times,* July 9, E-1.

Hakken, D. 1999. *Cyborgs @ cyberspace: An ethnographer looks to the future.* New York: Routledge.

Jones, S. G., ed. 1997. *Virtual culture: Identity and communication in cybersociety.* Thousand Oaks, CA: Sage.

Office for the Advancement of Telehealth [OAT]. 2000. Services. Retrieved May 11, 2002, from *http://telehealth.hrsa.gov/services.htm.*

Sinha, A. 2000. An overview of telemedicine: The virtual gaze of healthcare in the next century. *Medical Anthropology Quarterly* 14(3): 61–91.

Thompson, T. G. 2001. Report to Congress on telemedicine. Presented February 2001. Health Resources and Services Administration, Department of Health and Human Services. Washington, DC: Government Printing Office.

U.S. Department of Commerce [DOC]. 1999. *Falling through the net: Defining the digital divide. A report on thetelecommunications and information technology gap in America.* Washington, DC: Government Printing Office.

13

Conclusion

Sue Gena Lurie, Ph.D. Assistant Professor, Department of Social and Behavioral Sciences, School of Public Health, University of North Texas Health Science Center, Fort Worth, Texas.

Gordon A. Lurie, A.B.D. (Sociology), University of Toronto.

The relationship of ethnicity and culture to health-seeking behavior is complex, and must be addressed in particular social and cultural contexts. In this volume, case studies of variations in health-seeking behavior within and among ethnic groups in developed and developing societies, and effects of acculturation on health and illness experiences of immigrants, attest to interactive effects of culture and social environment. Complexity in influences on health-seeking behavior is thus found in comparison of the United States and cross-national studies on acculturation, mental and physical health, and health care in immigrant populations. There are even major differences in concepts and measures of acculturation that are applied to diverse ethnic groups (Salant and Lauderdale 2003). Research on health-seeking behavior among ethnic groups in a variety of national and international settings has also confirmed the significance of health and social policy. Social needs and access to care, including effective medications, influence medical pluralism in health-seeking behavior that combines self-care and alternative or complementary treatments with mainstream health services (Stevenson et al. 2003).

In the ethnically heterogeneous United States, culturally sensitive, accessible, integrated, and comprehensive health care for diverse patients is as essential as improving health-behavior change in order to prevent illness. Social and epidemiological research on health behavior has shown socioeconomic position, race, and ethnicity account for the majority of psychosocial, environmental, and biomedical risk factors for individual exposure (House 2002). This relationship can explain the persistence of large-scale disparities in health across social and ethnic groups and socioeconomic determinants.

The related challenges of eliminating health disparities and changing lifestyles and behavior, support the value of comparisons of health-seeking behavior and social networks in contemporary contexts. Although health status varies by race and ethnicity, the goal of eliminating disparities reflects values of social justice with recognition of social and economic determinants of health. Proposed solutions to disparities range from changing policy on access to health care to health promotion for behavior change and community empowerment.

Enhancing ethnic minority empowerment through social capital has been posited as a self-generated solution for health disparities. Public health research in urban U.S. neighborhoods has analyzed the effects of social mediators, including stability, immigrant concentration, "collective efficacy," and physical environmental factors on health (Cohen, Farley, and Mason 2003). Yet health and socioeconomic inequities of ethnic groups within nations and local communities are primarily affected by long-term, macro-level social processes. Political-economic differences are linked to the "social roots of disease": poverty, inequity, power differences, marginalization, racism, and violence. Comparative research should link cultural practices, social networks, and political-economic competition to health inequality, among diverse ethnic, racial, and national groups.

Community health is a key focus of the "New Public Health" that combines health promotion, prevention, treatment for disease, and rehabilitation for the individual and community (Tulchinsky and Varvikova 2000). Although contemporary emphasis is placed on the community as the locus of health behavior, the application of corporate planning models to governance in urban management and political and administrative redesign has important implications for health of communities.

In international health, policy makers and political leaders have emphasized efficiency as the goal of health-care reform, with less attention to the need for equity. However, increasing debate over equity has been stimulated by the World Health Organization report in 2000 that compared health-care systems on capacity for comprehensive care, and by evidence that inequality within a society affects health negatively. To understand the various social and political contexts of health system change, anthropologists, sociologists, and health practitioners need to direct research toward analysis of health and social institutions, political cultures, organizational dynamics, and interorganizational relations. As political and urban anthropology have focused on economic development and gender issues, such research has become less emphasized. Comparative analysis of the changing roles of local and urban policies *vis-à-vis* national policies and programs is central in research on health policy.

Collaboration among community organizations and residents is central to national, international, and local health and social movements. Rhetoric of local empowerment to improve social conditions for health is espoused by health and urban planners, who promote participation of community "stakeholders" in planning, implementing, and evaluating health and social programs. However, ethnic minority groups tend to have relatively less influence in this process. Research on ethnic identity, social capital, and health inequalities has assessed effectiveness of participation in community networks by marginalized groups for reducing inequalities (Campbell and McLean 2002). Social exclusion of multiethnic groups limits community participation and lessens the impact of policies for social capital to improve health. Broad social change is essential to increase multiethnic participation.

Social reform, in tandem with a transnational health movement, is also illustrated by international case studies. In Hong Kong, formerly a British colonial city, reform of the health-care system and the response of the nursing profession to a new model of community health care from a transnational movement was stimulated by political centralization, mobilization of community groups, and reform of the social welfare system, local government, and civil services (Lurie and Lurie 2001). Social justice issues, including how to help the poor and politically disenfranchised, intersected with "health justice" through the transnational community health movement. Although the majority of the local residents had similar regional Chinese ethnicity, this case study offered a model for contemporary analyses of health and social justice that situate ethnicity and social class in specific political contexts.

Social and cultural values are the basis for health and human rights. Societies vary in solutions to dilemmas of rights and needs for health care. Research by medical anthropologists, sociologists, health psychologists, and practitioners seeking to better understand health behavior, and develop solutions for health-care needs, is needed for social justice. Ethical decision-making is affected by the dynamics of multiple justice and ethical spheres or domains: distributive justice, health justice, political spheres, and economic inequities and priorities given to specific issues. Ethical choice and distributive justice issues are neither self-contained nor isolated, but interact with other co-existing issues and domains (Walzer 1983). Along with utilitarian and communitarian ethical perspectives on health planning and policy (Emanuel 1991), this approach is valuable in integrating diverse views of health and social justice.

Although ethicists may assume a national consensus in the United States on the meaning and moral value of health care, there is a range of community meanings and moral values concerning the extent to which health care should be viewed as a social good: which groups are included and what is "just" (Emmanuel 1991; Galarneau 2002). Local views differ as to the extent and causes of health disparities and potential solutions. In efforts to arrive at consensus to improve health for various groups, community decision making must at least address issues of membership, representation, and power (Galarneau 2002).

In conclusion, multiculturalism promotes the value of diversity through treating members of all groups with respect, as equals. Cultural diversity in health research, prevention, and intervention is integrally related to ethical and legal issues of social justice, empowerment, autonomy, and informed consent for individuals and communities. These issues are crucial in decision making for health care, especially when this involves diverse values of individual choice and family-centered and communitarian perspectives.

This perspective is essential to inform research on ethnicity and health-seeking behavior in the social context. The broader challenge is to integrate effective health education and promotion with health policy change for the benefit of ethnic minority and majority groups, immigrants, residents in the United States, and across the global community.

REFERENCES

Campbell, C., and C. McLean. 2002. Ethnic identities, social capital and health inequalities: Factors shaping African-Caribbean participation in local community networks in the UK. *Social Science and Medicine* 55: 643–57.

Cohen, D., T. Farley, and K. Mason. 2003. Why is poverty unhealthy? Social and physical mediators. *Social Science and Medicine* 57: 1631–41.

Emanuel, E. 1991. *The ends of human life: Medical Ethics in a liberal polity.* Cambridge, MA: Harvard University Press.

Galarneau, C. 2002. Health care as a community good. *Hastings Center Report* 32(5): 33–39.

House, J. 2002. Understanding social factors and inequalities in health: 20th century progress and 21st century prospects. *Journal of Health and Social Behavior* 43(2): 125–42.

Lurie, G., and S. G. Lurie. 2001. Social justice and the constellation of ethical domains. Paper presented at American Society for Bioethics and Humanities Annual Meeting, Nashville, TN. October 25th-28th.

Salant, T., and D. Lauderdale. 2003. Measuring culture: A critical review of acculturation and health in Asian immigrant populations. *Social Science and Medicine* 57: 71–90.

Stevenson, F., N. Britten, C. Barry, C. Bradley, N. Barber. 2003. Self-treatment and its discussion in medical consultations: How is medical pluralism managed in practice? *Social Science and Medicine* 57: 513–27.

Tulchinsky, T., and E. Varvikova. 2000. *The new public health.* New York: Academic Press.

Walzer, M. 1983. *Spheres of justice.* New York: Basic Books.